Diversions

TO KNOW   TO UNDERSTAND   TO PARTICIPATE
THE CANADIAN HERITAGE IS YOUR HERITAGE

**ALBERTA HERITAGE
LEARNING RESOURCES
PROJECT**

A Project of Alberta Education
Funded
By
The Alberta Heritage Savings Trust Fund
and
Dedicated to the Students
of Alberta
by the
Government of Alberta
1979

Grateful acknowledgment is extended
to those who assisted in the development
of the Alberta Heritage anthologies

Members of the Selection Committee

Theresa Ford / *Edmonton Catholic School District*
Michael Allen / *Calgary Catholic School District*
Tom Gee / *Alberta Education*
Marg Iveson / *Edmonton Public School District*
Gloria Limin / *Calgary Public School District*
Lorne MacRae / *Calgary Public School District*
Maureen Ross / *Edmonton Catholic School District*

Western Canadian Literature
for Youth

Diversions

Theresa M. Ford
Managing Editor

Alberta Education
Edmonton

Alberta Education
Devonian Building
11160 Jasper Avenue
Edmonton, Alberta
T5K 0L2

ISBN 0-920794-08-4

Project Director / Dr. Kenneth Nixon
Design / David Shaw & Associates Ltd.
Publishing Consultants / Hurtig Publishers, Edmonton
Illustration / Uplis (Haralds Gaikis)
Photography / Nancy Shanoff
Typesetting / The Albertan, Calgary
Printing / Lawson Graphics Western Ltd., Calgary
Binding / Economy Bookbinding Company Ltd., Calgary

To the Reader

Throughout history, people of all ages have recognized the need for fun, relaxation, and entertainment. On some occasions we prefer to be alone; on others we enjoy the company of one close friend or even a pet; for other events "the more the merrier", as we enjoy being part of a group.

This anthology, *Diversions*, presents a selection of short stories, essays, and poems which depict the various ways in which Western Canadians have spent — and often still spend — their leisure time.

Opportunity for relaxation is also part of your heritage. It is important for the development of your character and personality. So sit back, read, and relax!

Contents

Gatherings

Sports

Animals

Leisure Postscripts

Festivals

Celebrations

Happiness, Hard Won
Roy William Devore

I was sixteen when, in 1906, our family moved to the brush-covered homestead at Caroline, in central Alberta. That first year we had little time to become lonely. We were kept too busy battling the elements, hunting snowshoe rabbits, bush-partridge, and prairie-chicken, and fighting mosquitoes. We early lost the calendar, so that Sundays, Mondays, birthdays, and holidays were all the same — we had uniformity.

To the east of us lay the community named Raven, and as soon as we "Caroliners" had made some headway in our struggle with nature, we lost no time in joining battle with these neighbors of ours. Our first summertime engagements with the "enemy", in 1908, took place at picnics, the stellar attraction being the long-awaited baseball game between our boys and those scavengers, the "Ravens". The United Nations never assembled more ungraciously than did those two ball clubs on the mosquito-infested ball diamond. Diplomacy was something reserved for commonplace occasions; spectators came not to shout themselves hoarse, but to beat tin pans and shake cans half filled with pebbles, anything to rattle the opposing players. And such games! The boys were little practised, and in addition their muscles were stiffened by work.

They would drop the ball more often than catch it. The contests were hilarious marathon exhibitions. On one such occasion, when excitement had reached a near record pitch, a passerby enquired of one of the Caroline supporters:

"What's the score?"

"Fourteen to nothing in their favor."

"Gosh! Putting it over you rather badly, aren't they?"

"Oh, I don't know; we haven't been to bat yet. Wait till we get our innings."

Our first winter recreation had begun with the season 1907-08. We were settled by then, also lonely, and each homesteader reached out for companionship to break the white monotony. Our amusement had to be built from the ground up, and much of the material was truly raw. The initial efforts were local folk-dances — polkas, schottisches, minuets, waltzes, etc. These affairs began at eight o'clock at night and lasted until eight o'clock the next morning. Our music was supplied by two fiddlers, two guitarists, and a gentleman who could really "rattle the bones". During the midnight refreshment period a hat was passed on behalf of our musicians. The customary contribution was twenty-five cents, with one exception. A young gentleman, whom I shall call "Johnson", had brought in a twenty-dollar note from the "outside", and invariably presented it to be changed. Since there was seldom half that much in the hat, Johnson danced free all winter.

Being largely endurance tests, these dances grew monotonous to the middle-aged. Some different diversion had to be found for this element, so the Caroline Literary Society was formed. It could scarcely have been called "literary" much of the time — I repeat, our material was raw. There were songs and prose and poetry recitations, but the outstanding feature was the weekly debate. There was little method in the choosing of contestants; husband might be ranged against wife, and youth against middle-age. We really "went to town" in those debates.

One of them unearthed a real character in Zebine Vallier. "Zeb" came to Caroline country from the Ozarks of Arkansas. His dwelling was a semi-dugout affair, from which he rarely emerged on cold winter nights. But he made an exception for this debate since he had been chosen leader of the affirmative. He was to prove a far from shy person despite having what Mark Twain might have called "discrepancies". Zeb's coarse black hair and beard were luxuriant. His one coat, once black, had taken on a "sheen". It had one button, recently sewed on with clean, white thread, while padding peeped forth from the arm-pits. Promptly after rising to speak, Zeb proved himself a strategist who knew his way about. Our subject for debate read: "Resolved that man descended from the lower animals." The affirmative captain at once declared that there were no animals lower than man, the only one to plot destruction of his kind. "Descended" was acceptable to him; he maintained that man really had gone downhill. It was soon obvious that Zeb faced a hostile audience, especially the female sector, but like a boxer he pivoted on his toes to face and jab at each heckler. "If you feel inside the rim of your outer-ear," teased Vallier, "you will find a little lump, all that is left of a former peaked ear with which some ancestors flicked away flies."

At this juncture certain members of the audience were seen lifting a hand toward an ear, then suddenly lowering it in flushed embarrassment. "You can't tell me!" one listener shrieked. "The Bible says. . . ."

After bowing his head politely and waiting until the storm had passed, the speaker continued: "Also, we are descended from fish, and it might have been far better had we remained fishes, for three-quarters of the earth's surface is water and not much of the remaining one-fourth is fit even for homesteading."

It was Vallier's night. The opposing speakers simply did not belong in the same league with him. But while he dominated the argument, Zeb's side lost the decision. The outcome was never in doubt after one worthy judge was heard to mutter: "My mind is made up. Don't confuse me with facts."

Unlike Bret Harte's "Society upon the Stanislaus" our weekly debates did not collapse, nor was Zeb through as an orator. Our none-too-beloved neighbors, the Ravens, had also turned literary and had developed, according to rumor, one deadly debater who had been "mowin' 'em down". This gentleman displayed nothing but contempt for those brush savages to the west who thought they had a man who knew how to debate. The Ravens condescendingly hurled a challenge in our direction that was accepted with alacrity. We felt that if we could lure Zeb out of hibernation for the event, there would be nothing for the rest of us to do but cheer.

From the outset it was a contest between two champions. A site was chosen near the common border of the two settlements. At first, a measure of bickering took place regarding the three judges required, their geographical habitat, relationship to the contestants, etc. Zeb lessened this tension by offering: "Let him have his wife, father-in-law, and mother-in-law for judges."

Two Caroliners had scouted the champion of the Ravens, heard him debate, then reported back: "There's nothing to be frightened over." The advantage of surprise rested with us, for Zeb had passed unnoticed through the Raven area before building his burrow at Caroline. He was an unknown quantity.

Zeb was none too impressive on arrival at the scene of verbal combat that memorable evening. He had not dressed for the occasion but merely wore the only clothing he possessed. The warring factions sat on opposite sides of the hall, and as Zeb lumbered up the aisle toward the improvised platform, exuberant Ravens openly smirked, winked broadly, and nudged each other. This hillbilly would be "duck-soup" for their champion. When the object of their derision hoisted his two hundred and twenty pounds onto the platform, nodded to the chairman and to his opponent, assumed the seat provided for him, and then proceeded to ignore the audience completely, his sobering critics had a better look. Even the more stupid must have sensed that beneath the hair, beard, perhaps grime, reposed a personality.

The Ravens' celebrated Cicero had the affirmative side of the subject and so spoke first. The first sentences of his address (obviously well memorized) were rendered fairly well. When he came to the end of this rehearsed portion, words became rather difficult and he commenced to flounder. There seemed no place to put either of his hands, and the "ah's" and "uh's" became frequent. Then, when the Caroline rooters joined him briefly in a chorus of "uh's", the gentleman grew angry and substituted vehemence for clarity and fluency. He also glanced now and then in the direction of his opponent, as though expecting heated interjections from this quarter. Zeb was anything but heated. He took no notes on what his adversary said, but sat with hands resting upon knees, shoulders drooping, and head bowed. To all outward appearances the man was enjoying a nap. Frustrated and infuriated, the redoubtable Raven, instead of using the peroration he had planned, summed up with utterances more like croaks than crescendos. To complete his humiliation, a shrill-voiced Caroline boy shouted: "Take 'im to the Doctor!"

When Zeb rose to speak, his broad grin showed white against his dark skin and beard. His greeting to the audience consisted of a heavy wink beneath a bushy eyebrow. Numerous boos were given in answer by the Ravens, but these soon died away. Zeb had a way of commanding attention. Words were no worry to him; they poured forth like water from a faucet. When he strode across the platform his gait somewhat resembled that of a grizzly bear. Before long the Raven supporters were not only listening, but some were even beginning to applaud, albeit feebly. When Zeb sat down, there seemed no need for the formality of a vote by the judges — there had been no contest. However, the vote was taken, and after some delay the decision came: "Unanimous in favor of Raven!"

At first a weak, shamefaced applause came from the roosts of the Ravens; but this was soon "smothered" by the Caroliners' angry roars of "rotten", "dirty", "crooked". The chairman's task seemed hopeless. But he received unexpected assistance from Zeb, who rose and walked to the centre of the platform. An absolute silence now reigned. No doubt everyone present was expecting an outburst of unparalleled profanity, but Zeb played a far different kind of trump. At the "risk of boring them" he repeated his thanks to everyone present, particularly to the Raven section for their studious attention. He complimented the judges on the scholarly way they had arrived at their verdict. The decision could not have been easy. Then he expressed the hope that in the not too distant future he might again have the opportunity of addressing this fine audience, with this same panel of judges on hand for the event. He had enjoyed the present occasion immensely.

Seconds later, a subdued and silent flock of Ravens watched Zeb walk back down the aisle and out of the "Hall of Justice".

Thus it was your early homesteaders, young and old, entertained themselves. Crude? Primitive? Rough-hewn? Yes, it was all that. But nonetheless it was a happiness — and a part of it clings to me still.

Horror of Haunted Hallowe'en

Eleanor Pronik

'Twas Hallowe'en night at the old haunted house
So we thought we would pay it a visit.
We crept out at night 'neath the cold yellow moon;
The trees by the house swayed and slipped in a swoon
And the wind whispered through them,
   "What is it?"

But we both were brave and had no fear of ghosts
So we opened the rusty old gate,
The steps, how they creaked!
The wind, how it shrieked!
And we felt the cold fingers of fate.

The door closed behind us, it made us whirl back,
Then we heard a soft moan in the room;
In the shifting moonlight,
In thick, muffled fright,
Saw a witch and her long, magic broom.

A ghost softly floated above our poor heads,
A bloody head rolled on the floor,
The eyes were gouged out,
And I saw round about
Two clutching hands, lone, near the door.

A door slowly opened and through it we heard
A cluck and a cackle and peck,
In came a man,
With a club in his hand
And a double head perched on his neck.

Behind him we saw through our horrified eyes
A man hanging from an old pole;
His puffed face was blue,

His fingers were, too;
He was led by a terrible troll.

And next came a boy who was beautifully dressed
But no features had he, just a blank,
No mouth, nose or eyes,
As he let forth soft cries;
And into more horror we sank.

Then loud, eerie laughs and some goblins came in —
So ugly I cannot describe them;
We let out a cry
As we heard a soft sigh
And saw such a beautiful woman.

Her gown was of silver, her hair was gold,
She came forth and took my hand;
Her beauty just shone,
Her eyes like a fawn
And her manner was gracious and grand.

Suddenly as we looked at her lovely face
The beauty slipped down and grew grey,
Her face shrivelled up!
And then wrinkled up!
And it slowly rotted away . . .

We turned our faces, saw the creatures close in!
And that was all that we knew.
Next morning we were
Found dead on the floor
AND NOW WE ARE GOBLINS TOO!

Another Hallowe'en
J. O. Thompson

He put on his
mask and it bit

back. So then he
howled and all the

doors on the street
opened and from

each door was thrown
sticky candy

which he gathered
and ate, weeping.

Special Occasions
J. C. Charyk

When special days came the rural schools were ready for them. Victoria Day, Arbor Day, St. Valentine's Day, and Hallowe'en were appropriately celebrated.

Queen Victoria's birthday was observed on the twenty-fourth of May no matter on what day of the week it happened to fall. The children had a deep feeling for this day, for not only was it a school holiday but it meant that summer had officially arrived. They could now exchange their long heavy winter underwear for something lighter and they could go barefoot for the first time if they wanted to. This was the day when the children also vocalized, "If you don't give us a holiday on the twenty-fourth of May, we will all run away and hide in the hay." Of course it had to be sung loud enough for the teacher to hear.

The afternoon of the school day preceding the twenty-fourth of May was for the most part observed patriotically. Readings, songs and playlets or pageants unfolded the story of Queen Victoria and the British Commonwealth of Nations. The history and the meaning of the British flag received special emphasis. It was not unusual to present each student with a small flag. The children and the spectators could not help but be impressed with all the flag-waving and the reciting of numerous patriotic selections. In some schools the program was presented on May the twenty-fourth as a part of the district's celebration of the Queen's birthday. In addition, such patriotic community picnics included a full schedule of races, ball games, horseshoe pitching, and many trials of skill. The event was eagerly anticipated by both young and old.

Arbor Day was observed as a time for planting and spring cleaning. The teacher and students worked hard for the whole day. They raked the yard, moved the pile of ashes and rubbish that had accumulated during the winter, cleaned the barn, scrubbed the outhouses, put in their school garden, and if conditions were favorable, planted or replaced a few trees. The inside of the school was tidied and given a thorough washing, including the floor, the wainscot, the windows, the desks and cupboard, and the blackboards. The stove and the few pipes that could be reached were made resplendent by a new coat of polish. Even the drinking and washing facilities were made sanitary once more. Some school boards supplied a can or two of paint, and this enabled the older students to improve the outside appearance of the barn or the toilets. The Little White Schoolhouse glowed with some of its former freshness every Arbor Day. Then came the teacher's treat — a real coconut and the milk too. It was such a nice day but, "Why did they make the school grounds so large?"

One Arbor Day in the Mountain Chase School District 1373 was remembered for a long time. It happened in the Thirties, the decade when Russian thistles flourished as at no other period in Canada's history. The students, in their eagerness to dispose of the weeds, overloaded the pot-bellied stove with so many of the dry-as-tinder plants that the mopping-up operation ended on a disastrous note — the school burned down.

The first Arbor Day in most country schools was observed by planting a tree for each child enrolled. The trees were picked according to the sizes and characteristics of the students and planted in suitable parts of the school grounds, sometimes in attractive clumps and at other times in convenient straight rows. Some of these trees are still growing, after surviving sixty years of climatic inconsistencies and the carnage of thoughtless children. Another point of interest is that many rural folk believe that a tree planted for a particular child would reflect the vicissitudes of his life. If the person were successful and retained his health his tree showed unusual growth and beauty, but if he were having a hard time of it the tree exhibited the degree of his adversities in its appearance. In fact, the pioneers of Craig School District 1793 (Innisfail, Alberta) tell a story about a tree that was planted for Melvin Opstad in 1909. It grew impressively during the years that Melvin was a successful veterinarian in Vancouver, but when he passed away in 1927 his vegetable twin in the Craig schoolyard began to deteriorate rapidly and died that same year.

One of the most ambitious tree-planting projects undertaken by a one-room school was organized by a Miss Legg, who taught in the Little Red Deer School District (Innisfail, Alberta) in 1911. Nearly a thousand native spruce were dug up from along the banks of the Little Red Deer River, hauled five miles by wagon and then set in the ground to completely ring the schoolhouse and yard. The enrollment that year totalled forty-four pupils spread over eight grades so it was not difficult for Miss Legg to find boys who would rather haul and plant trees than do book work. Several of the older lads brought farm teams and soon everybody pitched in. Sam

Scarlett and Doug Scott, two students who participated in this mammoth tree-planting session, remember only one accident that attended this marathon Arbor Day — a runaway. No damage resulted except for the loss of a hundred seedlings which were scattered as the horses dashed madly across the homestead country.

It took several days of heavy work before the ambitious Miss Legg was satisfied that there was a sufficient number of healthy trees in place on the four sides of the school grounds. This was only the first phase of the job, for periodically throughout the balance of that season the schoolboys and their conscripted fathers hauled water in barrels on stoneboats to ensure that the newly planted trees received ample moisture.

Miss Legg must have known her tree-planting science, for today the towering evergreens sheltering the Little Red Deer schoolhouse show that almost every sapling survived. Thus this conspicuous and beautiful landmark becomes a fitting memorial to the imagination and public service of a teacher and her pupils in pioneer days.

School gardens were a special war project between 1914 and 1918, but the idea of a garden was revived every Arbor Day after that, war or no war. The plots were prepared from sod on the school grounds, or the garden was planted in the plowed fireguard surrounding the schoolyard. Each scholar was responsible for looking after so many rows. The gardens received some attention during the months of May and June, but by the end of the summer holidays the native grass had made a good recovery.

The week before St. Valentine's Day was always a busy one for the rural students. Every spare moment was used for making valentines. The days became a round of folding, cutting, gluing, drawing, painting and lettering. Some were works of art finished with lace or ribbons, while others displayed the results of indifference. The teacher assisted the primary students, but at best the love tokens emerged as misshapen hearts bearing the words "Be My Valentine" crudely lettered in colored crayons. The few store-bought valentines that appeared in the ornately decorated post-office box were destined for the teacher, or for the "one and only". The entire activity of making and addressing the valentines was shrouded in mystery, silence and intrigue. Subterfuge followed subterfuge any time an individual was questioned about a valentine to a particular person. Reciprocal agreements were quite common! "If you make one for me I'll make one for you." Any day a change in human relations occurred, the original name on the valentine was effaced and another substituted in its place. The teacher's valentines were no exception to this capriciousness, but she made sure, sometimes in an unorthodox manner, that every child received a valentine from the box. Since she could not show favoritism it was necessary for her to buy or make a valentine for every pupil. The big boys scoffed at the sissy practice of making valentines but often changed their minds the last day. There were always sympathetic people who helped them out in their last-minute rush.

The opening of the St. Valentine's letter box was the signal for much excitement. A couple of students, acting as cherubs, flitted about the room and delivered the valentines to the young hopefuls whose names appeared on the outside. The pupils accepted their cards in a matter-of-fact manner and appeared surprised to get them. In reality they had fully expected to receive certain valentines and would have been sadly disappointed otherwise. Invariably some pretty girl with a friendly smile and personality received a stack of the love tokens, while some poor unkempt and rough-spoken lad was fortunate to boast of more than one such greeting.

Older people feel a slight twinge of nostalgia when they remember the Hallowe'en parties in the rural school. They used to be such novel and exciting affairs. Materials were scarce but ingenuity was not, so practically every child came dressed in some form of costume. Many of the students were so well disguised that even their closest friends failed to recognize them for the first few minutes. Prizes were awarded to the students with the best or funniest costumes. These were simple little gifts worth just a few cents but of great sentimental value to the winners.

Once the costumes had been judged the students played traditional Hallowe'en games. Apples were a special treat in those early days so many contests were devised that involved them. They were suspended on long strings and the students with their hands clasped behind their backs tried to take a bite out of the swaying fruit. If they were successful in seizing the apple with their teeth it became theirs. Another stunt was to float the apples in a tub of water and the children endeavored to snatch the bobbing delicacies with their lips or teeth without using their hands or using the sides of the tub as arresters. A common gimmick was for each child to peel an apple and to toss the strip of peel over the left shoulder. The letter formed when it landed on the floor indicated the first initial of the name of the person that the caster would marry. The manner in which the children went about playing this game led any observer to assume that they believed this Hallowe'en sorcery. Some youngsters kept tossing their ribbon of apple skin repeatedly before they finally succeeded in obtaining the right configuration, that is, right as far as they were concerned.

There was no end to the variety of contests. For instance, there was one in which the children were given only a single opportunity to plunge their heads into a large basin of water to see how many of the small five-cent pieces scattered about on the bottom they could pick up with their lips. The vision of impending wealth enticed more than one boy or girl to remain under water longer than good judgement dictated. The spewing and the sputtering that followed such an asinine display provided fun for everyone but the suffocating make-believe frogman.

The youngsters enjoyed pinning on the donkey's tail while

blindfolded. Watching this game was as much fun as actually participating in it, for some of the competitors always managed to veer off course and miss the mark to such an extent that they involved themselves in any number of hilarious situations.

A peanut hunt or a peanut scramble enabled everyone to win something.

Probably the most popular event on the Hallowe'en program was the treasure hunt. The teacher hid a suitable article and supplied a map showing the whereabouts of its hiding place. The ensuing hubbub had all the earmarks and thrills of searching for a real pirates' cache.

Everyone looked forward to having their future foretold. The students drew their fortunes from the many that were placed beforehand in the bowl of prophecy. These utterances of the prophets when read aloud to the class created much merriment and teasing.

Since mirrors were supposed to be associated in some mysterious way with Hallowe'en an interesting competition was provided by asking each pupil to draw a picture of a simple object while peering into the looking glass rather than directly at his paper. The inverted-image situation perplexed the students and they enjoyed the novelty. In addition there was a handsome prize for the one making the best sketch.

Hallowe'en was a time for tricks and upon occasion the schoolhouse became the butt of these. The first arrivals at the school on the morning after were often greeted solicitously by a cow or horse tethered in the cloakroom. Chickens are at home in a coop, but when pranksters released a few of them in a classroom the resulting commotion and the fouling up of the surroundings were enough to satisfy any malcontent. The children enjoyed the noisy roundup but not the mopping-up operations that followed such frivolities.

A strange sight was to see a buggy or waggon straddling the ridge of the roof. It took some strategy and hard work to position it there but it required just as much effort to remove it. Who put it up? No one seemed to know! Who was going to haul it down? Everyone was cognizant of the fact that since the school board was responsible for the property it was up to the trustees to perform their "duty". There was just as much fun watching the restoration as there was in perpetrating the devilment, so an enthusiastic gathering was on hand to offer advice, laugh in derision, and have a good time generally at the expense of officialdom, but never to volunteer assistance.

The settlers of the Lawrence Lake School District 4909 (Smith, Alberta) could well attest to the possibility of such anomalies taking place. One post-Hallowe'en morning they witnessed three stalwarts remove a heavy farm implement from the top of their school house. It was feared that the new roofing had been damaged, but the trustees, with infinite care and patience, succeeded in getting the binder down success-fully.

Plugging the chimney with a sack was considered a clever prank by some scamps, but when the school filled with smoke and the children had to hasten out of the building to escape asphyxiation it was going beyond the jocular stage.

A customary Hallowe'en stunt was to push over the school's outhouses. Next morning, all the children shared in the unpleasant task of restoring the "conveniences" to their upright status. There was no help from the school board in such trivial matters.

Occasionally the Hallowe'en fun turned out to be a matter for the police, like upsetting desks, books, ink bottles, and other school supplies and then churning the whole into a hodgepodge. It required days to repair and straighten things out before school could be resumed. A less serious trick was to shatter a bottle of ink against the wall of the school. No amount of scrubbing ever removed the ugly blotch completely.

Some stunts involved horses.

The school board of the Lind School District 2170 (Coutts, Alberta) was in the habit of holding meetings in the schoolhouse on the last day of the month. October the thirty-first, 1918, was no exception. The trustees drove to the school with teams and buggies and as usual tied them up beside the barn for the duration of the meeting. But on this particular evening a couple of youngsters on horseback passed that way and upon seeing the horses thought it was a good time to do a little interchanging. The four teams were unhitched and then coupled again so each pair now consisted of one horse belonging to the buggy and the second from another team. The uproar that ensued after the meeting was wild compared to what had taken place during the official conclave. It required over half an hour of hard work and copious outbursts of profanity to restore things to their customary status quo.

The pupils in another school were excited to see one of their classmates ride into the schoolyard on a new horse. A fresh mount in those days aroused as much interest as does a late-model automobile today. The boy concerned failed to share the enthusiasm of his fellow students. During Hallowe'en night someone had sneaked into the pasture and curried the horse with either ink or bluing. The old gray mare was now a dappled blue. It took the better part of two months before nature restored the animal to its original color. In the meantime the horse, never known for her speed, had earned the impressive title of "Blue Flash".

The Curtain Goes Up
Myra Paperny

The community hall had never held such a huge crowd. Every single chair in the place was occupied and the janitor, with the assistance of some students, was hauling up wooden benches from the basement to make room for the people who were still flooding through the door.

"My gosh, there are more people here than at the flower show or the giant Bingo. Never knew there were so many people in the district."

"Can you imagine it, there are folks here from as far away as Hillbury?"

"Where on earth will we sit?" Mama asked in dismay. Lisa put one arm around Mama and hesitantly reached for Ben's outstretched hand with her other arm as she led them toward the front of the room. Tom had reserved seats for the entire family in the second row. Mama was pleased, and didn't even notice that there had been no place saved for their father. Lisa and Teddy sat down but found it difficult to concentrate on any conversation. Finally the lights dimmed and the curtain descended on the stage.

"What a strange curtain," Ben remarked. It really was different from the usual velvet stage curtain. The curtain was canvas and looked like a patchwork quilt with a mass of colored squares. Instead of dividing in the middle, the curtain rolled upwards like a store awning. Each huge square advertised some type of store or product. The curtain must have been very old, for some of the products listed didn't even exist in Chatko any longer.

There was the Gaylord Blacksmith Shoppe; Mackie's Shoe Repairs, which featured a giant high-heeled boot; Dr. Robinson's Rebirth Potion, which naturally displayed a medicine bottle, and a host of other colorful ads. In the center of the curtain was an enormous buffalo head with a huge staring eye. Lisa told Ben about the hole in the animal's eye. Using this secret peephole, the performers could peer unseen at their audience before a program began.

"Do you have to go now?" Ben whispered as they sat down at the conclusion of singing "God Save the King".

Lisa shook her head. "We're in the second half of the show. Don't have to leave until after intermission." She still couldn't believe that Ben was sitting here beside her. In the past number of months she had exchanged so many letters with him, but now that he was next to her she found it difficult to open her mouth.

Now the benches were also packed as heavily clad citizens entered from the still wintry street. Fathers herded their children in Hudson's Bay blanket coats, white with wide green and red stripes; brown woolen stockings bulged over their ankle-length combination underwear.

Toddlers sat patiently as their mothers unbuckled galoshes from their feet and tugged off bulky leggings. The pool hall owner proudly escorted his two costumed daughters. Their flower petal hats with crepe paper stems made them look like some strange variety of insect.

A pale young violinist with greased-down bangs was supported by his parents, each clutching one of his elbows. Every parent whispered advice to his particular prodigy while the crackling of paper sacks containing home-made fudge and popcorn balls added to the din.

Several girls from school walked down the aisles distributing ballots and programs to the audience. The mayor, a pudgy man, appeared on the stage to welcome them. He told the audience that they were privileged to have a panel of judges from the city . . . an actor, a school inspector and an alderman. There was a round of applause for the judges when they acknowledged the introduction.

"However, these ballots are for you. There will also be a prize for the most popular act . . . perhaps one that does not have the professional merit to be the judges' choice but one that appeals to you, the community.

"A special thanks to Mrs. Beddlington who has been so co-operative in organizing the show with me. And now without further ado . . . I give you the Chatko Falls Follies."

Lisa glanced down the list of names on the yellow program Ben handed her. There they were, number twenty-five on the program. It merely listed their names and called them a "Combined Performance".

"Liseleh, they've made some mistake. Go call the mayor.

They have all of you listed together. Oh dear." Mama peered more closely at the program through her glasses.

"Must just be a typographical error, Mama. No need to disturb the mayor," Suzanne quickly replied.

Fortunately the curtain was rolled up once again before Mama was able to call the mayor. The first act was a juggler, but he lost most of his rubber balls on the stage and one of his Indian clubs sailed down to the audience. Giggles of laughter followed.

This performance was followed by the Perkins twins reciting "My Shadow". "I have a little shadow that goes in and out with me," the number one twin droned, gesturing with a rigid arm toward number two standing slightly behind him.

The lesser shadow sidestepped to avoid being hit in the face by his identically dressed brother. The mutual wigwagging motions continued. Number two shot up "like an india rubber ball" on cue and then curled up a "sleepyhead" as they mumbled the conclusion. Then, counting to three out loud, they bowed and left the stage.

Then some girl in lemon velvet shorts did a tap dance standing on her head. A small elevated platform served as her upside-down stage.

"Never saw anything like that before," Mama said. "Poor little girl will get a headache." Ben was bent over double laughing. At first Lisa wanted to join him, but immediately she had visions of him laughing in the same way at their coming performance.

Next there were four boys in aprons who called themselves a barbershop quartet. The only problem was that the smallest boy drowned out the voices of the others. But the audience warmed to the performers, and as the appreciation increased the clapping was less sporadic and more enthusiastic.

There were several sopranos, all carrying long hankies, on the program, and Ben asked if they had colds or something. The poor Finch boy gave a thunderous version of "The Charge of the Light Brigade" and then forgot the final stanza. He stood there mute until Mrs. Beddlington's voice could be heard loud and clear prompting him from the wings.

At this point Lisa got the shivers. She pulled her coat more tightly around her shoulders but still she shook. She was unable to hear the dancers and instrumentalists that followed. She was petrified. What if they forgot their lines? Who would help them? Oh, it had all been a big mistake. There was still time to have Mrs. Beddlington scratch them from the program. Nobody knew what they were doing anyway. She turned to Teddy but he was watching the stage. Ben seemed to understand her fears for he awkwardly patted her shoulder and winked. Mike was making horrible faces at her from the other side of Mama, motions that suggested he was about to be sick. However, when Mama looked down at him he straightened his shoulders and gave her an innocent smile.

"Oh, isn't Marion gorgeous? Look at her, Lisa," Suzanne whispered. Marion wore an unbelievable pair of spangled green tights with a sparkling bodice. She also had green stockings and green ribbons in her hair. She cart-wheeled her way across the stage and then stopped long enough to go into a great spin, like a top. The audience gasped when she completed a series of handstands by flipping right over in the air. Absolutely weightless. For her finale she did a full backbend. With great suppleness she bent backwards and reached for a green silk scarf placed on the floor. She picked it up with her teeth, then flipped up on her feet with the piece of silk still intact in her mouth. There was a great gasp. Marion bent forward in a curtsy and then raised her arms to the audience, as Lisa had suggested. The boys in the audience whistled and clapped wildly.

"Oh, there's just no use trying now, Teddy. She'll win it . . . she's a shoo-in," Suzanne said.

"Boy, that girl sure is talented, and what looks," Ben replied. Lisa felt a pang of envy. If only Ben would use that tone of voice in speaking of her! For a moment she regretted that she wasn't doing something solo so she might at least look attractive. She crouched down in her seat. Perhaps Mrs. Beddlington had forgotten them. As the audience stretched during the intermission she called to Teddy to suggest they forget the whole thing.

"Ah, there you are, Steins. Backstage immediately. Quietly now. Through the side door there. Really, did you forget? I said that as soon as the curtain falls, second act performers backstage. Anyone see Jerry Bashford? I can't find him either. Hurry, everyone, hurry."

Mrs. Beddlington had grasped Lisa's arm before she could even blow Mama a kiss. She was steered with the boys and Suzanne through the stage door while Ben whispered good luck to their backs. They fumbled their way down the narrow cement steps to the dressing rooms below the stage. There were two dressing rooms upstairs, but it was far too cramped for all the performers to gather there.

What bedlam backstage! Not at all like the professional theater she had seen in the city. A fat girl was having trouble doing up the zipper of her fluffy organdy dress and called to Lisa for assistance. Mrs. Macrae stood applying bright red lipstick to Shirley's lips.

"Shirley, purse your lips tightly, that's better . . . no, no, don't smirk. Is your kilt pin straight? Never mind those other children. This is your show. Just concentrate on winning."

Shirley picked up her gilt-coated swords, fitted her velvet tam on her head, and tossed her short yellow curls at Suzanne. Lisa thought the curls looked like wood shavings, glued to her head. What a nasty girl.

"Gee, I wish I could be seen in a lovely dress instead of scrunching up behind our stage in the dust," Suzanne said longingly.

Lisa shrugged her shoulders as she searched for Teddy and

Tom. Finally she found Teddy at the very back of the basement. He motioned for her to join him backstage.

"Just enough time to check our theater before the next act goes on. Come on Lisa, stop shaking. We're the best and you've all got to believe that."

It was dark on the stage now and Lisa tripped as she followed him. Picking herself up from the grimy floor, she wiped her hands. The stage had a second set of curtains near the back and the puppet theater stood behind them. Lisa checked the puppets with Teddy, pausing to fondle a favorite before she returned to the dressing rooms.

"Oh, bring us luck," she whispered, giving the doll a kiss.

"Number twenty please, onstage now. Number twenty-one follow. Will the next four numbers line up here in the wings . . . now, now."

Mrs. Beddlington seemed to be everywhere at once. "Now don't forget your numbers. Yoohoo, Miss Jones, you are to accompany the following two performers, so check your music and for goodness sakes remember that Larry has 'Danny Boy' and the Kantowitz girl needs the Ukrainian melody for her dance. Remember, you forgot during rehearsals."

Again the house lights dimmed as the curtain began to creak its way up. Larry Harrigan had a mellow tenor voice and his "Danny Boy" was wonderful.

"He'll win, for sure he'll win."

Lisa turned to speak to the girl behind her. The girl had her hand clapped over her mouth. "Oh, I can't go on . . . quick someone give me a towel, I'm going to be . . ." The girl rushed toward the dressing room, pushing past the row of waiting children.

While Mrs. Beddlington announced that number twenty-two would be unable to perform, Lisa grabbed Suzanne's hand. "Now look straight ahead," she hissed, surprised at the note of command in her voice. "That won't happen to you. You have a cast-iron stomach, Mama says." Suzanne nodded, but her face was drained of all color.

"Oh dear, the poor Hindley child. Anyone have some aspirin?" Mrs. Beddlington asked.

Shirley Macrae pranced onto the stage, and as the footlights were turned up, she began her precise sword dance. Such confidence. And her nose was raised so high. Perfectly executed.

"Just look at that turned-up nose," Suzanne whispered.

And then as she was completing an intricate step across her sword, Shirley's dainty black slipper misbehaved. Her hopes, along with the golden sword, went flinging wildly across the stage. A great gasp from the audience. Shirley stopped moving; the pianist, hidden in the corner, blithely continued to play the Scottish tune. The children in the wings gazed at Shirley in alarm.

"Oh shut up, you fool," Shirley shrieked at the accompanist as she retrieved her swords. Hysterical giggles from below appeared to enrage her further and, grabbing her swords, she stamped off the stage.

"How awful, not to complete her dance. Whatever you do, finish the play, no matter how many goofs you make. Don't ever insult an audience. The show must go on," Teddy told them.

Lisa was certain that number twenty-four had just gone on, but Mrs. Beddlington was pushing them toward the stage.

"Number twenty-five. Do hurry. I told them to hold the curtain longer this time to give you a chance to move your theater forward. Good luck, children."

Then they were alone on the empty stage, pushing the theater carefully toward the closed curtain. It took their combined strength to move the heavy puppet theater and it swayed with each step.

"Oh, it won't work, Teddy. It's going to fall over."

"Nothing I build ever falls," Tom said.

"My throat's all closed up. I can't talk."

"Did you remember to tell Mrs. Beddlington to start the Circus Parade song as soon as the curtain begins to go up?" Lisa asked Teddy. Teddy nodded and then turned his warm smile on all of them, as if this was just a performance in the attic. Now Lisa was relieved that their faces would be hidden behind the curtains. At least with puppets, the audience didn't see you. You could almost pretend that you weren't really there . . . like an invisible person.

"Quick, Lisa, take a peek through the eye."

"You do it, Teddy."

"Got too many butterflies."

Lisa tiptoed to the vacant eye of the buffalo, and peered through it. What a mass of cabbage heads the audience seemed, all staring intently at the curtain. She couldn't even see Mama. She heard the creak of the curtain as it began to rise and rushed back to her position behind the theater.

"Think of them as cabbage heads, just rows and rows of cabbages," she whispered to the other four children. "That's all they are." Suzanne's hunched shoulders dropped and Teddy even managed a smile. Perhaps this would help them.

The sudden glare of the lights focusing on them from all directions caused them to blink. Then the music began.

"Hurry, hurry, hurry, ladies and gentlemen . . . get your tickets now before it's too late — for the Greatest Show on Earth. The Big Top," shouted the lion tamer, swishing his whip as he crossed the stage.

The acrobats somersaulted across the stage with Mike's dilapidated lions rolling behind. The clown plopped down on the stage while the trapeze artists gestured to the audience. "And now, ladies and genemummms, we present the Bigtop Buskins in a heart-stirring performance of *The Sleeping Beauty,*" Teddy announced from behind the curtain as the ringmaster again cracked his whip.

There had been a sudden lull as the audience realized that

they were seeing a puppet performance. Now as the circus performers bowed and turned to the stage, there were oh's and ah's but no applause. Oh dear, were the people sitting on their hands? Obviously they didn't care for marionettes. Lisa ducked down, reaching for the good fairy. The wicked fairy flew about the stage, her wings flapping violently as Teddy snarled at the stricken king and queen. What a hideous laugh that was! Then it was Lisa's cue to make her pronouncement of the long sleep for all the members of the court, the spell which would finally be broken by the kiss of the brave prince.

By the time the prince had climbed the enchanted hedge and kissed Sleeping Beauty, lying on her lovely canopied bed, Lisa sensed that this was the best performance they had ever given.

"But no one's clapped at all. It's so silent out there." Teddy whispered.

"Maybe everyone's gone home, including your city cousin," Tom replied as Lisa's godmother swooped down to bless the happy bride and groom. At this point they were all far too occupied to converse since they had to manipulate the many dolls of the court as they awoke from their hundred-year sleep. All the members of the cast bowed or curtsied to the audience. The velveteen curtain was finally closed and they all sighed with relief.

"Now they'll all clap," Suzanne gasped. But there was silence. A long painful silence. Mike already had tears in his eyes.

"More, we want more," someone shouted. And suddenly there were great gusts of applause. And stamping and shouting and whistling. The thunder of the response seemed to fill the hall. The five children stood grinning at each other. Then they drew together in a spontaneous embrace.

"I guess they liked us after all," Teddy said as they waited for the big curtain to fall. When it dropped they raced off to the wings. Still more clapping and the curtain creaked upwards again. The five of them stood smiling in the wings.

"Don't be dummies," Mrs. Beddlington said. "Go onstage. They want to see you. That was excellent, just perfect."

She pushed them out onto the stage. Lost without their protective covering, the five of them hesitantly walked toward the center of the stage, arms linked. Eyes downward, they bowed very low. Another burst of applause and they ran off the stage.

Lisa wasn't even aware of the acts that followed them. All that mattered was that the people had liked their puppets, really thought that they were good. When the final performer left the stage many of the participants returned to their seats as the judges headed for the stage. The Steins conferred and decided they'd better wait backstage until it was over. Maybe Mama would go ahead home.

"Come on now, children. Everyone back to their seats. What are you skulking back here for? Shoo. Out with you." Mrs. Beddlington pushed them through the door.

"Do you think we have a chance at a prize?" Mike asked.

"Maybe, maybe, but Marion was so good and did you see the way everyone looked at that violin player?" They searched for Mama and hastened toward her. Mama had tears in her eyes and did not appear to be angry.

"My babies, how wonderful. When did you do it. Why didn't you tell me? I was so proud of all of you." Mama kissed each of them, including Tom, as they settled into their chairs.

"Gee, that was absolutely the greatest," Ben said, and kissed Lisa on her cheek. Blushing, Lisa looked up to see Tom frowning in the distance. Didn't Tom like Ben? The curtain was up again as the judges, the mayor and Mrs. Beddlington walked across the stage to chairs behind a long table.

"It has been so difficult to make a decision today . . . you were all so very good," one of the judges began. In the distance there was a low murmuring, followed by an audible muttering as some commotion at the back of the hall increased in volume.

The judge raised his voice to be heard above the noise coming from the rear. Still the racket persisted. "And so we will start with the number three selection first. To that most skilled dancer, Miss Marion . . ." his voice was drowned out as the disturbance drew closer to them. It was obvious that someone was pushing violently through the crowd. "How dare you elbow me like that?"

"You shoved my wife."

"Please lower your voices, friends," called the mayor.

Lisa gave Suzanne a squeeze as the clapping muffled the competitive sound. "Gee, I'm so happy for Marion. I think she should have been first, she was so . . ."

"Honest with her parents," a foghorn barked in her ear. "Not like some children I know. Pretending they were playing instruments, telling lies. Nothing but falsehoods."

And then the source of the turmoil reached them as Papa, looking deranged, loomed in back of them. His face was an over-ripe tomato as he raged at them.

"Aha, take your time, Papa, don't rush back from the farm. Wanted me to miss it, eh? When did you make those fantastic puppets, when you were supposed to be studying for exams? Doing your chores? Well, answer me, why don't you?" His bald head was covered with beads of perspiration and his hands shook as he spoke.

Mama tried to shush Papa, to make him lower his voice. It was useless. Dimly, in the distant world, Lisa heard the judge talking. "And to that very talented tenor, the singer of 'Danny Boy', the second prize. Come up here, young Mr. Harrigan, and receive your justly deserved award."

There was applause and a few cheers. Someone demanded that Papa sit down and stop blocking the view. Papa reached for Mike's arm and lifted him from his chair.

"Home, right now you will come home. Telling lies to your father, making a fool of me."

"Please, Irving, let them wait until it is over, only for a few more minutes and then you can punish them," Mama pleaded in vain. Even Teddy was too shocked at Papa's unexpected appearance to risk speaking back.

"*Now,* this very instant we go home." Papa pulled them down the aisle with Mama and Ben bringing up the rear. Even Tom seemed to feel that he had to obey Papa's wishes.

It was difficult to break through the audience to reach the rear doors of the hall. Many people were standing up against the walls to have a better view of the judges. People whispered words of praise, clapped them on their shoulders and tried to shake their hands as they marched meekly down the side aisle. Papa was going to make them the laughingstock of the school in addition to punishing them.

"And now for our grand winner," the judge said. "Without a doubt this was the most talented, original act we have seen in some years. This was brilliant theater. There were many fine performances tonight but all the judges concurred on this one. Yes, friends, this one really deserved to win. It had that star quality. So without any further ado I will call upon that brilliant Stein family and their partner Tom to come forward and accept first prize for their magical puppet theater! Congratulations and we'll look forward to seeing more of this family when they tread the boards again. A fine young group of thespians."

They were almost at the door when they halted to hear the judge. Mama and Papa had also stopped. Despite Papa, the five of them threw their arms around each other. Ben was jumping in the air with them. Oh, they had won even if Papa wouldn't let them receive their prize. They had *won* it.

"We made it."

"We won. We did it, we won the prize."

"Irving," Mama's tone was harsh. "Let them get the prize. So maybe they were wrong but you must let them receive their prize."

Papa paused and sucked in his cheeks. "Go," he said

pointing to the stage. "Go up there. We won't insult this town. Get your prize but come back immediately. Then I'll decide what to do with you."

Teddy turned recklessly from his father and dashed toward the stage as if a hive of wasps were after him. "He is a tyrant," Teddy stormed to no one in particular, "but he's not going to break me or tame me." The applause was deafening and Lisa barely heard Teddy as he continued to seethe.

Lisa didn't think she had ever felt so many different sensations at the same time. Tears streamed down her cheeks. It was a strange feeling, since she never cried. Friends hugged them as they pushed their way back through the mob to the stage. Teddy was way ahead of them now and had stopped shaking his head in a violent manner. Tom cleared a space for her and Mike to slip through while Suzanne skipped behind them.

As they climbed the steps to the stage the tears continued to dribble down her cheeks. They shook hands with the officials and received a broad grin from Mrs. Beddlington. The stamping from the crowd made it impossible to think clearly. Lisa wondered briefly if her tears came from delight at having won the grand award or from shame at having deceived Papa.

Arby's Pinocchio
Charles Noble

Pinocchio carved was a playful puppet;
until he raised real issues and tissues
he had strings attached

and this is an unreal game
you think I play
glorious and notorious things I say
childish extremes but wild screams
these running rules my tools for escape

but my doll has come alive,
moving and we're overlapping,
singing, having shot the gap
we've sparked a life, displacing
my early carving knife,
and feeding spoon,
nourishing now,
and I play in the sun
or under the moon
no longer make-believing

Pinocchio living, lied, grew a large nose
and please, when mine grows,
notice, just measure,
the size, amazing, larger-than-life!

Vacations

Summer Vacation, or
Nothing Ever Happens Around Here

Agnes Copithorne

Dear Mom,

There's nothing much to write about. But Gramma says I have to send you a few lines even if it's only Hello, how are you, goodby.

Things are pretty quiet around here. Gramma has Arthrytis in her knees. She moves around real slow. Grampa tripped over a coil of barb wire, fell down and hurt his shoulder. He walks around cranky with one arm hanging down lower than the other but he won't go to a doctor. Gramma says if one of the cows got hurt he'd send for the vet right quick. But he figures humans can doctor themselves.

The old woman who lives alone in the shack across the road had to go to Edmonton to look after her father. He is 99 years old and failing fast. She has (or had) five brown Leghorn hens and a cat and didn't know what to do with them. Gramma said, "Bring 'em over here, I'll look after them." So the old woman whose name is Mrs. Gootch, stuffed the Leghorns in a gunny sack, carried them over here and turned them loose in the henhouse.

Well now, you'd 'a thought they'd been dropped into a den of chicken thieves. Taking one horrified look at Gramma's big white Wyandottes, they flew to the very top of the roost squawking their heads off. There they sat huddled together, a pretty scared looking bunch of chickens.

Brown Leghorns are supposed to lay brown eggs. I waited and waited for a brown egg. I even whacked away at those dumb hens with a broom handle trying to get them down off the perch and into a nest. But they just screeched like I was trying to kill them, dug their claws into the pole and hung on.

There they sat for five days. On the morning of the sixth, they were all laying on the floor under the roost stone dead. Gramma looked them over and said there wasn't a pick on their bones. They had starved themselves to death. Which goes to show how stupid hens are. I still don't know what a brown egg tastes like and I guess I never will now.

Gramma doesn't know what she's going to say to Mrs. Gootch when she comes home and finds all her hens dead.

There are a lot of pigeons around. They fly in and out of the hayloft. They've got nests up there on the rafters. And do you know what? You'd never guess in a million years so I may as well tell you; when the baby pigeons are hatched and a few weeks old, the mother pigeon lays a few more eggs and makes the young ones hatch them out. Grampa says a thing like that could go on forever until there'd be nothing but pigeons left in the world. He's going to invite the neighbors over for a shootout and we'll have pigeon pie. Gramma said, "Who's going to pluck 'em? Not me." I didn't offer to help neither.

Be sure Bunty looks after the Gerbils real good.

Love from Arnold

P.S. If you are wondering how I manage to spell some of these words and I know you are, I've got a dictionary right at my elbow. Gramma told me to.

Dear Mom,

There's nothing much to write about, but when Gramma says get busy and write I don't argue.

A stray dog, black and white and kind of skinny, stopped in here one day, decided he liked us and wouldn't go away. Grampa gave me Heck for feeding him; said it would only encourage him to stay and we needed another dog around here like we needed a hailstorm. "Besides," he said, "this mutt looks like a stupid you-know-what and will probably give our Buster wandering notions."

But I sneaked him table scraps and we got to be real good friends. I named him Mutt because it kind of suited him. He took a great fancy to Sam too. Sam is the hired man. Twice a day when Sam mixed up a bucket of oat chop and skim milk for the hogs, Mutt ate right along with the pigs and pretty soon he was a good looking dog with a nice shiny coat.

Sam had a runaway in the hayfield the other day. It was terribly windy. The wind blows all the time here but this day it was BAD bad. He had hooked up Spook and Boxer to the mower. Spook was a new horse Grampa bought at an auction sale. He shies a lot. Gramma didn't think much of him when she saw him. "He's got a mean eye," she said. "And Spook's a good name for him."

Anyway, as I've already told you, it was windy. A big flap of tar paper came sailing through the air from nowhere. It hit Spook mid-center and drove him plum wild. Dragging Boxer along with him, Sam told me afterwards, they galloped around and around the hayfield like there was fire under their tails. And there wasn't a thing he could do to stop them. And he was having a hard time staying aboard the way the mower was bouncing over rocks and badger holes. Mutt wasn't any help either, tearing alongside barking his fool head off.

Finally a wheel fell off and that's when Sam and the mower parted company. The horses were headed straight for a barbwire fence, so he flung the lines in the air and threw himself off backwards.

And that's where he proved himself a whole lot smarter than Mutt, who, dumb dog, got crazy with excitement and ran in front of the cutting bar and do you know what? He got his hind leg sliced off. Howling and yelping he streaked across the field to home on his three legs. The cut-off one dangling by a piece of skin.

Sam was kind of shook up. But he finally got to his feet and walked over to where the nags were standing, all tangled up in barb wire. Spook snorted and pawed, getting his legs all cut up and bleeding like everything. But Boxer had more sense. He waited quietly until Sam got there, straightened them out and led them home.

Gramps sent for Mr. Crooks, the vet. He came right away and sewed up Spook's legs. Now he's limping around the pasture not much good for anything; Spook I mean.

I asked the vet to have a look at Mutt, who was hiding under the back porch whining and moaning something awful. Mr. Crooks snipped off the piece of skin, poured disinfectant on the stump and bandaged it up tight.

Grampa said, "Shoot him, he'll be no more good. He never was any good." I was about ready to cry. Mr. Crooks patted me on the head and said, "He'll be okay, Kid. He'll heal up real fast." And that was the truth. He did heal up fast and he gets around on three legs good as he ever did on four.

Love from Arnold

P.S. If Bunty has the Chicken Pox tell her to stay away from the Gerbils. They might catch 'em. Tell her Chicken Pox ain't so bad. All she has to do is sit up in bed and scratch.

Dear Mom,

Remember I told you about Mrs. Gootch's cat? When she first came here Floss made herself right at home. She was a big cat, almost as wide as she was long. And spoiled, you can't imagine. All she did was get under our feet, eat, sleep and snitch things off the table when nobody was looking. She was fussy about her meals, fussy about where she slept. Mostly she liked to eat ham and the white meat of a chicken. And if Gramma wanted to sit down and have a rest (she liked to drive back and forth in the old rocker beside the kitchen stove), there was the cat filling up the whole seat and Gramma has to yank the cushion from underneath her to make her move.

Anyway, one day she disappeared. I scouted around inside and out and down the cellar; no cat. Gramma was sure worried. After what happened to the Leghorns, she said it would be the last straw if Floss turned up dead or missing. Mrs. Gootch would never speak to her again.

Gramma always makes tea on the dot of four every afternoon. In case of company dropping in, she likes to put on a clean white apern. This particular afternoon she asked me to run upstairs and fetch her a fresh apern from her bureau drawer. Which I did and guess what. No, you'd never guess in a million years so I may as well tell you. The middle drawer of the bureau was half open and there, on top of Gramma's aperns was Floss and six new-born kittens.

She looked up at me with her round yellow eyes and said, "Miaow." And I'd bet my last dollar (if I had such a thing) that she was smiling.

I yelled for Gramma, she came fast as she could with her Arthritis. I showed her what was in the drawer. "Blast that dern cat," she said, throwing up her hands. "I knowed she had made a bed somewhere but never imagined it would be in my bureau drawer." Gathering up the kittens in her apern (the old dirty one she was wearing) and paying no mind to Floss's fussing, she carried them downstairs.

"Get me Gramp's old wooly sweater hanging in the woodshed," she said to me, which I did. "Now fetch me that round vegetable basket from the celler," she ordered. And I did. We lined the basket with the sweater and Gramma tumbled the kittens into it. Floss jumped in after them and started washing them to beat the band. When they were shining clean she stretched out. How they did it I don't know because they were stone blind, but each one found a little fawcet and began nursing.

After supper Gramma and I went out to the garden to pour water on the cabbages to make them grow, and pull a few weeds. It was almost dark when we came in and guess what; Floss and the kittens were gone. Vanished. Vamoosed.

I hustled upstairs to see were they back in the drawer but Gramma had closed it and all the other drawers, tight. I looked upstairs, downstairs and in the cellar. No luck. Grampa, who was reading a newspaper at the kitchen table looked up over his glasses and said, "Quit worrying. Floss has got her kittens hid where no one will monkey with them again."

The next day I climbed up into the hayloft. I wanted to see how the young pigeons were making out with their hatching job. I heard tiny little mewing noises coming out from a pile of hay. I knew right away it was the kittens. Poking around, I found them. Just like Grampa said, Floss had carried them all to the haymow. There she had made a nest for them. They were cozy as could be, with Floss curled up around them. I thought she looked at me kind of pleading. So I took myself away from there very quietly.

We were all happy about finding them. Even if Mrs. Gootch is short five hens, she now has seven cats.

Love from Arnold

P.S. How are Jack, Pete and Sandy making out at camp? Being here on the farm with Gramma and Grampa sure beats going to camp. I can eat when I want to, and if I don't wash my feet every night the world won't come to an end.

Dear Mom,

Thanks for the birthday present. The baseball and mitt will sure come in handy. Some kids from the next farm came over last night. We played Scrub and Anti-i-over until dark. It was quite a change from playing field hockey with brooms and road apples.

There's nothing new around here, except I had my first run-in with a setting hen.

Gramma had been complaining about being short of eggs. She said to me, "Seeing you've got nothing else to do, Boy, scout around the farm and find out where the hens are hiding their nests. Likely they're all set to raise another batch of chicks." Gramma didn't want baby chicks hatched out this time of year. She wanted eggs to trade for groceries at the store.

Clucking hens are pretty dangerous. When you hear a hen going cluck, cluck with her feathers all ruffled up, it's a sure sign she's got a nest of eggs hid away and is on the job producin' more chicks. At this stage she gets real cranky if anybody comes near. I learned that much pretty quick.

First off she finds a good hiding place. Then she scratches out a nest and lays twelve eggs or maybe fourteen. Which isn't a good idea. Too many eggs in a nest means some are apt to get broke, or chilled. If an egg gets chilled, she may as well kick it out of the nest. Don't ask me why. Then this hen sits on the eggs day and night for three weeks to hatch out the chicks. Sneaking out once in a while to get a drink and something to eat.

I prowled around granaries and strawstacks with no luck. Behind the barn there's an old binder half buried in shoulder high grass and thistles. I figured this might be a good bet. I armed myself with a willow dropper (long stick) and whacked my way through the forest of weeds pretending I was an explorer beating my way through the jungles of Africa with a machete.

I scrunched down to look under the binder. POW! Before I had time to throw up my arms to protect myself, I was hit by a bomb of feathers and claws. I was so scared I threw away the stick and ran. My attacker, neck stretched out and beak wide open, right at my heels.

I made it safe to Gramma's kitchen door where I fell into a chair shaking like a leaf. When I told her what happened she plumped herself into the rocker and laughed. She laughed and laughed, driving that old rocker a mile a minute, tears rolling down her cheeks. I didn't see anything funny about it.

After some lemonade and cookies Gramma took my hand and we went back to the binder. I picked up the stick and showed where the big white bombshell was hid. She reached in and grabbed the hen by the neck, dragging her out flapping and squawking. Then Gramma switched her grip to the legs and carried the hen, her head trailing on the ground, to the horse trough. You shoulda heard that chicken fuss. But I wasn't a bit sorry for her.

At the trough Gramma dunked her underwater three times. I thought she was trying to drown her. But I learned later that this is an old time way to cool off a broody hen. It's a sort of brain-washing to make her forget about hatching chicks. And get back to the business of laying eggs.

But the dunking doesn't always work. If not, she's captured again and shoved under an upside-down apple box with a rock on top. Here she stays until she comes to her senses — usually a week or so. Then we let her out and after a while she's ready to go back to what she's supposed to do.

It will soon be time to go home. I don't suppose the school has burned down or anything since I left. School isn't all that bad, but I'll miss Mutt, my three-legged dog. And Floss with all her kitties. But I won't miss the chickens. If I ever get to be a farmer, I won't have a hen on the place.

Love, Arnold

Melvin Arbuckle's First Course in Shock Therapy

W. O. Mitchell

Last year like thousands of other former Khartoumians, I returned to Khartoum, Saskatchewan, to help her celebrate her Diamond Jubilee year. In the Elks' Bar, on the actual anniversary date, September 26, the Chamber of Commerce held a birthday get-together, and it was here that Roddy Montgomery, Khartoum's mayor, introduced me to a man whose face had elusive familiarity.

"One of Khartoum's most famous native sons," Roddy said with an anticipatory smile. "Psychiatrist on the West Coast. Portland."

I shook hands; I knew that I should remember him from the litmus years of my prairie childhood. As soon as he spoke I remembered: Miss Coldtart first, then *Pippa Passes* — then Melvin Arbuckle.

I was tolled back forty years: Melvin Arbuckle, only son of Khartoum's electrician, the boy who had successfully frustrated Miss Coldtart through all our Grade Four reading classes. Then, and today it seemed, he was unable to say a declarative sentence; he couldn't manage an exclamatory or imperative one either. A gentle-spoken and utterly stubborn woman with cream skin and dyed hair, Miss Coldtart called upon Melvin to read aloud every day of that school year, hoping against hope that one of his sentences might not turn up at the end like the sandal toes of an *Arabian Nights* sultan. The very last day of Grade Four she had him read *Pippa Passes* line for line after her. He did — interrogatively down to the last "God's in his Heaven? — All's right with the world?"

And forty years later it seemed quite fitting to me that Melvin was a psychiatrist, especially when I recalled Melvin's grandfather who lived with the Arbuckles, a long ropey octogenarian with buttermilk eyes, the sad and equine face of William S. Hart. I liked Melvin's grandfather. He claimed that he had been imprisoned by Louis Riel in Fort Garry when the Red River Rebellion started, that he was a close friend of Scott whom Riel executed in 1870. He said that he was the first man to enter Batoche after it fell, that he'd sat on the jury that condemned Riel to hang in '85. By arithmetic he could have been and done these things, but Melvin said his grandfather was an historical liar.

Melvin's grandfather had another distinction: saliva trouble. He would gather it, shake it back and forth from cheek to cheek, the way you might rattle dice in your hand before making a pass — then spit. He did this every twenty seconds. Also he wandered a great deal, wearing a pyramid peaked hat of RCMP or Boy Scout issue, the thongs hanging down either cheek, a lumpy knapsack high between his shoulder blades, a peeled and varnished willow root cane in his hand. Since the Arbuckles' house stood an eighth of a mile apart from the eastern edge of Khartoum, it was remarkable that the old man never got lost on the empty prairie flung round three sides. Years of wilderness travel must have drawn him naturally towards habitation; Melvin's after-fours were ruined with the mortification of having to knock on front doors in our end of town, asking people if they'd seen anything of his lost grandfather. All his Saturdays were unforgivably spoiled too, for on these days Melvin's mother went down to the store to help his father, and Melvin had to stay home to see that his grandfather didn't get lost.

No one was ever able to get behind Melvin's grandfather; he sat always in a corner with two walls at his back; this was so in the house or in the Soo Beer Parlor. Melvin's mother had to cut her father's hair, for he refused to sit in Leon's barber chair out in the unprotected centre of the shop. If he met someone on the street and stopped to talk, he would circle uneasily until he had a building wall or a hedge or a fence at his back; sometimes he would have to settle for a tree. He had a very sensible reason for this; they were coming to get him one day, he said. It was never quite clear who was coming to get him one day, but I suspected revengeful friends of the halfbreed renegade, Dumont. He may have been an historical liar as Melvin said, but there was no doubting that he was afraid — afraid for his life.

I sincerely believed that someone was after him; nobody could have spent as much time as he did in the Arbuckle privy if somebody weren't after him. From mid-April when the sun had got high and strong to harvest he spent more time out there with four walls closing safe around him than he did in the house. I can hardly recall a visit to Melvin's place that there wasn't blue smoke threading from the diamond cutout in the back-house door. Melvin's grandfather smoked natural leaf Quebec tobacco that scratched with the pepper bitterness of burning willow root. He had the wildest smell of any man I had ever known, compounded of wine and iron tonic, beer, natural leaf, wood smoke, buckskin and horses. I didn't mind it at all.

He was a braggarty sort of old man, his words hurrying out after each other as though he were afraid that if he stopped he wouldn't be permitted to start up again and also as though he knew that no one was paying attention to what he was saying anyway, so that he might just as well settle for getting it said as quickly as possible. Even Miss Coldtart would have found many of his expressions colorful: "she couldn't cook guts for a bear"; "spinnin' in the wind like the button on a back-house door"; "so stubborn she was to drown'd you'd find her body upstream"; "when he was borned they set him on the porch to see if he barked or cried". Even though you felt he was about to embarrass you by spitting or lying, I found Melvin's grandfather interesting.

Yet I was glad that he was Melvin's grandfather and not mine. Even though he kept dragging his grandfather into conversation, Melvin was ashamed of him. He was always reminding us of his grandfather, not because he wanted to talk about him but just as though he were tossing the old man at our feet for a dare. I can't remember any of us taking him up on it. Perhaps now that he is an analyst out on the West Coast, he has decided what compelled him to remind us continually of the grandfather he was ashamed of.

The summer that I have in mind was the year that Peanuts moved to Khartoum from Estevan, where his father was an engineer for a coal strip-mining company. Some sort of cousin of the Sweeneys, Peanuts had migrated to Canada from England just a year before. He'd only had three months in Khartoum to pick up the nickname, Peanuts. He was not a Peanuts sort of boy, quite blocky, very full red cheeks, hemp fair hair and flax blue eyes. At ten years of age, I suppose John Bull must have looked a great deal like Peanuts. His given name was actually Geoffrey.

He was quite practical, fertile for all kinds of reasons that a project could not work; this unwillingness to suspend disbelief tore illusion and spoiled pretend games. He had no sense of humor at all, for he seldom laughed at anything Fat said; English into the bargain, he should have been the most unpopular boy in Khartoum. However, he had piano-wire nerves which made up for his shortcomings. When we held our circus that July, he slipped snake after snake down the throat of his blouse, squirmed them past his belt and extricated them one by one from the legs of his stovepipe British wool pants. They were only garter snakes, but a week later to settle a horticultural argument in Ashford's Grove, he ate a toadstool raw. Just because he didn't die was not proof that he was right and that we were wrong, for immediately after he pulled up and ate two bouquets of wild horse-radish with instantaneous emetic effect.

Now that I think back to a late August day that year, I can

see that Peanuts has to share with Melvin's grandfather the credit or the responsibility for Melvin's being today a leading West Coast psychiatrist. It was a day that promised no excitement. The Khartoum Fair was past; Johnny J. Jones' circus had come and gone a month before, posters already nostalgic and wind-tattered on shed and fence and barn walls. We couldn't duck or bottom it in the little Souris River, for it was filled with rusty bloodsuckers and violet-colored algae that caused prairie itch. The bounty was off gopher tails for the rest of the year so there was no point in hunting them.

There was simply nothing to do but sprawl in the adequate shade of McGoogan's hedge, eat clover heads and caragana flowers. With bored languor we looked out over Sixth Street lifting and drifting in the shimmering heat. Without interest we saw the town wagon roll by, darkening the talcum-fine dust with spray; moments later the street was thirsty again, smoking under the desultory August wind.

Fin pulled out the thick glass from a flashlight, focused it to a glowing bead on his pant leg. A thin streamer of smoke was born and we idly watched a fusing spark eat through the cloth until its ant sting bit Fin's knee. He put the glass back into his pocket and said let's go down to the new creamery and chew tar. Someone said let's go look for beer bottles and lead instead; someone else said how about fooling around in the loft of Fat's uncle's livery stable; someone else said the hell with it.

About that time we all got to our feet, for an ice dray came down the street, piled high with frozen geometry. When the leather-chapped driver had chipped and hoisted a cake of ice over his shoulder and left for delivery, we went to the back of the dray. We knew we were welcome to the chips on the floor, and as we always did we popped into our mouths chunks too big for them. The trick was to suck in warm air around the ice until you could stand it no longer, then lower your head, eject and catch.

Someone said let's go over and see Melvin stuck with his

grandfather; inhibited by ice and the cool drool of it, no one agreed or disagreed. We wandered up Sixth Street, past the McKinnon girls and Noreen Robins darting in and out of a skipping rope, chanting: "Charlie Chaplin — went to — France — teach the — ladies — how to — dance . . . " At the corner of Bison and Sixth we turned east and in two blocks reached the prairie. I think it was the tar-papered and deserted shack between the town's edge and Arbuckles' house that gave us the idea of building a hut. By the time we had reached Melvin's, we had decided it might be more fun to dig a cave which would be lovely and cool.

Melvin was quite agreeable to our building the cave in his back yard; there were plenty of boards for covering it over; if we all pitched in and started right away, we might even have it finished before his grandfather had wakened from his nap. Shovel and spade and fork plunged easily through the eighteen inches of top soil; but the clay subsoil in this dry year was heart and back breaking. Rock-hard, it loosened under pick and bar in reluctant sugar lumps. Stinging with sweat, our shoulder sockets aching, we rested often, reclining at the lip of our shallow excavation. We idly wished: "If a fellow only had a fresno and team, he could really scoop her out . . . "

"If a fellow could soak her good . . . run her full of water — soften her up — easy digging then."

"If a fellow could only blow her out . . . "

"How?"

"Search me."

"Stumping powder — dynamite . . . "

"Oh," Peanuts said, "yes — dynamite."

"Whumph and she'd blow our cave for us," Fin said.

"She sure would." Fat said.

Melvin said, "Only place I know where they got dynamite — CPR sheds."

"I have dynamite," Peanuts said. "I can get dynamite."

We looked at each other; we looked at Peanuts. Knowing

Peanuts, I felt a little sick; Fat and Fin and Melvin didn't look so happy either. We had never even seen a stick of dynamite; it simply did not belong in our world. It had been quite imaginary dynamite that we had been tossing about in conversation.

Fat said, "We can't go swiping dynamite."

Fin said, "We don't know a thing about handling dynamite."

"I do," Peanuts said.

"Isn't our yard," Fin said. "We can't set off dynamite in Mel's yard." Peanuts got up purposefully. "Can we, Mel?"

"The cave's a hundred yards from the house," Peanuts said. "Nothing dangerously near it at all." He turned to Melvin. "Are you frightened?"

"Well — no," Melvin said.

"My father has a whole case of sixty percent," Peanuts said. "From the mine. While I get it you have them do the hole."

"What hole?" Melvin said.

"For the dynamite — with the bar — straight down about four feet, I should say."

"The whole case!" Fin said.

"Dead centre, the hole," Peanuts said and started for his house.

"He bringing back the whole case?" Fin said.

Fat got up. "I guess I better be getting on my way . . . " His voice fainted as he looked down at us and we looked up at him. "I guess I better — we better — start punching — down that hole," he finished up. "Like Peanuts said." It was not what Fat had started out to say at all.

Peanuts brought back only three sticks of dynamite, and until his return the hole went down rather slowly. He tossed the sticks on the ground by the woodpile and took over authority. He did twice his share of digging the dynamite hole; from time to time he estimated how much further we had to go down. When it seemed to suit him he dropped two of the sticks down, one on top of the other. There was no tenderness in the way he handled that dynamite, inserted the fuse end into the copper tube detonator, crimped it with his teeth, used a spike to work a hole into the third stick to receive the cap and fuse. He certainly knew how to handle dynamite. We watched him shove loose clay soil in around the sticks, tamp it firm with the bar. With his jackknife he split the free end of the fuse protruding from the ground. He took a match from his pocket.

"Hold on a minute," Melvin said. "where do we — what do we — how long do we . . . "

"Once it's going there'll be three minutes," Peanuts said. "Plenty of time to take cover."

"What cover?" Fat said.

"Round the corner of the house," Peanuts said. "You may go there now if you wish. I'll come when the fuse is started. They're hard to start — it will take several matches."

We stayed. The fuse took life at the third match. Fat and Fin and Melvin and I ran a hundred yards to the house. We looked around the corner to Peanuts coming towards us. He did it by strolling. I had begun to count to myself so that I could have a rough notion of when the fuse was near the end of its three minutes. I had reached fifty-nine when I heard the Arbuckle screen slap the stillness.

Melvin said, "He's headed for the back house!"

Fat said, "He's got his knapsack and his hat and his cane on — maybe he's just going out to get lost."

Melvin started round the corner of the house but Fin grabbed him. "Let him keep goin', Mel! Let him keep goin' so's he'll get in the clear!"

"I'll get him," Peanuts said.

"He's my grandfather!" Melvin said.

Fin said, "There ain't even a minute left!" I had no way of telling for I'd stopped counting.

The site of our proposed cave and, therefore, of the dynamite with its burning fuse, was halfway between the back of the Arbuckle house and the privy. Melvin's grandfather stopped by the woodpile. He shook his head and spat. Peanuts launched himself around the corner of the house, belly to the ground towards the old man. Melvin's grandfather must have thought the running footsteps behind him were those of either Louis Riel or Gabriel Dumont, for without looking back he covered the open ground to the privy in ten seconds, jumped inside and slammed the door. Right in stride, Peanuts pounded past and out to the prairie beyond. There he was still running with his head back, chin out, arms pumping, knees high, when the dynamite let go.

The very first effect was not of sound at all. Initially the Arbuckle yard was taken by one giant and subterranean hiccough, an earth fountain spouted; four cords of wood took flight; the privy leaped straight up almost to six feet; two clothes line posts javelined into the air, their wires still stretched between them in an incredible aerial cat's cradle. Not until *then* did the lambasting explosion seem to come. For several elastic seconds all the air-borne things hung indecisively between the thrust of dynamite and the pull of gravity. Gravity won.

At the back of the house we looked at each other wildly; we swallowed to unbung our ears, heard the Japanese chiming of glass shards dropping from the Arbuckle windows, the thud of wood chunks returning to earth. I saw Melvin lick with the tip of his tongue at twin blood yarns coming down from his nostrils. No one said anything; we simply moved as a confused body in the direction of the privy. We skirted the great shallow saucer the dynamite had blown, and I remember thinking they would never fill it in; the dirt was gone forever. At the very center it was perhaps ten feet deep; it would have taken all the lumber from a grain elevator to roof it over for a cave.

"Grampa — Grampa — " Melvin was calling — "Please, Grampa. Please, Grampa."

"We'll have to tip it up," Fin said, "so's we can open the door."

"You're not supposed to move injured people," Fat said.

Melvin squatted down and put his face to the hole and his frightened voice sounded cistern hollow. "Grampa!" Then he really yelled as the varnished willow cane caught him across the bridge of the nose. He straightened up and said, "He's still alive. Give me a hand."

It took all of us to upright the privy and Melvin's grandfather. He swung at us a couple of times when we opened the door, then he let us help him to the house and into his own room off the kitchen. Seated there on a Winnipeg couch, he stared straight ahead of himself as Melvin removed the Boy Scout hat, slipped off the packsack. With an arm around the old man's shoulders, Melvin eased him down on the pillow, then motioned us out of the room. Before we got to the door the old man spoke.

"Melvin."

"Yes, Grampa?"

"Sure they're all cleared out now?"

"Yes, Grampa."

He released a long sigh. "Get word to General Middleton."

"For help, Grampa?"

"Not help." The old man shook his head. "Sharply engaged enemy. Routed the barstards!"

We were all whipped that evening, and the balance of our merciful catharsis was earned over a month's quarantine, each in his own yard. When his month's isolation was up, Melvin gained a freedom he'd never known before: he didn't have to knock on another door for his grandfather never wandered again. He sat at the Arbuckle living room window for the next three years, then died.

"One of Khartoum's most famous native sons," Roddy Montgomery had called him at the Chamber of Commerce birthday party in the Elks' Bar; "Dr. Melvin Arbuckle, Portland psychiatrist and mental health trail blazer." In shock therapy — of course.

Holiday Handicapping

Mervyn J. Huston

It is quite a problem to know how to compete with your friends who have been to some glamorous place on their holidays and want to talk about it. Particularly if you spent yours at Dried Meat Lake with the kids, outdoor plumbing, and Aunt Sarah who is deaf and doesn't believe in liquor. But don't despair. Get in there and fight. You can hold them at bay or at the very least you can sabotage their pleasure in the telling.

One way is of course to shout them down with local trivia. This is not very sporting, but is used effectively by housewives whose voices have been honed by years of ennui. A variation of this device, but one still requiring a pungent voice is the "Oh that reminds me" gimmick. There doesn't need to be any relationship between the two events. Supposing they are telling about a posh night club just out of San Francisco and are making it sound distressingly fascinating, you interrupt with "oh that reminds me," and then proceed to tell about all the jolly excitement at the lake when the neighbour's cow fell down your well.

If you have ever been to the place they visited, even if it was fifteen years ago, you are in a strong position. Anything they saw or did you can compare unfavorably with your own experience. You can gradually take over and monopolize the conversation with an account of your own trip. If you have never been there, then use someone else's account. You are almost sure to know someone who has been there and insisted on talking about it. You may have suffered at the time but you can put this to good use now by recounting the reactions and impressions of Edna and Buster Ergot who have *lots* of money and didn't have to *skimp* and saw and did just everything. (Strong innuendo here.) So much the better of course if good old Edna and Buster thought the place was terrible. In this case you can call into doubt your friend's good sense, good taste and sanity.

If you don't know anyone who has been there you can fall back on a book. Indeed, if you know in advance where your friends have been it is a good idea to get a book and bone up on the place. In this way you can be the authority and can question them closely. You will be sure to find some things they don't know, like the average rainfall or the percentage of the populace who have sewing machines or the illegitimacy rate, and you can imply quite clearly that they certainly didn't get much out of their trip.

A useful device is to find some place they haven't visited or something they haven't done, and then pour it on. After I came back from New York one time and had seen four musicals and three plays, a friend of mine wormed out of me the admission that I hadn't seen *Chugalug*, the new musical comedy by Tennessee Fishrot based on the story of Jack the Ripper, which is hilarious. He made me feel that my trip was a complete failure and I might just as well have stayed home. I found myself apologizing for my stupidity and wallowing in hopeless explanations. I spent the rest of the evening in eclipse and I must confess in a bit of a sulk.

Supposing your friends the Fleeps have just come back from Hawaii, then the conversation can go something like this:

You — There are so many interesting and fascinating spots to go to, aren't there? You'll have to tell us just all about it. I suppose you were at John the Breach Clouter's?
Horace Fleep — Oh, of course. We thought . . .
You — The Open Mu Mu?
Mildred Fleep — Yes, yes. It was just . . .
You — The Pregnant Mermaid?
Mildred Fleep — Yes. We went there on the Friday night and . . .
You — Prince Mahi Mahi's?

Mildred Fleep — Prince Mahi Mahi's? Nnno . . . I don't think so. However, we did get to . . .

You — You didn't get to Prince Mahi Mahi's? Oh, what a shame!!

This is what you have been looking for. Some place they haven't been. If you get desperate, there doesn't even have to be such a place . . . you can just make it up. However, this may backfire. Experienced travellers may not admit a thing. I have heard friends describe in considerable detail and great enthusiasm the wonderful time they had in non-existent places I just made up. This is frightfully dishonest of them and just makes you wonder about some people's ethics — doesn't it?

But to continue:

You — Prince Mahi Mahi is a real Polynesian prince and his place is one of the very few spots where you can still see authentic native customs and foods. He . . .

Mildred Fleep (loudly) — Another place we . . .

You — These other places are just tourist traps really. Not authentic at all. All the tourists go to them, of course. But you really have to be in the know to find Prince Mahi Mahi's. It's very exclusive and you have to have an entrée, etc. etc.

You are on to a good thing with this tourist emphasis. All tourists hate to be called tourists for some obscure reason. The other people on the trip were tourists but they were travellers or visitors or something . . . but not tourists. Also all tourists hate to feel that they went only to places where tourists go. You can rub it in by saying, "Of course you went to Koko Head, all the tourists do." They will writhe and confess with great reluctance that they did.

A related device is to emphasize commercialism. "Waikiki is so commercialized now. Not like it was in the old days. I understand it's just like Coney Island. But take Dried Meat Lake . . . it isn't commercialized at all." Actually, everything throughout the world that is worth seeing has an admission gate and some character beside it with his palm out. But you can ignore this and blast away at vulgar commerce and your friend's naivete.

If by any chance they did get off the beaten path and start yammering about authentic local color you will have to shift ground. The thing to do here is to congratulate them on their great courage and rashness in venturing into the septic hinterland. Talk delicately about sewage disposal, yaws, beri beri, leprosy and chiggers and draw away slightly from them. When they enthuse about unsullied scenery and quaint local customs, enquire about creepy things in the salad and did they check the mattresses carefully. By the end of the evening you will have them surreptitiously taking their pulses and furtively scratching . . . in fact, everyone will be doing the latter. This indicates you have been a success and they haven't.

Here are some other simple but effective procedures I have heard used. Find fault with the time of year they went, "Venice is so hot and smelly in June, I don't know how you stood it." Enquire why they didn't go some place else instead, "If I was going to spend all that money I certainly wouldn't go to Rio, I'd go to Stockholm." If they did something unusual, be sniffy, "I suppose it's all right if you like that sort of thing" — but if they did the usual make it mundane, "Just everyone is going to Acapulco now, aren't they? It's the obvious thing to do." (This word "obvious" is real murder . . . use it a lot.) Be critical of the means of transportation, "It's too bad you went by air, you don't really see the country that way do you?" or "Why on earth did you drive, it takes ages to get anywhere. Of course, it's cheaper, isn't it?" Then there's the matter of children. "Oh, you took the kids with you. My aren't you brave and dutiful! But you can't have much fun with children along can you? They always want to go to the bathroom or the zoo or something." Or contrariwise, "You didn't take the children? I always think holidays should be family affairs. I always say

families should do things together. That's what I always say."
You can also do some switch hitting on entertainers. "I'm
surprised you say you enjoyed Bing Johnson at Vegas. I never
cared much for him on television. We always turn him off.
Anyway, why go all the way to Vegas to see someone you can
see on TV at home?" or contrariwise, "No, I never heard of
Bing Johnson. I guess if he amounted to much he'd be on
television."

There is no simple way to deal with friends who are
equipped with movies or slides of their trip. This calls for heroic
measures. You can stick a hair pin in the nearest socket and
blow the fuses or wait until the lights are out, hit your wife on
the head with a beer bottle and call an ambulance, making
vague and worried comments about Beatrice not feeling well
lately. But get that ambulance there in a hurry.

Christmas

A Moment's Silence
Tom Gee

Tumbling its flotsam of shoppers,
the tide of chilly evening air sweeps me
through doors, past counters,
into cloying warmth and humidity.

This final hour of frantic Christmas buying
breaks
like a wave against me
and I am conscious of the noise:
the incessant jingling of Sally-Ann bells,
the wheezing of pneumatic doorstops,
the susurrant cacophony of shoppers blend in a harmony
punctuated by jangling cash registers.

Ringing call-bells summon one
harried manageress to authorize cheques.
Dog-eared streamers and tired cardboard Santas
twist slowly beside signs proclaiming the season
and fifteen-minute specials.

Thank God I've only a small purchase
quickly made. I hurry,
armed in egoism, down the aisles of produce.

Queued for the checkout
behind an Indian whose odor combines woodsmoked clothing
and urine-tanned mukluks,
I inspect the contents of her shopping cart:
coarse cheap jeans faded blue
for the kids,
heavy work socks for the old man,
a large net bag of candies wrapped in multi-colored foil,
Copenhagen for Grandma,
red corduroy from the remnants counter. . . .

She is tiny even for an Indian woman.
Her head is wrapped in a frayed woolen shawl
and her dumpy body bulges a worn, spotted overlong coat.
Her mukluks are encased in rubber overshoes
tied with binder twine.
As she lifts the contents of her cart
onto the counter, she smiles ingratiatingly
around a mouthful of bad teeth.

I am startled from my revery
by the harsh, over-loud voice of the checkout girl.

Can you pay for all that, she spat.

The mumbled, yes I have money,
is lost on other customers who look up,
hostility shining bright in their eyes.

Are you sure you can pay?
Do you have money in your purse?
pursues the clerk in an even louder voice
as she reaches threateningly toward the squaw's handbag.

We stand now in a pool of silence
which ripples further and further out into the store.
When the squaw's whispered reply comes
it is loud in the silence. I have a clothing voucher
for twenty-five dollars, she says,

and she reaches into her purse and extends the chit
towards the sales girl.

Snatching the slip of paper,
the clerk raps viciously on the call-bell.

Its strident ring comes as a signal . . . ,
and sound surges back like tide on a barren shore
obliterating from all time and consciousness
that moment of silence.

The manageress comes;
the chit is authorized;
my own purchases rung up and paid for.
My gaze sweeps past the sign hanging over the exit,
idly turning in the fetid air
as I shoulder through the door.
Peace on earth, good will to men, it reads.
And the voices of unseen carolers float to me
on the brisk evening air . . . ,

and every heart prepare him room. . . .

Hark, the Herald Angels . . . Sing?
Max Braithwaite

Although not specifically spelled out in the course of studies,
in the prairie rural school of the dirty thirties the Christmas
concert was far and away the most important event of the year.
It involved everyone in the district, from the oldest grandmother to babes in arms.

But most of all it involved the teacher. In fact, to a large
extent he was judged by his ability to put on a good concert.
He might let the children run over him, neglect their reading,
get muddled in math, make a bad call against the local team
while umpiring ladies' softball, or even fail to court the

chairman's daughter, and get away with it. But let him fail to stage "the best concert we've had yet," and he was dead.

It was in my next school after Willowgreen that I staged my most memorable concert. Memorable? Chaotic is a better word. In fact, it is the only word. The memory of it lies in my mind like a rock in a sack, and I still squirm like a worm on a hook when I hear "Hark, the Herald Angels".

Compared to Willowgreen, this school which I shall call Haldane was in the heart of civilization. Not more than five miles away was a hamlet of seventy-one persons with all the amenities such a community affords. Haldane was built on the same general plan as Willowgreen — most prairie schools of that era were — except that the district had run out of money before installing chemical toilets in the basement. So, the facilities were outside about fifty yards from the schoolhouse, up against the fence. Also I didn't live in this school but boarded with a farmer about a mile down the road. These facts are essential to the story or I wouldn't mention them.

Anyway, early in November I began training my twenty-eight children for the concert. An irrevocable rule of this institution is that every child, regardless of ability, sex, size, or inclination, must be given exactly as much to do in the concert as every other child. Parents, grandparents, uncles, aunts, godparents and friends insisted that this rule be observed. They drove to the school in below-zero weather to see their favourites perform and would brook no partiality by any smart-alec schoolteacher.

If memory serves me right, we had no less than thirty items in this concert, consisting of recitations, sketches, solos, pageants, plays, skits, pantomimes, dances, drills, monologues, magic acts, Santa Claus, and choruses. Oh Lord . . . those choruses!

A very few times in each generation the fates, in a sardonic mood, so muddle up the genes in an individual that he is born completely without a sense of music. I don't mean he isn't a good singer. He's no singer. He can't even whistle or hum a tune. It's the opposite to perfect pitch. It's a nothing pitch.

Such a one am I.

I consider anybody who can pick out any kind of a tune on anything a genius. My mind becomes a dead thing when confronted with those little black dots with stems on them that other people see as notes representing sounds. At the Normal School the music teacher, a Madame Perry who enjoyed a considerable local reputation as a singer, once asked me to teach a song by rote. I still don't know what this could possibly mean, except that it is different from "by note", which also baffles me. I went up to the front of the room, scratched my seat, drew five lines on the blackboard, turned and looked at her with such suffering that she told me to sit down.

She already knew about me. Like every other music teacher I'd had in every grade, she'd listened to me try to sing a note once and then told me henceforth to shut up.

Well, at least fifty per cent of any Christmas concert is music. I kept away from it as long as possible, concentrating on skits, recitations, and the rest, but finally I had to face up to it.

"Can anybody play the organ?" I asked the class.

A hand from a seat near the back went up. It belonged to Marjorie Quick who was freckle-faced, snub-nosed, and in Grade Nine.

"Good," I said. "We'll begin practising our Christmas carols. What can you play, Marjorie?"

Marjorie shrugged and slouched over to the organ and began to play "Hark the Herald Angels". At least it sounded like that, but there was something wrong, too. It didn't sound exactly right. I hesitantly suggested this to Marjorie . . . people with nothing pitch are pretty deferential about such things . . . and she swivelled on the stool and asked, "How does it go then?"

This was like asking a Zulu fisherman how to knot an ascot

tie. Marjorie played completely by ear and had I been able to hum the tune all would have been well. As it was she had to go with what she had.

So we practised this with the kids singing as loudly as they could. Then we did "Jingle Bells" and "King Whats-his-name" and several others. They all sounded all right to me. But the angels. Somehow there was something wrong.

As we approached the Friday before Christmas, the traditional date for concerts, the school time was given over completely to practices. Besides, there were a thousand details to be arranged, not the least of which was the finding of a Santa Claus.

I solved this by making a deal with a friend who was a principal of the continuation school in the town. I'd be his jolly man and he'd be mine. Now the playing of Santa Claus at school concerts follows a set, unchangeable pattern. The suit is red and scruffy, the boots rubber and high, the beard a wispy bit of white cotton dangling from the chin. The general demeanour is rather diffident and quiet, the whole idea being to try and prevent all the children from figuring out in the first few seconds which local personage lurks behind the beard. They'll catch on soon enough, but these first few seconds seem important.

Well, I decided that this wasn't good enough. There should be some life, some sparkle, some humour in the old boy. And that cotton beard wouldn't do at all. So I cast about for a better one. It turned out there was none in the district, but when I'd been visiting the farm of Sam Melville, who kept sheep, I'd seen the hide of a ram thrown over a fence. The very thing.

I cut off a piece of this hide, combed the wild oats and dust out of it, made a hole for my mouth near the top and shaped a passable moustache and beard. But I didn't do anything to remove the smell, and this oversight later almost cost me my life.

Came the evening of my friend's concert. The town hall was

packed with every man, woman, and child from a radius of ten miles, and the place was hot as an outdoor phone booth in July.

I waited outside the door, observed and sniffed by a couple of dogs who had never before encountered such a Santa Claus. Then the fake telegrams had all been read, and I was on. With a ringing of bells and a great deal of ho-ho-hoing, I bounded down the aisle and onto the stage.

"Hellllo boys and girls!" I roared.

Dead silence.

Then back with my head and out with a blast of lusty ho-ho-ho's.

More silence.

So I pranced up and down the stage, clicked my heels and bellowed about how cold it was at the North Pole.

Nothing.

I still had a bag of tricks. I'd composed a monologue filled with terribly funny comments about local residents and some jokes left over from my Nutana Collegiate triumphs. As I delivered these in my most comical manner I noted a certain restlessness in my audience, but no laughter.

And I was quickly becoming aware of another problem that transcended my poor reception. The heat of the building plus that of my blushing countenance had got to the uncured hide of Melville's ram, and it was beginning to stink. Now a beard, by its very nature, must be worn in close proximity to the nose and, in fact, I had to breathe through it in order to survive.

This, along with the fact that I'd dropped my paper of witty sayings and the rope I was using for a belt had come untied, made me lose some of my earlier enthusiasm for my skit. Dance and jollity and jokes all came to a grinding stop in the middle of the stage, and I called upon my elves — some teachers and Sunday School leaders standing self-consciously by — to distribute the goodies from under the tree. I got the hell out of there. Never did fresh air smell so good.

But to go back to my own concert. A week before opening

night a half dozen farmers moved in, fetched planks from the basement, and laid them on sawhorses to make a narrow stage across the front of the room. Then they shoved most of the desks back against the wall and laid planks over the others to make benches. The old school had become a theatre.

The next five days were solid rehearsals. And not one child, not one of the entire twenty-eight knew more than a couple of words of what he was to say. But I had standards. This thing of a prompter behind the curtain hissing louder than the performers wasn't good enough. So, I drilled and shouted and paced up and down between the benches clutching at my forehead. And they looked at me with watery eyes wondering why all the fuss. They'd been in lots of concerts. They knew how things would be. But this was my first time.

The night of the concert came and with it the worst blizzard of the year. The wind velocity increased all day, and by six o'clock it was a real snorter.

"Well," I said, pressing my nose against the frosty window pane and noting the swirling snow, "I guess nobody'll venture out on a night like this."

"Get away with you," my landlady scoffed. "A little snow like this won't keep folks away from the Christmas concert!"

She was an ex-schoolteacher and I had a bad feeling she knew what she was talking about.

She and I and her husband, all the presents and candy for under the tree, plus assorted bits of costume, a wooden telephone for a skit, and a couple of recently completed shepherd's crooks were all to be picked up by Alvin Carmen and his family who would arrive at seven via a trail across the field. Seven o'clock went by, and eight and eight-thirty. No Carmens. Outside the storm grew steadily worse.

Then, about nine o'clock we heard a noise in the yard, and in a moment Alvin Carmen appeared at the back door looking like a snowman. There was snow in his eyebrows, eyelashes, and moustache. "Come on," he puffed. "We'll be late for the concert."

"What happened?"

"Got lost in the field. Kept going round in circles. Never would have got straightened out if Tommy hadn't noticed a frozen rabbit we'd passed twice before." Then he added philosophically, "Worst night I've ever been out in."

Nothing, I'm sure, could have brought anyone out that night except a Christmas concert.

So we loaded the stuff into the sleigh box where Mrs. Carmen and the three kids were huddled down in the straw. The road from there to the school was straight and between fences. So, we made it without trouble. To my surprise the school yard was full of rigs, the barn full of horses, and the school full of people. They filled every inch of planking and stood at the back and along the sides. And still they came. Each time the door opened, snow blew half way across the room. Inside, the air was thicker than soup. Above, the gas lamp sputtered and hissed. The tiny candles on the tree tilted crazily. If fire had broken out there, sixty people would have perished without a chance. But they never even gave that a passing thought. It was the Christmas concert.

In the cramped space behind the curtain I went crazy with costumes, make-up, and props. It wasn't easy to keep my huge cast under control. The little girls primped, swished about, giggled, and posed. The boys grinned, poked each other, shoved, and wrestled. All of them were so hopped up with excitement that they'd forgotten everything they were to say or do.

There was a commotion in the audience. A large woman, packed in against the window on the side of the room furthest from the door, lifted a two-year-old child from her lap and passed it over her head to the man behind. Without a word, he took it and passed it into the outstretched hands of the woman behind him. So, like a medicine ball, the child was passed from hand to hand over the heads of the audience to a man leaning against the door jamb who took it outside for what had to be done. Back inside again, the child was passed over the heads to the mother. She plunked it onto her knee, gave it a little jiggle and looked sternly towards the stage.

We were ready to begin. Marjorie Quick, who alone of all the cast had kept calm, struck a chord on the organ and the audience struggled to its feet for "God Save the King". Then the chairman of the board in blue serge suit came onto the stage and counted it a pleasure and a privilege to thank each and every one who had contributed to making this concert the great success he was sure it was going to be. Then he added that, for him, the best part of any Christmas concert was hearing those eager young voices singing those . . . "dear old Christmas carols we remember so well from our childhood."

I didn't pay much attention, because I had other problems, not the least of which was the absence of my friend who was to be Santa Claus. Nobody but a fool could be expected to go out to somebody else's concert on a night like that, and he was no fool. This meant another session with the fleece of Melville's ram.

I shoved the first child onto the stage, a six-year-old who recited a thing about being just a little boy who hadn't much to say except to wish them a happy Christmas day. He remembered two-thirds of it and drew prolonged applause from the corner of the house where his relatives predominated.

Then the entire ensemble wiggled and giggled its way on stage and sang "Jingle Bells". So far, so good. More recitations, some skits, an action song, a drill, and we were ready for "Hark the Herald Angels". I could have used a couple of those angels myself — guardian type.

Marjorie struck a chord. The children opened their mouths. From behind the curtain I peeked at the audience. As the singing began a most unusual expression spread over their collective faces. A combination of wonderment, horror, disbelief, and a sort of over-all sadness at the terrible things that can happen to people in this world.

There was no applause at the end, just stunned silence. I was completely baffled at this and quite hurt. It wasn't until I got home for the holiday and heard "Hark the Herald Angels" come over the radio that I understood their reaction. The two tunes had nothing in common.

And to this day, when the joyous season is upon us and the air is filled with carols, I get up and quietly leave the room where the radio is playing. My kids look after me and wonder what's wrong, for I've never told them what happened. The memory of "Hark the Herald Angels" is far too painful, altogether.

Christmas
Emily Carr

Victoria Christmas weather was always nippy — generally there was snow. We sewed presents for weeks before Christmas came — kettle holders, needle books, penwipers and cross-stitch bookmarkers. Just before Christmas we went out into the woods, cut down a fir tree and brought it home so alive still that the warm house fooled it into thinking spring had come, and it breathed delicious live pine smell all over the house. We put fir and holly behind all the pictures and on the mantelpiece and everywhere.

Plum puddings were dangling from under the pantry shelf by the tails of their boiling cloths. A month ago we had all sat round the breakfast-room table, stoning raisins while someone read a story aloud. Everyone had given the pudding a good-luck stir before it went into the bowls and was tied down and boiled for hours in the copper wash boiler while spicy smells ran all over the house. On Christmas Day the biggest pudding came out for a final boil before being brought to the table with brandy fire leaping up its sides from the dish, and with a sprig of holly scorching and crackling on its top.

Christmas Eve Father took us into town to see the shops lit up. Every lamp post had a fir tree tied to it—not corpsy old trees but fresh cut firs. Victoria streets were dark; this made the shops look all the brighter. Windows were decorated with mock snow made of cotton wool and diamond dust. Drygoods shops did not have much that was Christmassy to display except red flannel and rabbit fur baby coats and muffs and tippets. Chemists had immense globes of red, green and blue medicine hanging from brass chains in their shop windows. I wished some of us could be sick enough for Dr. Helmcken to prescribe one of the splendid globes for us. The chemists also showed coloured soap and fancy perfume in bottles. Castor oil in hideous blue bottles peered from behind nice Christmas things and threw out hints about over-eating and stomach-ache. A horrid woman once told my mother that she let her children eat everything they wanted on Christmas Day and finished them up with a big dose of castor oil. Mr. Hibben, the stationer, was nicer than that woman and the chemist. He hid all the school books behind story books left open at the best pictures. He had "Merry Christmas" in cotton wool on red cardboard in his window.

It was the food shops that Merry Christmassed the hardest. In Mr. Saunders', the grocer's, window was a real Santa Claus grinding coffee. The wheel was bigger than he was. He had a long beard and moved his hands and his head. As the wheel went round the coffee beans went in, got ground, and came out, smell and all. In the window all round Santa were bonbons, cluster raisins, nuts and candied fruit, besides long walking-sticks made of peppermint candy. Next to this splendid window came Goodacre's horrible butcher shop — everything in it dead and naked. Dead geese and turkeys waggled, head down; dead beeves, calves and pigs straddled between immense meat hooks on the walls; naked sheep had bunches of coloured paper where their heads ought to have been and flowers and squiggles carved in the fat of their backs. Creatures that still had their heads on stared out of eyes like poached eggs when the white has run over the yolk. Baby pigs looked worst of all — pink and naked as bathing babies, their cheeks drawn back to make them smile at the red apples which had been forced into their toothless, sucking mouths. The shop floor was strewn deep in sawdust to catch blood drips. You heard no footsteps in the shop, only the sharpening of knives, sawing of bones, and bump, bump of the scale. Everybody was examining meat and saying, "Compliments of the Season" to everyone else. Father saying, "Fine display, Goodacre, very fine indeed!" We children rushed out and went back to Santa while Father chose his meat.

The shop of old George, the poulterer, was nearly as bad as Goodacre's, only the dead things did not look so dead, nor stare so hard, having shut the grey lids over their eyes to die. They were limp in necks and stiff in legs. As most of them had feathers on they looked like birds still, whereas the butcher's creatures had been rushed at once from life to meat.

The food shops ended the town, and after that came Johnson Street and Chinatown, which was full of black night. Here we turned towards James' Bay, ready for bed.

There was a high mantelpiece in the breakfast room. And while we were hanging our stockings from it my sister read:

'Twas the night before Christmas
and all through the house
Not a creature was stirring,
not even a mouse.

On the way to bed we could smell our Christmas tree waiting in the dining-room. The room was all dark but we knew that it stood on the floor and touched the ceiling and that it hung heavy with presents, ready for tomorrow. When the lights were lit there would be more of them than any of us children could count. We would all take hands and sing carols round the tree; Bong would come in and look with his mouth open. There were always things on it for him but he would not wait to get his presents. He would run back to his kitchen and we would take them to him there. It seemed as if Bong felt too Chinese to Christmas with us in our Canadian way.

The Presbyterian Church did not have service on Christmas morning so we went to the Reformed Episcopal with my sister; Father stayed home with Mother.

All the weeks before Christmas we had been in and out of a sort of hole under the Reformed Church, sewing twigs of pine onto the long strips of brown paper. These were to be put round the church windows, which were very high. It was cold under the church and badly lighted. We all sneezed and hunted round for old boards to put beneath our feet on the earth floor under the table where we sat pricking ourselves with holly, and getting stuck up with pine gum. The pricking make the ladies' words sharp — that and their sniffy colds and remembering all the work to be done at home. Everything unusual was fun for us children. We felt important helping to decorate the Church.

Present-giving was only done to members in one's immediate family. Others you gave love and a card to, and kissed the people you did not usually kiss.

New Year's Day had excitement too. It was the custom for ladies to stay at home, sitting in their drawing-rooms with decanters of wine and fine cakes handy. Gentlemen called to wish them the "Compliments of the Season". Right after lunch we went up to Mother's room where you could see farthest down the street, to watch for Mother's first caller, and it was always the shy Cameron brothers, coming very early so as to avoid other visitors.

Gentlemen paid their respects at Government House, too, on New Year's Day, and Naval officers made a point of returning the hospitality of those who had entertained them while stationed in Victoria.

A Boy's Unforgettable Christmas Dinner

J. G. MacGregor

The sleigh track cut across the snowy whiteness of a little meadow, scarcely a hundred yards across, surrounded with a frieze of willows and backed with its wall of evergreens. Countless rabbit tracks, mere shaded dimples in the soft whiteness, criss-crossed its powdery snow. On the fringe of willows and the spreading alders the mystic tracery of hoar-frost clung undisturbed in the breathless, sunny air, till the vibration of the passing sleigh shivered it off in dripping cascades of starlight to find repose on the white blanket. The meadow was still and silent. Motionless under every snow-piled branch or log sat a snowy cotton-tail, its presence revealed only by its black eyes, and nothing broke the silence till the invasion of the swishing sleigh. In stillness and snowy whiteness the rabbits celebrated their Christmas. For it was Christmas in the cathedral of the forest.

Quickly we slipped along, and almost before we knew it we emerged from the forest into Johnstone's field and swept on to the warm welcome of Johnstone's hospitality.

Christmas dinner at Johnstone's! That was an experience never to be forgotten — an experience, alas, no longer possible to duplicate. Yet the recipe for it is simple. Take the hungry stomach of an active farm boy that gnaws again an hour after any meal. Give it a breakfast cut short by the excitement of new toys. Bundle stomach and boy into heavy clothes, and whisk them in a farm sleigh two miles through the crisp spruce-scented air. Let the boy run into Mrs. Johnstone's kitchen. Let the aroma of roasting turkey fill his nostrils and the crackling of the basting fat assail his ears. That is your recipe.

Garnish, if you wish, by letting his eyes dart about the kitchen. See — there on the shelf are six pies, two blueberry, two mince, and two low-bush cranberry, still hot from the oven, their acrid smell blended with the odour of hot lard. On the stove, bubbling away in the big pot, is the Christmas pudding, its savoury steam competing in gusto with all the other smells. Let this boy stand looking through the doorway with his back to the crackling kitchen and before him the long log room (usually part dining-room, part sitting-room, but today all dining-room). Let his eyes take in the red Christmas bell in the centre, with its green paper streamers sweeping off to the corners of the room, and then the long table set for ten, and loaded with colourful, cheery Christmas goodies. Look at the piles of home-made crusty bread, the plates of cookies, plain or iced with red or green, and the red candles flickering their welcome. Look at the green of cucumber pickles, the yellow of the mustard pickles and the glowing red of pickled beets. And there, on the sideboard, right there enthroned in the very centre — that is Mrs. Johnstone's chocolate cake. What a cake! Made as only Mrs. Johnstone can make it. Five inches high — two layers, chinked with jam and roofed with a quarter inch of chocolate icing. And there to keep it company stands the huge bowl filled with preserved wild strawberries and flanked by two piles each of five ruby glass dessert dishes, while tucked into every vacant space on the sideboard are bowls of nuts, oranges, apples and candy, a plate of jelly-roll and a pile of cinnamon buns. Over all presides Mrs. Johnstone, beaming with friendship and with Christmas time and with pride in her handiwork.

Let this boy walk slowly around the table and see all the side dishes — here a dish of low-bush cranberry jelly waiting for the turkey, there a jar of high-bush cranberry jelly, and there some spiced black currants. Finally the glistening bowls awaiting the arrival of potatoes and carrots, and beside each of the ten white plates, flanking each knife and fork, red, yellow, and green Christmas crackers.

Then, amidst all these smells and sights, make him wait nearly an hour while the turkey roasts to its brownest crackling excellence. Then seat everybody. Otis Johnstone at the head, his face beaming and his bald head shining, while he whets away at the huge carving-knife made from a piece of scythe blade and hafted with deer horn. Next, a chair for Mother, still busy in the kitchen, and beside it, Bill's chair. Then Pearl Johnstone, placed so as to be able to tend both Bill and her younger brother Charlie. And so on around the table; Mrs. Johnstone and Dad and Lloyd, with me sitting beside him; then Charlie Rose with the iron-grey beard, and Grandfather Johnstone with his white one.

Then let Mrs. Johnstone carry in the turkey, while Mother brings bowls piled high with mashed potatoes, white and fluffy, and with rich golden carrots, and the steaming dark brown gravy. Have Otis stand up and, with deft strokes, lay bare the white meat of the turkey breast and the dark meat of drumstick, and scoop out the dressing. Let no grim visage nor solemn discourse mar the pleasure of passing back for second helpings and then following these with cake and cookies, pies and strawberries. Finally, lay before Otis the steaming Christmas pudding with its blue brandy flames flickering and following each other round and round about.

There's your recipe for Christmas dinner at Johnstone's — a boy's unforgettable Christmas dinner.

For hours afterwards Mother and Mrs. Johnstone washed dishes, and before they were all dried Lloyd and I were eyeing oranges and cracking nuts with a hammer. Soon Mrs. Johnstone dug out the ice-cream freezer; and this luxury, strange to a farm boy, would fill in any chinks that had developed as his enormous dinner settled. Then, as the early dusk dimmed the room, old man Johnstone brought out his fiddle and all joined in singing the old favourite songs — "My Old Kentucky Home", "Sweet Genevieve", "Kathleen Mavourneen", "Killarney", and many more. All the while Otis played the accordion and Lloyd chimed in with his Jew's harp.

Finally the coal-oil lamps were lit, and Mrs. Johnstone

began to prepare supper. But who, except the children, could eat any more? The adults had a cup of tea or coffee, and, for courtesy's sake, nibbled at some Christmas cake. The children, of course, did not miss the chance to start again; but, alas, as Mrs. Johnstone said, their eyes were bigger than their bellies. Sighs of satisfaction succumbed to sighs of surfeit, while heavy eyelids testified to the toll taken by Christmas. It was time to go home.

Chappie and Charlie were soon hitched up to the sleigh, and amid repeated shouts of "See you at New Year's!" they picked their way along the trail, winding through the twisted birches and the stark tamaracks. Bill and I were soon settled down in the bottom of the sleigh-box, while Dad and Mother sat watching the trail ahead as it wound into the recesses of the forest.

Thieving Raffles
Eric Nicol

Anybody know how to make a delicious Christmas dinner out of old turkey raffle tickets?

That's what we've got at our house. No turkey. Just raffle tickets. Big raffle tickets, little raffle tickets, blue ones, red ones, yellow ones. My wallet is full of them. No money. Just raffle tickets.

The turkey raffle tickets cost more this year, too.

Two bits each, some of them. This year we paid more for the turkey we don't get to eat than we paid for the turkey we didn't get to eat last year. Never before have so few paid so much for sweet nothing at all.

I've had a book of raffle tickets to sell at a dime each. Every time I put the bite on somebody he bites back with his tickets at a quarter each. And some of those boys are awfully fast on the Christmas draw. I'm still reaching for my raffle book when they have theirs whipped out and are wetting the point of their pencil on my tongue.

For many years I have bought my turkey raffle tickets according to a system. The system is infallible. It never wins.

Sometimes I buy the last ticket in the book. Sometimes I buy a ticket with a number whose figures add up to three, the way I add. Once I bought a ticket from a girl because *she* had a nice round figure. That one cost me plenty before I was through. I could have bought a whole turkey farm with the big fat upshot of that raffle ticket.

Anyhow none of these devices works. The turkey is always won by some playboy who didn't even consult his astrological chart before making the investment.

Some people are born lucky. They usually look like Bing Crosby, have a golf handicap of four and are married to a lovely woman who has given them two children — a boy and a girl.

I am not one of these people. It was while I was bending over to pick up a pin that I was hit by that dolly in the department store. I have had to work for everything I've got. This situation seems even more poignant when I realize that I haven't got anything.

But to get back to the turkey raffle tickets. I remember we did win once. That was about fifteen years ago, and we won two turkeys for the same Christmas. Instead of Lady Luck's smiling on us regularly, she turned around for this one belly-laugh.

That wouldn't have been so bad if one of the turkeys hadn't weighed about forty pounds. We tried to invite some people to help us eat the thing, but we'd won it too late. Everybody had made plans for Christmas. So there we were, my mother and my father and I, with this huge bird lying naked in the kitchen like Edward Arnold.

We found we didn't have a pan large enough to hold the turkey, so we bought a new pan. Once we got the turkey into the pan we found it wouldn't go into the oven. The top of the oven caught the turkey a good two inches below the crest of the breast bone, so for a while there it looked as though we might have to build a fire in the bathtub.

I think we finally got the turkey in by laying it on its side. Or maybe it was by laying the stove on its side. Anyway, we cooked it and stuffed ourselves with it and on Boxing Day it still looked in better shape than any member of the family.

That turkey was around so long we grew to hate all forms of bird life. After the first week Mother didn't even bother to camouflage it as chicken a la king or Irish stew. We just tore at the great carcass in cold fury, uttering low, inhuman cries.

I forget what happened to the second turkey.

Well, that has never happened again. This year we have had to buy a wild duck for Christmas dinner. It isn't really a wild duck. Actually it's a tame duck that went mad with hunger. We found it hanging in the butcher shop with a note beside it explaining why it did it. "Life isn't all it's quacked up to be," the duck had written.

Some of you people won't believe that was what the duck wrote and will say I just made it up. These are the same people that don't believe in Santa Claus. There are too many cynics in the world, and too many turkey raffle tickets. I'd like to see anybody disprove that.

An Angel After All
D. P. Barnhouse

Chris frowned at the basket. It was only half full of eggs. Nothing's gone right, she thought, since the day Daddy went to the hospital. First there was the blizzard and the vegetables freezing in the root cellar and now the hens weren't laying. Yesterday she'd dropped the big enamel kettle and chipped it in a dozen places. Chris knew her mother felt like getting mad or crying — but she didn't.

"Well," she said, "it looks a mess all right, but thank goodness it still holds water." That was like Mom, always looking on the bright side of things . . . even when they were all so down in the dumps about Daddy.

"Cheer up," she'd said that time. "Now we'll find out what we can do on our own."

Chris tried to find a bright side to not being in the school concert but she couldn't; nor could she stop her knees from getting rubbery with excitement whenever she thought about it. To be the Christmas angel! How wonderful! . . . and how impossible!

"A long white robe," Miss Hart had said, "with perhaps some silver and your hair hanging down. You've just the right sort of hair for an angel."

"I just can't bother Mom about a costume," Chris thought. "She's already got enough worries to fill Pandora's box. If she can do without a new kettle on account of the hospital bills, I guess I can do without a silly old costume. When I see Miss Hart at church tomorrow I'll ask her to choose someone else."

To drown out the sharp twinge of disappointment, Chris tried to fasten her mind on other things; the beaded Indian belt she was making Toby for Christmas; the knitted shawl for Great Aunt Jocelyn.

Aunt Joss was a bit deaf and a bit of a "romancer" and Chris was glad she was. She could listen for hours to the old lady's stories about when she was a girl in the "old country" and about the "treasures" she kept locked up in the yellow pine chest in her room.

Chris and Toby had the stable nearly finished now. They'd pooled their money to buy the whitewash. This was to be Daddy's surprise when he got home.

But what about Mom? What could they possibly give Mom

that was good enough? Chris carried the egg basket into the kitchen. Its rattling wakened Aunt Joss who was napping in her chair by the fire.

"You'd better get on down to the post office," she said. "There might be a letter from your dad — and don't forget my cough drops from Doc Bates."

Doc Bates was an animal doctor. Chris loved to visit his store. On its crowded shelves, veterinary supplies rubbed elbows with paint brushes, raisins and hunting caps. His fascinating assortment of merchandise was guarded by a huge yellow cat named Hortense who slept on a sack of peanuts on the counter.

Doc Bates was talking on the phone when Chris came in. She played with Hortense who was curled up in her usual spot.

"Gosh, Joe," Doc was saying. "I can't close up the store right now because I'm expecting an important delivery from town. The mail truck's late today. All you can do is keep that mare warm till I can get there and get some more of that medicine down her — you hear? Hey, wait a minute!" He turned and stared at Chris . . . "Are you in a hurry?"

"I'm waiting for the mail truck," Chris said.

"How would you like to keep store for me while I save a horse from choking to death with pneumonia? Doc Bates didn't give Chris a chance to answer but hollered into the phone. "Okay, Joe, I'll be there in twenty minutes . . . Got me an assistant."

While he was stuffing supplies into his bag he rapped out orders. "You can sort the mail and have the driver put the other stuff in the back room. If any customers come in have them help themselves. Most folks can find things easier in the store than I can anyway." The door banged shut behind him and Chris heard his old pick-up explode into life.

Chris felt quite important. It's like an adventure, she thought.

Mr. Moodie came in for a sack of flour and showed her how

to ring it up on the cash register. She tidied the little glass cubicle marked "Post Office" so there'd be room to sort the mail. Then she swept up the candy bar wrappers and pop bottle tops and watered the scraggly little lemon tree in the window. Before she knew it, the sun was going down and Doc Bates came bounding in red cheeked from the cold. She could tell by his smiling face that the mare would be all right and he remarked on how tidy the place looked.

"You did me a whopper of a favour," he said. "Now for your wages. I want you to pick out something you really like — anything — except *that*, of course." He indicated a red canoe that hung from the rafters.

Chris laughed at his joke. "It was fun keeping store," she said. "You don't need to pay me anything." Her eye fastened on a bolt of white muslin on the top shelf . . . "Unless . . . "

"Come on Missy," Doc Bates urged. "Try hard."

Chris pointed without speaking. Her knees were going limp again. Doc got down the bolt. Sure enough it was soft and wispy; just perfect for an angel costume.

"How about something fancier," Doc said — "With flowers maybe."

"Oh no," Chris breathed. "That will do just fine."

"You're the doctor," Doc grinned. He flopped the bolt over and over, measuring out lengths of material. On the shelf behind him there was a gleam of copper which bothered Chris. For a moment she couldn't tell why. Doc picked up the scissors.

"Wait!" Chris said, so sharply that Hortense opened one eye in astonishment. "Excuse me," she said, "but is that a copper kettle?"

"Not real copper," he said, "but it shines just as pretty doesn't it?"

"Is it very expensive?"

"No," he said. "It's really quite cheap — doesn't tarnish like copper either."

"Could I change my mind?" she said slowly.

"Why not? It's a woman's privilege." Doc went in the back to find a box and Chris wound the white material neatly back on the bolt. It would have been nice to be an angel, she thought, but it would be even nicer to watch her mother's face when she saw that beautiful gleaming kettle on Christmas morning.

Mother and Toby were already doing the evening milking when Chris got back. She took her dinner from the warming oven and carried it up to Aunt Joss's room. The old lady loved excitement. Chris told her how she'd "kept store" for Doc Bates and then she unwrapped the kettle. They both gazed at it admiringly. Then, because it was settled in her mind and easier to talk about, Chris told her about the Christmas concert and about having to tell Miss Hart that she couldn't be in it.

"Save your breath, Missy," Aunt Joss said. "If you'd tell a person what was going on, you'd save yourself a heap of trouble."

"You don't understand," Chris said and raised her voice a little . . . "I have to tell her that I can't be . . . "

"You needn't shout. I'm not as deaf as people seem to think. Who says you can't be an angel?" She unlocked her chest and lifted out a heap of white silk. "I knew there was a good reason I kept this all these years. This gown once curtsied to a queen," she said proudly.

"How can you bear to cut it?" Chris asked. She saw at once that this material was much more beautiful than the muslin in Doc's store.

"Too much stuff in here anyway." The sharp black eyes twinkled at Chris as though sharing a private joke. "My jewels are getting crowded . . . Come here. Let's see how tall you are . . . Yes, there's plenty to spare. We'll bend a coat hanger for a halo and bind it up with tinsel. You know that silver star on Dolly's halter? That's as pretty a star as ever I've seen. If you were to give her a few sugar lumps, I'll bet she'd let you borrow it. Now I'll tell you a secret . . . A certain party is going to be at that Christmas concert — if he has to go on crutches. You do him proud, mind!"

"Oh Aunt Joss . . . you're not just romancing?"

"Didn't get a letter today, did we?"

"No, there was nothing for us at all."

"You know why? 'Cause the doctor phoned from the hospital and said your father could come home tomorrow . . . providing you kids don't pester him to death."

Even if the pestering part was romancing, Chris knew the best part was true. She threw her arms around the old lady and hugged her tight.

"It can't help being a wonderful Christmas then," she cried. "Just like all the others. And thanks to you, Aunt Joss, I'll be an angel after all."

Stage Fright
Ken Wotherspoon

It was slightly more than fortuitous that the opening line of my monologue at the Runneberg School Christmas Concert was from the well-known essay that began, "Whenever I go into a bank I get nervous."* That was just about all I uttered before my mind went blank. I couldn't remember what I was standing there for. I saw individuals in the front row gradually merge into the blur of the crowd. I was unaware of what was going on around me; the prompter's voice was merely some annoying static emanating from a great unseen void somewhere behind me; two large gas lanterns hissed above my head; the place was in silence and I had forgotten not only my lines, but my own identity. I had stage fright.

The advantage of being caught in the throes of stage fright

*Stephen Leacock, "My Financial Career".

is that of the accompanying numbness. I would not blush or giggle uncontrollably or start to cry because of the protective layers of anonymity engendered by the ego during this traumatic experience. Obviously all of the visible and invisible rehearsals merely postponed the grim reality of this stage appearance. In my mind I had gone through the performance over and over again. Actually I had survived the agony of the dress rehearsals and the countless unnerving times I stood beside my desk and rattled through the short address, my voice quavering and my knees knocking to my mortification each time. But I had on each successive trial convinced myself that I was making progress. Although my neck reddened with anxiety and my mouth craved lubrication I did not break down and cry.

Crying in front of my classmates was an infelicity I never wanted repeated again. It was the ultimate humiliation. The first time it happened was in the first week of my first year in school. My pencil had rolled out of the groove on the desk top and on to the floor. I was proud of that pencil with its bright gold and red colors, its large eraser and its length. It was the first time in my life I owned a new pencil. Mom and Dad brought it home one day from Melville with my new scribbler that had the arithmetic tables on the back. I didn't want to use it until school began so it was kept in its shiny condition until the first day when I grasped it avariciously in my hand and guarded it carefully from harm. Now when it hit the floor I envisioned a broken point.

It was worse than that. I leaned out of my desk and attempted to retrieve it. But just as my fingers touched it, it rolled beyond my grasp and under the desk across the aisle. An older boy who was enjoying my discomfiture placed his foot on it and rolled it back and forth beneath his shoe. I could hear the crackling crunch announcing its annihilation. I was shocked and felt desperate in the face of such open cruelty. I started to cry. I didn't want anyone to notice but the more I smothered my sobs, the more the increased pressure broke through my nose and forced my hands away from my mouth. I blubbered and snorted and the sobs broke into uninhibited wails. Now even the sympathetic teacher couldn't bring my open grief under control before it had run its course.

Having once lost face before your peers it's extremely difficult to replace an undesirable image with a more heroic one. I would have preferred a bully's image to that of a sissy but having cried once it was easier to cry again and again. Hence whenever it was time for voice tests and singing, my spirits sank very low. Fear of making a mistake and being ridiculed often made a fool out of me. When it came my turn to sing, because we had no alternative but to go through the words of an entire song, I frantically requested the teacher to let me do the bee song. It had only two lines and one could get through the entire ditty without varying pitch or key. I marched stifflegged to the front of the class on those crushing occasions, stared dead ahead and proceeded as quickly as possible with:

Bees gather honey,
Paying poll and money.

Then rushing back to my seat I'd slink down praying that my performance would suffice albeit unsuccessfully. If questioned by my teacher at this point or criticized I'd burst into tears. This practice approximated my art of speechmaking also. Except when speech classes called for my participation, my fear of standing alone before the mixed group of Grades one to ten often caused me to forget subject, text and audience. In the earlier grades, tears were the painful remedy and during the latter grades plain ordinary stage fright resulting in a nonsensical stupor was the manner in which my human organism protected itself from the unfriendly audience.

The blurred figures in the front row were beginning to get restless. Nervous coughs accompanied by scraping winter boots on the floor of Banner Hall were awakening me to my hapless position. This indeed was the Christmas concert. I was one of that class of rugged eighth graders and I was standing before this expectant audience making them as uneasy as hens in a chicken house invaded by a skunk. They were empathizing with me but were unable to do anything to help me. My parents must have felt like dropping through the floor not from shame or disgust but realizing the importance of a breakthrough for me at this point in despair because I'd blown it again.

The lamps hissed on. The prompter's voice broke through my fuzzy trance.

"Start again!" "Whenever I go into a bank I get nervous!" I suddenly regained composure. I felt a surge of self-confidence pervade my entire being such as I had never felt before. My knees steadied, my eyes sparkled with the mild amusement of an orator about to break an original story on his audience, my heart beat loosened to a healthy, regular thump and the palms of my hands dried. I freed my fingers which had been tightened into two little balls and lifted my right arm in a waving gesture. I was amazed at the new sense of freedom that allowed my entire body to relax. Moving my feet from their rigid side by side position I set my left foot just a little ahead of my right, poised for a dramatic address. Lowering my eyes which had been staring glassily above the audience I concentrated on people whose faces began taking shape in the front row where the gas lanterns from the stage cast a few reflections in the darkened hall. Clearing my throat I began,

"Whenever I go into a bank I get nervous." I said it, clearly, distinctly and with the resonance of a CBC announcer. I couldn't believe my ears. Was that really my voice? Did I say that? Even though the words of the great Canadian essayist flowed back into consciousness I felt an indomitable desire to wade into some off the cuff dialogue. I wanted to break into the core of this captive audience and move them off their seats. I wanted to open my being to them and expose all the pent-up philosophy that had been ground out in quiet suffering in erstwhile predicaments when my voice had been choked by fear and shame. Now I wanted to free them in the spirit of my own newly discovered freedom. The gas lamps hissed on. In actual time I had been standing there for only an embarrassing number of seconds; in the depths of my life I'd been out into eternity and back. I'd go over that line again.

"Whenever I go into a bank I get nervous. Well maybe you'd get nervous, too, if you didn't have any money in the bank and you had my credit rating and you were going to ask for a loan." I paused because I figured the farmers could identify with that line I'd just made up and there would be an appreciative response. There was gentle and relieved laughter. That added fuel to my newly discovered self-confidence.

"Well. . . ." I was already developing my own style. The audience appreciated the drawl and showed it with a ripple of laughter.

"Well . . . the things that go on in banks you wouldn't believe. The last time I was in town I saw this farmer taking a pig into the bank. I went up to him as he was holding the door open and asked why he was taking his pig into the bank. He said he was made to feel nervous in the bank the last time he'd been in because he asked for a loan and the manager said he couldn't give him one. He asked the manager why that was the case. The manager told him he didn't have enough security. 'You bring home the bacon and share some with this bank and I'll get you a loan.' So the man told me he was going to bring some real live bacon in for that unwilling manager."

I paused for laughter because I figured I deserved it. The crowd hollered in joy and stomped their feet and clapped their hands. Actually looking back now I see how dumb that joke really was, but I guess they were really pleased with my performance. I was a new person. I noticed Mr. Thompson move from his chair at the side over to one of the centre seats. He couldn't believe it was me.

"Well . . . anyway, whenever I go into a bank I get nervous.

You see banks appear to be more than they really are, if you know what I mean." I was plunging into some homespun philosophy the like of which I'd heard the recorded voice of Will Rogers give. It must be his style I wanted to emulate. But where was it going? What was I going to say after this kind of provocative beginning? "You see, it's not really the big door at the front or that row of little cages behind which you see those efficient-looking ladies, that gives you the heeby-jeebees. It's the guy on the other side of the little wooden fence in the office. The manager. He's so good at clearing his throat and saying 'no' that he reminds you of some mean, unhappy uncle you know. You're taught to be scared of him and he knows that. If he ever figures for a moment that you're not scared of him, he closes his door and you can't get in to see him. But most folks don't get that brave; so for most of us who go into banks we get nervous. It's not the money or the place, it's all because of that guy who seems to be what he isn't, you see. So the next time you go into a bank and feel nervous, you think of what I'm telling you and when you feel your stomach getting like it was crawling with ants, just march up to one of those wickets and say, 'Pardon me ma'am but I want to speak to the manager on an urgent matter.' That'll get you in. Then when you get ushered to this guy's door, don't let your scared feelings tell you what to do; listen to me." The direction my monologue was going was engendering amongst my hearers a sympathetic response. The funny part of the monologue with its incongruities between my unsureness and the contrasted over-confidence which let the people laugh in gratitude for my deliverance from complete humiliation was presently giving way to actual interest in the content of what I was saying. Still there were the surprised and mildly shocked and amused faces of my teacher and my peers in the eighth grade who were witnessing the transition from a crowd-frightened milksop to an orator of sorts who enjoyed his new image of crowd-pleaser.

"Don't wait to be invited in; just enter and sit down in the chair opposite his desk as if you owned a good portion of the bank. This will upset the manager a little and will give you the opportunity to move in on him." The words were coming out as if I'd just read the script. I tried not to think of this because I was afraid I'd get lost in my own narration. "He'll likely try to say something about this point, but don't let him. Hush him up by holding your hand up like this." I held up my right hand in a traffic cop's stop signal. "Then rush out with words such as 'This country's in bad shape. You bankers are letting things get out of hand. You're not keeping up on where the people are and you can't deal with money matters unless you understand where the people are because they're telling you what's important and what's not important in the community. You guys spend too much time behind closed doors. The whole world out there changes a little every time you close that door. I'm here to help you before it's too late for you to do anything about it.' By now, you see, you've got this fellow scared about himself. Just maybe he can't take a chance on you bluffing him. Now he'll likely try to speak again, but it won't be to get you to leave. He'll likely say he'd like to know what you think he should do about it. Then the rest is up to you. You can string him along about some little job you've got started and how everybody else whose opinion matters is really stirred up about it and how you need a little money to keep it going. Then you're telling him. He isn't sitting there clearing his throat and getting ready to form his lips into a loud 'no'. That's how to get over feeling nervous when you go into a bank." I said that line as if it was the conclusive clincher but the applause was so great that instead of bowing and moving off the stage I hung on for one more glorious moment.

"Well . . ." I dragged it out and basked in the accompanying appreciative applause. "Well . . . when I go into a bank I get nervous. But then what else can be expected from a kid who grew up in a community like this?" Sweeping my arms around in an arc that comprehended the school district I continued in a vein that excited the audience by its unknown possibilities. Even I the speaker had arrived at the point where I was over-extending my good fortune. I didn't want to become insulting and, much less, boring but I simply couldn't shut up.

"Yeah, well . . . what do you expect of a kid that's spent his whole life going to this knock-kneed school and collecting rabbits' hides for war savings certificates in the winter and gopher tails and crow's eggs for bounty payment in the summer? Where's it all getting to anyway?" There was a serious air descending upon the gathering and I was wishing for an easy escape. Why had I added these inconsequential remarks? "Anyway folks, that about says the whole thing for all of us. The moral is I guess it's better to be collecting the hides and tails and things than it is to be the rabbit or the gopher or the crow. So in the words of my favorite animal and to save me from arching my back, may I conclude by saying instead of doing, 'Bow-wow'." A pun is truly cheap humor. For me at this juncture, however, it got me out of a predicament and freed my audience to show they were grateful that a case of stage fright evolved into a new and risky experience for another of the Banner Hall's local youths.

I was so light-headed and ebullient as laughter and cheers for my monologue rang out, that I forgot that my main job for the night was to work with Albert as stage hands for the main performance of the evening, a play about a girl and her hapless beau. Albert had to come down into the audience to retrieve me from the hugs of my parents and the accolades of relatives and neighbours. Dad was laughing it off with some friends by saying "Always said that kid was a ham. He'll never be a farmer, so might as well let him clown," when Albert yanked me by the arm and said, "C'mon. Mr. Thompson says it's time to set up for the play."

This was the play in which Sally was to be the big star. She had won the part over Joan who was another kid in seventh grade. Sally got the part, Albert and I knew, because she out-maneuvered and outsmarted poor little Joan. Sally had a lot to say when Mr. Thompson was casting the play. She went up to offer to clean a section of the blackboard and we noticed how she worked on Mr. Thompson. Although we both thought Joan said the lines as well as Sally, Sally had ways of making Joan look bad. For example, when she was cleaning the board she was going on to Mr. Thompson about how she was worried about Joan's health since she had the flu because Joan's mother had said to Sally that she hoped Joan wouldn't have too heavy a part in the concert this year. We figured she'd be saying a lot of other sly things like that and knew how it would all come out because Mr. Thompson was such a wonderful person he wouldn't hurt anyone. At least we understood that even if Joan didn't get the part, he'd work in a song or recitation or something for her. There weren't any of us who got away without doing something public at the Christmas concert, just like in the singing and speech classes.

Albert and I, therefore, decided it was our duty to even the score for Joan against Sally and make it look like it was God or some higher power who was getting even. Maybe that's why God gets blamed for so much badness. There was a place in the play where the young lady hears her boy friend knock on the door and she steps out to greet him, then brings him in by the hand. It was a kind of gummy play where the boyfriend is away fighting a war or something and the girlfriend, Sally, paces around the living room expecting him to arrive back after several years' absence. Most of the words are spoken by this lonesome female who is getting really excited about their reunion. It's supposed to be some town in the Western United States in the winter time.

As she speaks her lines her voice is to show more and more emotion building up to quite a bit of excitement when a train whistle announces the soldier's return. Why she doesn't run to the station we couldn't figure out except maybe it would involve a lot more stage scenery. Anyway her voice gets higher and the words come faster as a dog starts to bark. This dog was really Clifford barking off-stage. Then the knock comes and Sally rushes to the door, opens it and runs out into the blinding snowstorm into her boyfriend's arms. The boy's voice and Sally's are then heard as if coming from outside. They don't re-enter the room as the curtains close with them saying nice things to one another in spite of the horrible weather.

The two of us stage hands besides setting up the living room, had to manage the train whistle which we simulated by blowing through a long narrow pipe and we had to knock on the door at the right time and release some white confetti when Sally rushed through the door. This was the snow driving in against her, indicating how strong her love must be for this soldier because she runs right into it. Albert and I figured that we'd give Sally something to think about besides what a great actress she was and how smart she had been in outwitting Joan in getting the part.

We didn't tell anybody else about it, but we filled a pail full of snow mixed with water which we thought we'd use instead of confetti. We set it against the back door of the hall where the wet snow wouldn't melt. When Sally's voice was getting higher and Clifford started barking, Albert went for the pail while I did the knocking. When the door opened and Sally ran into the back stage area I threw a handful of white confetti through the door onto the stage and Albert dumped the slush over Sally's head. It came off with quite a bang. Sally, who figured she'd really pulled off a great stage performance, ruined her last sentences with a shrieking sound that must have left Mr. Thompson and the others wondering what was coming off.

Christmas concerts in Banner Hall were fun. It was the crowning event to the old year and an occasion for parents to talk about how well we did our parts. We got to love and to hate each other more in school during the practices, the rehearsals and performances. And Mr. Thompson became even a greater friend as we got to know him during the trials and foibles of the break in the usual school routine. But I guess the highlight of the whole event was when the program ended, Santa Claus had visited our tree at the front of the hall with its candles actually lit and we all went home with our brown bags of hard candy, an orange and a few nuts. The trip home in a team-driven sleigh box over snow banks and across fields was serene. The muffled voices of the adults brought contentment to us tired kids as we huddled together under a dyed cowhide robe on the straw, our eyes fixed on spaces between stars and our thoughts filled with the joys of school ended and Christmas turkey and toys just ahead.

Miss Henchbaw
W. O. Mitchell

Miss Henchbaw she got up, and she stood there with her hands folded together across her stomach; her mouth was sort of turned up at the corners, like when she's got something to tell us and it's good. Jake he claims she always looks like a hungry goshawk, only he isn't fussy about her, not with her all the time saying he didn't capture Looie Riel and Chief Poundmaker singlehanded.

Miss Henchbaw she looked down at us; her grey hair, that's piled up like one of those round loaves of bread, was under the writing on the board:

The girl plays with the dog. It is fun to play.

She waited for Una to quit whispering to Violet, and the pencils to stop their dotting sounds, and Fat to finish grinding on the pencil sharpener. Fat he's always sharpening a pencil.

Steve Kiziw, that sits in front of me, he was leaning back lazy in his seat, twirling his ruler on the point of his pencil. Steve has two brothers in the Air Force. Me I got my dad that's in the South Saskatchewans. Steve and me have our trap line together; skunk and weasel been running good since the last of October.

"Children!" Her voice all the time goes up at the end. Steve's ruler clattered to the top of his desk.

"Just three weeks till Christmas." She smiled and you could hear the Grade Ones and Twos sighing all over the room. "Time we were getting to work on our Christmas concert." The Grade Ones and Twos sort of all squealed together. "Now I've — Steve, sit up in your seat!"

Steve he sat up.

"I've been thinking that we — instead of getting a play already made for us, we'd do something new this year." Everybody was looking up at her. Beside her you could see the orange flames flickering to beat anything in the school stove. "We're going to make up our own play this year. And — yes Una?"

Una took down her hand. " 'Bout the Babe in the manger, Miss Henchbaw?"

Miss Henchbaw sort of pulled her mouth up together. "Why, I think that —"

"Er — thuh Three Wise Men." That was Fat by the pencil sharpener.

"Them sheepherders," piped up Ike. His dad raises a lot of sheep. "Where they wuz watchin' their herda sheep an' they saw thuh northern lights — "

"The Star of the East, Harry — were watching — Sit down, Willis." She meant Fat. She turned to the board. On one side she wrote "Babe-manger", on the other "Three Wise Men". She turned around again. "We'll vote."

"Didn't put down no sheepherders," Ike muttered under his breath.

It turned out 11 to 10 for the Three Wise Men. We got 10 girls in Rabbit Hill. Ike he didn't put up his hand for either one.

Ike he got picked for one of the Wise Men along with Fat and Steve. Miss Henchbaw she made Steve in charge of all the stuff we needed for the concert: broomsticks for the camels' heads to go on, red tissue paper and a light bulb for the campfire, candles for all the Grade Ones for when they were all dressed up in green tissue paper to make a Christmas tree out of themselves.

I got to be the Wise Men's hired man, only Miss Henchbaw she suggested they better call me a camel driver.

We made up a pretty good play, all about where the Three Wise Men are figuring out what presents they're going to bring, and they end up where Fat brings gold and Steve some perfume called frankincents and Ike he was going to bring meer, whatever that is. Fat had the most to say.

After four Steve and me kicked our way through the schoolyard. She'd been snowing most of the afternoon, so the yard was spread white and the prairie had lost her edge. You could only see a glowey place where the sun was supposed to be low down in the sky. By our forts we built in the corner of the yard where the buck brush had its black arms held out, Steve burped.

He can burp whenever he wants to by taking down the air first. When he burps he can talk at the same time. Once he said five words and only used one burp. You ought to hear him pretend to sneeze too.

"You gotta pelt thuh next one," Steve said.

I didn't say anything. In our trap line we'd got eleven weasel and three skunks; Steve meant she was my turn to skin the next skunk. I didn't say anything.

We walked down Government Road, with the snow sort of squealing under our feet.

"Wonder if we got a badger this time, Steve?"

"Dunno — Oughta be a good play."

"Yeah. I didn't want to be in it much."

Steve said he didn't either, but he didn't mean it any more than what I did.

"Guess we ain't gonna have Henchbaw teachin' us next year," Steve said.

I stopped right in the middle of Government Road.

"Huh?"

"They're gonna git Miss Ricky that's at Broomhead — Old Man Ricky he's gittin' her."

Mr. Ricky he's down the road from us and he's tight. The last three years he's been chairman of the school board. I never heard about Miss Henchbaw leaving Rabbit Hill. I said:

"I never heard about her leavin', Steve."

"I heard my dad talkin' to Ma — he says Old Man Ricky's after the $15 a month board he'll git outa Louella. If she comes here to teach she'll hafta stay with her dad."

"What'll Miss Henchbaw do?"

"I dunno," Steve said. "Git her another school."

"Wonder if Ricky's daughter's like he is."

"Can't be no worsen Miss Henchbaw."

"No," I said, "guess she can't."

But I wasn't so sure. Jake and me we're not very fussy about Mr. Ricky. Take the way we can't even get a softball for the school out of him, and the way he's all the time kicking about us using up the chalk. He claims Miss Henchbaw lets us waste it, throwing it around all over. I never threw any. Every time he gets a chance he hints about Miss Henchbaw not being so good a teacher; Jake he sort of agrees with Mr. Ricky on that; he claims her history's shaky.

When I told Ma what Steve said she blew up. "Why, that's a shame! Miss Henchbaw's been at Rabbit Hill twenty years!"

"Twenty years too long," Jake said.

"She's been a very good teacher," Ma said.

Jake he muttered something under his breath.

"I don't think the people around here want to see her go."

"Well, I knowa one that ain't enny too — "

"This is her home," Ma said. "She — why I've never heard of anything like that in my life!"

"Ricky he's thuh whole school board," Jake said. "Got his own hired man, Art, on. Old Man Gatenby he ain't much good, him bein' deef. Ricky he jist runs that there school board."

"That isn't democracy," Ma said.

"Miss Henchbaw she isn't so democratic, Ma. The way she —"

"That'll do, son!"

Sometimes Ma isn't so democratic either.

The next week I sort of forgot about Miss Henchbaw getting fired. She didn't act any different in school that I could see. Steve and me were pretty busy with our trap line: two weasels, no skunks, one of Tincher's chickens.

Friday I went back to school to get my Health book I forgot, and I was almost to my seat before I noticed. Miss Henchbaw's head was resting bent forward on her desk, with her hands made into fists and them by her ears. I stopped. I didn't know what to do.

I scuffled some with my feet.

Her head came up. A hunk of her grey hair had come out and it was hanging down by her ear. Her face was streaky. Her eyes were just as red as the Santa Clauses sort of marching along the top of the side blackboard.

Old people look awful when they've been crying.

I got out of there without my Health book.

When I got home I looked for Jake.

"Jake."

"Yeah?"

"I — I'm not so fussy about — about the way Miss Henchbaw — "

"I ain't fussy about her either."

"No — I mean — about Mr. Ricky's gettin' rid of her."

"No skin offa my knuckles."

"Jake — I got to thinkin' — everybody makes fun of old maids, don't they?"

"Uh-huh."

"It isn't funny, Jake."

"Whut ain't?"

"Being an old maid."

" 'Tain't likely — "

"It must be awful lonely, Jake — she's lonely — "

"So's a goshawk."

"But he wants to be — she hasn't got anybody, Jake — she hasn't even got anybody in this war — she — once Ma told me she had a fella she — "

"Who? Her?"

"The last war — he was at Vimy."

Jake's mouth came open and it stayed there. Jake he was at Vimy Ridge too.

"She's always askin' about Dad or about Aunt Margaret's baby."

"Is she?" Jake he's fussy about our baby.

"Gettin' old and not having anybody give a whoop about you — Jake, that's worse than hail or rust — something you can't do anything about."

Jake he nodded his head slow. He isn't so young.

"An' if Ricky he — Jake — she was bawlin'!"

That night Jake went over to see Mr. Tincher. The next day they started the paper around for people to sign saying that they didn't want Miss Henchbaw to leave. It stirred up a lot of talk, all about how Mr. Ricky he was getting his hired man to tend the school stove and not paying him any extra wages but charging for a janitor all the same. Everybody signed.

In school we went right on like there was nothing wrong. We had our play all memorized. Ike he'd forgot all about the northern lights. Steve and Miss Henchbaw they had an argument and it was about chickens.

Steve he figured she'd be nice to have some chickens around the Wise Men's bonfire in our play. Miss Henchbaw she said no. Steve he kept bringing her up and Miss Henchbaw kept right on saying no.

It was about a week after we made up our Christmas play that Mr. Ricky came into the schoolyard. If he wasn't all the time coming to snoop he wouldn't have got Steve's snowball in the back of his neck, the one with the special centre Steve meant for Ike.

Mr. Ricky he got Miss Henchbaw to line all us kids up and he started in giving us a talking to about running wilder than hooty owls, and how we needed somebody to really give us some discipline. Every few word's he'd say, "Section so and so, paragraph so and so of thuh School Act." He said he didn't blame us so much as he blamed the teacher that would let us get out of hand the way we were, and Miss Henchbaw she was blushing real red.

Steve he sneezed the way he can do.

Mr. Ricky, standing there with his hat still on and the flaps down so he looks like a goshawk with blinkers on, he said:

"An' I wanta know who threw that there snowball?"

Steve he went, "AAAaaah — whooooo!"

"I'm a gonna keep yuh all here till I find out which one a yuh."

"AAaaaaa — whuhiiich!"

Mr. Ricky looked sort of startled at Steve. He began to say something, but Steve looked like butter wouldn't melt in his mouth. "Ain't no use in tryin' tuh git outa her — I'll find out ef we gotta stay here all night."

"AAAaaaaaah — huh-huh-hu-night."

"Say — " Mr. Ricky took a step toward Steve. "You ain't tryin' tuh — " "Aaaaaaay — huh — ho — noooooo!" She was a wet one.

Mr. Ricky leapt back and reached into his hip pocket for a handkerchief. "That's him!" His voice sort of cracked. "That's thuh boy that done it!" He reached out and lifted Steve up by the collar of his jacket. Steve's face started in working again. Mr. Ricky let him go quick. Steve's face straightened right out again.

Mr. Ricky he said likely the teacher wouldn't do anything about making sure it wouldn't happen again.

Mr. Ricky was wrong. I saw Steve's hands afterward.

After that Mr. Ricky spread all over about how bad us kids were, and he said seeing the teacher couldn't keep any control over us he had no way of doing his duty as chairman of the school board except by getting somebody else to take her place next school year. He said he felt the paper everybody signed didn't change things a bit; the folks didn't know how bad things were in the school and it was time something was done about it.

Ma blew up again.

She said, "Something has to be done, Jake!"

"Ain't nothin' a fella kin do," Jake said.

"But — can't — "

"Ed Tincher he said somethin' 'bout holdin' a ratepayers' meetin' — tellin' thuh board how they — "

"Then why — "

"Ricky'd run her — soon as thuh notices wuz posted he'd git her all figgered out how tuh throw a monkey wrench intuh her — all thuh time talkin' about that there School Act nobody knows about — fella feels like a fool ef he gits up tuh argue with him — can't open your mouth but whut she's wrong by section so an' so, paragraft such an' such."

"Why doesn't — can't somebody get a School Act and —"

"Why — I s'pose — "

"Does Mr. Ricky have to know about the meeting ahead of time?"

"There's somethin' about yuh gotta have her up three places — I remember when — how kin yuh hold a meetin' ef folks don't know about her — an' ef they know, Ricky he'll know too. He — say! Kid! When's that there Christmas concert?"

"Week from Thursday, Jake."

That's whut we kin do — folks'll all be tuhgether — hold our meetin' right after thuh concert — good time too right after a entertainment she got up — kinda softens folks up toward her."

All that week the weasels were running good. The night before the concert Steve and me took a badger out; his hair was real long and thick.

It was the night of the Christmas concert we got the skunk.

Steve he came over to our place for supper, and he helped me with my chores. He brought over his sheet for being a Wise Man all wrapped up in paper. Ma and Jake went over to Tinchers early so they could go to the concert with them. Steve helped me hitch up Baldy to the bobsleigh when she was about time to go. He threw his parcel into the back of the box. I went back to the house to get my Little Daisy .22; our trap line lies right on the way to the new Community Hall and we figured we might find something in her to shoot.

When I came back outside, Steve he had a funny sack in his hand and he was tying the neck up and there were some squawks coming out of it.

"What you doin', Steve?"

"Jist borra'd a couple of your chickens for that there play."

"But — "

"Ain't nothin gonna happen — "

"Miss Henchbaw she said you couldn't."

"It'll make it a lot realer to have some chickens up on the stage."

"But what'll Ma — "

"We'll bring 'em right back after the concert. They'll be all right."

I didn't argue any more. How'd I know he'd caught the barred Rock and the Wyandotte? They bust loose every time they catch sight of each other. They're roosters.

When we got to the fourth trap there was a skunk in it. Steve shot it and he took it out. He threw it into the box of the sleigh. We went on to the hall, and the smell of skunk came right along with us.

Because he had to fix up the light bulb with red tissue paper and sticks for the Wise Men's bonfire, Steve went in the hall ahead of me. He took the sack with the chickens, said he was keeping them in the kitchen till it was time to use them. He told me to bring his other parcel.

I tied Baldy up to the fence then went to get Steve's Wise Man sheet.

The Skunk was lying right on top of it.

The smell of skunk followed me to the hall real strong.

For a good 15 minutes before our play came on the folks out front could smell Steve's sheet, not so strong at first, Jake told me after, but when the curtain came apart she just leapt out at the audience. I know when I came onto the stage I could see the folks looking around sort of sidewise at each other, like they were wondering whether the skunk was somewhere in the hall or just outside.

Two of the Wise Men knew — Ike and Fat; when they came out on their camels there was a lot of distance between Steve and the other Wise Men. Even the two roosters Steve had turned loose just stood on the stage, looking dazed. When I came up to take the camels away the smell sort of caught at my breath.

The way he was supposed to Steve sat up close to the bonfire; on the other side Fat and Ike were just as far away as they could get without looking as though something was wrong.

"What are we going to give, O Wise Men?" Ike's voice came out sort of muffled. He was holding his sheet up over his nose.

"We must bring the best presents that can be brung." Miss Henchbaw had told him not to say "brung".

"And what are you — goin' — to — what — uh." Ike choked.

Steve got up and started around the fire the way he was supposed to. "Thuh bee-you-teeous perfume of thuh East. Frankincents."

"I-will-bring-the-gifta-meer." Fat ripped it out; he was way ahead of himself, but it was the speech he was to make before he went off. He left.

"Me, I better throw down a bundle to them camels." That was real smart of Ike; it wasn't what was written in the play at all, but with Steve coming for him Ike had to think quick. He turned and ran. The light cord for the bonfire caught his foot; he took off and lit flat on his face.

The barred Rock rooster let out a crow and leaped at the Wyandotte, his feathers up around his neck. Then they were going at it, just like a couple of balls you throw up in the air and catch and throw up again.

Smell or no smell I rushed out on to the stage to help Steve get those roosters. He'd got one, was holding it squawking under his arm whilst he tried to get the other. Just as we got the Wyandotte chased off into Fat's arms, the barred Rock got away again, and we had to go through her all over again.

We'd sure messed her up for Miss Henchbaw getting back again as teacher in Rabbit Hall. I told Steve that whilst we were out getting rid of his sheet and helping to open all the doors to air out the hall. It didn't seem to bother Steve; he had his mind on the Christmas candy and pop they were going to hand out.

When we came back in the front of the hall Jake and Mr. Tincher were up on the stage. Mr. Ricky was standing out in the audience.

" 'Tain't legal!" he was yelling. "Can't hold her unless yuh got yer three notices posted!"

"We posted 'em!" Jake yelled back at him.

"Where? I ain't seen 'em. Where was they posted?"

"Backa our cow barn," Jake said. "One on Totcoal's windmill — 'nother on Ed's granary in his East forty."

"But that ain't — I didn't — "

"We're here tuhnight," Jake said, "tuh make sure thuh folks in this district get thuh teacher they want teachin' their kids. So we have — "

"Section fifty-three — paragraph five says — "

"We have met tuh direct our school board tuh — "

" — only ratepayers kin — "

"Will Mr. Ricky set down an' shet up!" That was Bent Matthews.

"No, he won't," said Mr. Ricky. "I've set here tuhnight an' seen thuh most disgraceful display I ever — "

"Fine concert — what I saw," said Mr. Tincher.

"Them roosters!" shouted Old Man Gatenby. "Most comical thing I ever seen!"

"Ain't bin so much excitement sence thuh Fenian raids," yelled Phadrig Connor.

Then they were all yelling what a good concert it had been, and they meant it. When they had quieted down Jake said:

"We're gonna take vote — "

"Section fifty-three — paragraph five — "

"Johnny — Bent!" Jake called out. Mr. Totcoal and Mr. Matthews stood up on either side of Mr. Ricky.

"Kindly lead out thuh school board chairman — in — uh — accordance with section two hundred an' — uh — sixty — paragraft ten — which says — ennybuddy don't shet up when they're told three times, jist take 'em outa thuh hall."

"But there ain't enny such — "

I guess Mr. Ricky finished up outside.

I don't understand so well how they worked it, but Ma says Miss Henchbaw's staying. After the folks voted they asked Mr. Ricky to quit being chairman. He did. Even Mr. Ricky, Jake says, hadn't got the nerve to hang on after that meeting.

Lutiapik
Betty Lee

Don Baird had heard by radio that the RCAF would make its Christmas drop at Lake Harbour on December 12, so Georgie, Ishawakta, and Akavak went out to the bay-ice with oil drums to be used as flares.

The news of the drop generated an infectious excitement within the little settlement. Christmas meant mail and parcels from home. It meant temporary relief from isolation when the Inuit sledded in from camps for visits, games, and the services at the Anglican church. Christmas was an excuse to eat the best of the food supplies and to socialize more than usual. Christmas was an excuse to decorate the plain little house.

Dorothy had heard there were sometimes Christmas trees on the drop, but she decided to make her own from a triangular boot scraper she kept on the porch. With a box of tinsel and Yule decorations from the attic, she spent an afternoon setting up the scraper, hanging it with faded icicles and balls. The tree looked bare without parcels; she hoped there would be some for her in the mail. She wondered what she could give her friends in Lake Harbour and anxiously rummaged through her personal possessions and the attic shelves.

Mike might like a canned Christmas cake. She knew he missed Marg's baking. Don could have the deck of cards she had brought from Toronto and never used. She would give Hilda the bracelet she had admired. She puzzled over gifts for the two constables before deciding to buy cigarettes for them at the store. There was canned butter, jam, and bacon for the Inuit.

It was fun writing out her Christmas list. She was humming to herself when the door of her house opened and an Eskimo man came in from the icy darkness. She was surprised. The Inuit invariably stopped first at Ishawakta's home when they came from the camp seeking help. But she got to her feet and politely extended her hand. The man took it. He was handsome, grey haired and probably more than seventy years of age. "Lutiapik," he said, and his eyes crinkled.

She nodded at her name and smiled.

He pointed at his chest. "Kingwatcheak."

"Ah!" She nodded again. Mike had once told her about Kingwatcheak, the Cape Dorset leader and elder of the Anglican Church, who had been taken by Scottish whalers to Queen Victoria's Jubilee in 1898.

"He still handles his own dog team," the missionary had

said. "One day he'll turn up in Lake Harbour to say hello and visit. He always drops in to see everyone."

But was this a social or a professional visit, she wondered. *"Anneayoo?"* she asked the man, patting at her head, then her stomach.

He shook his head. *"Agai."* Then he laughed, walked into the kitchen and sat on a chair. The coal stove was blazing, but he did not remove his duffle-cloth parka. He pushed back the hood and the hoar-frost on the fur trimming quickly melted.

Dorothy was flattered. This was the first time she had received a personal call from an Eskimo, so she decided to make it an occasion. Kingwatcheak watched with interest as she went to a cupboard and brought out her best china tea service. Then she took some sweet cookies from a jar, arranged them on a plate, and poured the tea. Kingwatcheak helped himself to three heaping teaspoons of sugar. He took the cup delicately by the handle and sipped. "Queen Victoria's Jubilee," he said gravely.

"Ee," said Dorothy. *"Peoyook."*

Kingwatcheak sipped again, then munched two cookies. "Punch him in the nose," he said.

She was not sure how to respond to this, but she smiled and poured more tea.

"Sigalik?" she asked, offering a pack of cigarettes.

"Ee," he nodded graciously and took one, tapping it on the back of his hand. *"Peoyook."*

She wanted to ask the Eskimo if he intended staying in the settlement for Christmas, but did not know the right words. She decided to ask anyway, hoping he might understand. "Will you stay here for the Christmas celebrations?" she asked.

He shook his head, either to say no or to indicate he had not understood.

She tried other words. *"Sheetlitchea,"* she said. Fine weather. He stared at her with faint amusement for a moment, then he laughed and she laughed along with him.

"Ookoo!" she said, pointing to the stove. Hot. He laughed again.

He butted the cigarette in a glass ashtray. "Queen Victoria's Jubilee," he repeated and got to his feet.

She followed him to the door; again they shook hands. He left without saying good-bye.

Everyone listened all day for the sound of the RCAF boxcar. Ishawakta and Akavak had poured gasoline into the oil-drum flares and took turns, waiting on the sea-ice. It was late afternoon when someone heard the drone of the engines and shouted so loudly and urgently, the dogs began to howl in interested chorus. Dorothy struggled into her parka and ran into the chilly darkness, staring at the sky. The drone grew louder, and then she could see the wink of lights. Akavak lit the flares.

She sprinted excitedly towards the barrier-ice. Georgie had hitched the dogs to the Hudson's Bay *komatik*, and the sled slithered past her in the gloom, bumping and crashing through the hummocks. Don and Hilda were already standing on the flat sea-ice, bundled into parkas and stamping their feet in the bitter cold. She could see Gerry Heapy coming from the fjord with the RCMP *komatik*, while Mike emerged from the barrier-ice with his team as well.

The Inuit laughed and pointed as the aircraft banked and headed up the fjord towards the flares. Two bundles suspended from white parachutes drifted from the belly of the plane followed by a third, then a fourth. After a moment, two spruce trees dropped out of the sky and landed, upright, in the snow. Her eyes blurred a little at the sight of the familiar trees standing so straight and alone on the flat ice. The aircraft gained altitude and vanished over the hills. She wondered where the crew would be that night. In a Montreal restaurant? Walking along a crowded street? At home with their families?

"Let's go," said Don. "This is the closest thing to Santa Claus we'll ever get."

The drop had been made in large wicker baskets which were loaded on the sleds and taken to the mission house for unpacking and sorting. She jogged along behind the *komatiks,* feeling the same kind of anticipation she always felt when her brothers brought parcels home at Christmas. She swallowed hard at the thought of her family in Toronto and found herself a chair in a corner of the mission house kitchen as the men fished the fat mail bags from the hampers.

Gerry, as official government representative, was given custody of the red sacks of registered letters and parcels. She thought he was joking when he announced that everyone would have to come over to the detachment next day to sign for their mail. She started to laugh, but it was no joke. Registered mail was registered mail, even in Lake Harbour. The constable put the red sacks on the porch, then helped his four white neighbours work through the unregistered letters, packages, and periodicals.

Someone, probably at the Air Force base, had stuffed some paperbacks into one of the hampers. Don spread them on the table together with a giant card wishing Lake Harbour a Merry Christmas. The two trees, it was decided after a conference, would be put in the Hudson's Bay store and the mission, because the visiting Inuit would be most likely to see them there.

Mike had some small sacks stored on the porch, and Dorothy asked to borrow one to carry her mail. There were at least a dozen parcels and a small stack of letters addressed to her via Lake Harbour, Northwest Territories, Royal Mail Service, Ottawa. She had riffled through the pile while she waited. Nothing again from Health and Welfare, she noted with disappointment. Did her employers know she existed? She envied the mountain of mail that had come for the mission, the detachment, and the Hudson's Bay post. Perhaps, if she read one letter a day, hers might last until January. But she shrugged. She knew she would read the letters, one after the other, until they were finished. It was like the Inuit with their food. Mail was such a treat, she would consume it all at once.

When Don and Hilda climbed into their parkas, she decided to leave with them. She told Gerry a little formally that she would come to the detachment next day and sign for her registered mail. He grinned at her. Akavak was at the door, and after a short conference with him, Gerry came back across the room. "It's Kingwatcheak," he said. "He's sick. Akavak has taken him to Ishawakta's house. I hope it isn't too bad."

After examining the old man, it was difficult to tell. He had a slight temperature and was complaining of stomach cramps, but he was cheerful and sipped smilingly at a mug of tea. She was glad she had set up a hospital bed in her diningroom. "Ishawakta," she said, pointing to Kingwatcheak, then towards her home. "I will take Kingwatcheak over there."

The courtly old Eskimo seemed delighted when Ishawakta told him he would be staying at the *aniatitsiyuk's* house until he felt well again.

"Ee," he nodded. *"Naak."* And he rubbed at his sore stomach. He followed Dorothy down the gravel path to her home and sat quietly in the livingroom while she heated him a bowl of chicken soup. While he ate from the bowl with the shiniest soup spoon she could find, she checked the bed and put out more blankets. The problem of pyjamas worried her until she remembered she had packed a large flannel nightgown with the supplies transferred from the hospital.

"Kingwatcheak," she said, holding it for him to see.

He laughed, pointing at it and then at himself. "Kingwatcheak?"

She nodded, went into the diningroom, and laid it over the bed. He padded into the converted diningroom, and she left him alone. The parcels looked friendly and reassuring when she stacked them under the boot-scraper tree. She squeezed one or two of them curiously but resisted the temptation to see what her family thought she would like to have in the Arctic. Instead, she opened the first of her letters, reading about Ray and Sylvia and Fred and how the temperature in Toronto had dropped to a frigid low of twenty degrees in November. Aunt Nell was fine and so was mother and everyone was going to miss her a lot at Christmas.

She tore open a letter from a nursing friend, forgetting for a moment about Kingwatcheak. "Things are about the same at the hospital —" Then she heard a low, musical sound from the diningroom. The old man's song was really a chant, and she put down the letter to listen to it. She had no idea what it meant, but she was sure it was about life and loving and hunting, and the harsh beauty of the North. Perhaps, she smiled, it was also about his adventures in London at Queen Victoria's Jubilee. She picked up the letter again.

Two nurses she knew had left. Iris had become a stewardess with an airline; Shirley was working in a New York cancer hospital. She tucked the note back in the envelope, listening to Kingwatcheak's haunting chant. The nostalgia and the aching loneliness she had felt when the green spruce trees landed on the ice had gone. She went into the kitchen to heat her patient some milk before getting ready for bed.

Kingwatcheak hitched up his team a few days before Christmas, patted his well stomach, and departed smilingly for Cape Dorset. His *komatik* had scarcely disappeared from the frozen bay before the Inuit began arriving from the outer camps. Some built snowhouses close to the settlement, but others crowded in with Ishawakta, Georgie, and Akavak. After a talk with Mike, she opened and heated the hospital for any of the Inuit who cared to stay there. The old hut near the cemetery would also provide extra shelter.

Lake Harbour was alive again with the sound of laughter, children's voices, and the constant howl of dogs. The Eskimos jammed into the Hudson's Bay store, trading furs with Don, spending their credits on supplies. The men admired the .22 rifle donated by the company as first prize in the annual dogteam race. Women sat in small, giggling groups, doing almost exactly as they did in their home camps — sewing clothes, making meals, and feeding any child who happened to wander by.

There was an immediate rush of callers at Dorothy's porch door. She saw the first batch of patients in the kitchen, directing the rest to the hospital surgery. She felt comfortable and at home, working in the Quonset hut again. There was the ever-present impetigo to treat, ear infections, boils. She administered DPT shots and boosters to babies. With the help of the Inuit, she pulled several teeth. From Utye's camp, Kavanaugh brought Jamesee to the hospital as Dorothy had asked her to do. Apprehensively, she examined the boy's eyes. The keratitis nodules were no longer visible; there seemed to be no complications from the cortisone. *"Peoyook?"* she asked the Eskimo woman, pointing at her son.

Kavanaugh nodded *"Ee. Peoyook."*

"Peoyook!" shrilled Jamesee, grinning and blinking rapidly to show the itching and pain had gone. He jumped down from the examination table. *"Koveeashoobik!"* he said. Christmas.

Since the Inuit had always held celebrations in mid-winter it must have been easy for them to accept the white man's festival when they were converted to Christianity. As far as Dorothy could tell, it seemed to matter very little to an Eskimo whether he ate cookies and bean stew, or slices of raw seal meat during the Yule season. Scottish reels were as much fun as ancient drum dances. Christmas toys were as novel and amusing as other *kabloonah* toys. Religious ceremonies were expected. And games were part of the Inuit tradition.

Hilda called her on the settlement telephone. "We're all having Christmas dinner here at the post," she said. "I'm cooking the *Rupertsland* turkey."

"What can I bring? Oranges? Cake? Nuts?"

"Bring everything. We'll all share."

"How about the washing-machine beer?"

Hilda laughed. "We've been spared. The boys have been saving some Scotch."

The woman discussed the feast the settlement whites were planning for the Eskimos. Cauldrons of stew. Sacks of pilot biscuits and cans of butter and jam. Dozens of fresh cookies. Gallons of tea. During a lull in the stream of patients, she brought armfuls of supplies from the attic and dumped them in a corner of the kitchen until she could find time for cooking. Between splinting a fractured finger and bandaging a cut she baked a cake. She dispensed bismuth and aspirin to those who asked, then went back to the house to start on her quota of cookies. That evening, she flopped wearily into a living room chair and vowed she would turn in early. But the settlement telephone rang twice, and she rose to answer it.

"Dorothy," Gerry Heapy's voice came over the wire. "The Eskimos have got a dance going in the old hut. You want to come?"

She tried to tell herself it was just Gerry's way of spreading the Christmas spirit around, but it was impossible not to feel as excited as she had when a boy in Toronto had asked her to her first teenage hop. Of course she would go. She found herself laughing into the telephone and asking what on earth one wore to a dance in the old hut with a crowd of Eskimos?

"Well, I sure as heck wouldn't wear a crinoline and high heels if I were you," Gerry told her. "These dances can get pretty strenuous."

She had no intention of wearing the crinoline, but for some reason she felt disappointed.

"Well, what do you want me to wear? Slacks and nurse's shoes."

"Good idea. Pick you up in an hour."

She grimaced at the sight of herself in ordinary slacks and sweater, but she took some time with her hair and make-up and used some perfume. The new duffle-cloth parka she had asked Oola to make had been delivered that morning. When Gerry knocked at the door, she zipped herself into it, and they walked through the windless night to the building near the graveyard.

Mosesee's daughter, Noota, was playing an accordion; two Eskimo men were blowing energetically into mouth organs. The music had obviously been inspired by the Scottish whalers who had spent so much time in Lake Harbour. The Inuit men were performing some lively steps, but the women had gathered in a tight inner group and were shuffling in a slowly moving circle. Some had babies asleep in their hoods. Children darted among the dancers clutching playfully at their parkas and *amoutis*. No one seemed to mind.

"Well, let's get a proper reel going," said Gerry. He shouted to the men in Eskimo, and he and Dorothy began dancing hand-over-hand around the room. Noota pumped tirelessly at the accordion. The mouth organs droned on and on. The men and some of the teenage boys decided to join in the new dance. But the women still shuffled, their eyes fixed on the wooden floor.

"When do we stop?" Dorothy gasped as she caught up with Gerry during a frenetic turn around the room. The air was stifling and she wished Noota would play something slow. *Dream when you're feeling blue . . .* Gerry was on the other side of the hut again. His good-looking face was shiny with perspiration. *Dream, it's the thing to do . . .*

Hand-over-hand. Two giggling Eskimos, then Gerry. "When do we stop?"

"When you drop," he yelled back over the music and laughter.

For a moment, she thought she might join the circle of shuffling female dancers. "You must be kidding!" she panted. She wondered if Gerry knew how to do a slow foxtrot. "This has been going on for an hour."

It went on for another two.

Christmas was a non-stop holiday of feasting, carol-singing in the church, and games on the sea-ice. There were competitions in harpoon-throwing and snowhouse-building. There was wrestling and tug-of-war, and the women and children crowded excitedly into the old hut to scramble as Don and Mike up-ended baskets of candy and oranges.

A young Eskimo from Mingeriak's camp won the running broad jump and received Mike's prize of a new Bible. Young Sandy was a close second in the big *komatik* race that had a dozen crack teams skimming up the fjord to the finish line opposite the mission. No whips were allowed in the race. The drivers knew they must encourage their dogs by voice alone. She stood with Hilda on the ice, listening as the shouts of *"hraw! hraw!"* and *"hoit! hoit!"* came closer and the *komatiks* struggled out of the afternoon gloom. Some were overturned; almost all of the teams were tangled in their hide traces. A man named Lukasee won the .22 rifle and spent the rest of the day shooting a small fortune in cartridges at tin cans. Sandy won a sack of groceries.

She opened her parcels alone on Christmas morning, reading the messages inside and making a neat pile of stockings, boxes of candy, a new sweater, and copies of Nevil Shute's *On the Beach* and James Gould Cozzens' *By Love Possessed.* Both books, she was assured by her brothers, were bestsellers in the South. It was fun, opening the parcels, but the aloneness was depressing and she went back to bed.

Later, she took the candy, together with the cake she had baked and some fruits and nuts, to the *kabloonah* Christmas dinner at the Bairds. The roasted *Rupertsland* turkey was consumed to an appreciative chorus of *"ee . . . ahaloonah!"* and washed down with a bottle of wine hidden somewhere in the post since August. It was warm and friendly in the house, and she forgot her morning loneliness. There were songs and tall stories about the Arctic. To uproarious laughter and applause, Don found some reedy music on the radio. It was yet another Scottish reel.

Dorothy was still humming as she brushed her teeth in the frigid bathroom before going to bed. Next day, there would be a whip-cracking contest and a football game. Then there would be the big Boxing Day feast in the old hut. She washed her face with the expensive-smelling soap that Hilda had given her and decided she would read a chapter of the new Shute novel before turning out the lights.

"Lutiapik," she heard Ishawakta say softly from the kitchen. She was startled. She dried her face and went to him. The Eskimo pointed at the porch door. "Seemeega. Come from camp. With son. Iktoluka."

"Iktoluka *anneayoo?*"

Ishawakta shook his head. *"Tokovok."* He dies.

Seemeega was standing by his *komatik* in the black night. She switched on the porch light and saw his dogs were sitting or lying, panting in the snow. Something wrapped in skins was lashed to the top of the *komatik* load. She assumed this was the body of the boy. She waited for the Eskimo to say something to Ishawakta, but he simply stood, gripping the butt of his whip.

She knew it was useless to try questioning the Eskimo, so she walked back into the house and called Gerry on the settlement telephone. The RCMP should be informed of a death, in any case.

"Gerry? A man named Seemeega has come into the settlement with a dead boy. It's his son, Ishawakta says. I thought you should know about it. But could you talk to the man on the phone and let me know what happened?" Gerry sounded sleepy, but he agreed to interpret, so she went to the door and asked Seemeega to come inside. She pointed to the telephone, talked into it to show what it was for, then offered it to the Eskimo. He hesitated. Then he took it, smelled it carefully, held it at arm's length, and put it to his ear.

She watched his eyes widen when he heard Gerry's voice. *"Ee,"* he said, and listened again. After a few moments, he spoke into the receiver. There was another silence, then he gave her the telephone.

"Gerry?"

"It's his son, all right. The boy was hunting seal, then apparently got very hot, with much pain and coughing. He stayed on the sleeping platform for a few days. Then, when he got worse, Seemeega loaded him on the *komatik* to bring him to Lake Harbour. The boy died on the way. He doesn't say why he didn't come in for Christmas."

"How far away was the camp?"

"One sleep, apparently."

"But he left it too late!" said Dorothy. "He should have come earlier with the boy, or sent for me. Doesn't the man know that I would have come if he had sent a message?"

There was silence at the other end of the telephone. She turned to look at Seemeega. The Eskimo's eyes were slits above his high cheekbones. "Ayonamut!" he mumbled.

"Oh my God," said Dorothy, suddenly angry. "He says it can't be helped! But it could have been helped. Doesn't he know that? The boy probably only needed some antibiotics."

"Dorothy," Gerry said, "could you leave the body on your porch? I'll come around some time to check it over."

"Sure," she said. "Goodnight, Gerry." And she hung up.

She lay awake for a long time that night, grieving for young Iktoluka, realizing the boy's life had probably ebbed away on the cold sled while she and the other settlement whites had been eating their Christmas dinner. She turned her face unhappily into the pillow wondering again whether she, the Inuit, or even the Department of Health and Welfare really knew why she was there.

The Eskimos packed their *komatiks* two days after Christmas, shook hands around the settlement, and hitched their teams. Soon, the settlement was as quiet and deserted as it had been before the invasion. To add to the let-down, the weather broke and the snow rattled against the side of the house like pellets of gravel. She tried to cheer herself up by finishing the new books and making herself a dinner out of the leftover turkey that Hilda had given her. But she missed the friendly Inuit faces at the door, and she longed to be busy.

She called Gerry again to talk and to ask about the body on the porch. He said he had not been able to cross the bay. "Plenty of time," he said at the other end of the squeaky line. "It's cold enough for the corpse to keep a while. If you don't mind having it there, that is."

She did, but there seemed nothing she could do about it. Whenever she walked through the porch, Iktoluka's still form was a reminder of that night's anger and frustration. She tried to forget by writing her regular INHS report and long, somewhat rambling letters to her family and friends. She wondered bleakly when the messages would reach their destinations. The next mail to go out would accompany Hilda on the Hudson's Bay Beaver in a few weeks time. She preferred not to think about Hilda's going. She doubted whether she could be any lonelier than she was now, but she resented the diminishment of the little community. *One little Indian, two little Indians* she began counting compulsively. *And then there were only six.*

When the blizzard petered out next day, she bundled into warm clothes and walked through the squeaky snow to the hospital and back. The dogs were unstaked at this time of the year; King spotted her and raced to jump. She wanted to take him into the kitchen for food, but stopped herself. "King," she said, softly, "King," and turned from him. The animal lowered his head and walked away.

She kept walking beyond the house and began climbing the small hill. It was mid-afternoon; she could see the jagged outlines of the mountains and the white fjord in the glow of the Arctic twilight. There were a few stars in the north, over the peninsula. She could travel for half the length of Baffin Island with nothing but ice-locked lakes and empty tundra until she came to the small settlement of Clyde River. She remembered that tomorrow was New Year's Eve. There would be crowded celebrations in Toronto. There would be toasts in champagne and warm kisses and bittersweet choruses of "Auld Lang Syne".

Nineteen fifty-eight. "Happy New Year, Dorothy," she whispered to herself, pulling her frost-crusted scarf more closely around her cold face. Well, she had always boasted that she did something absolutely different on New Year's Eve. She wondered if anyone had decided yet where the *kabloonahs* would see the old year out. She laughed. There wasn't much choice. There was her house, Mike's, the detachment, or the Baird's.

Christmas on the Farm
Allan Anderson

The Christmas Parcel "When Christmas rolled around I'd had a lovely letter from home saying that there was a parcel on the way. And I knew that would be good. So a neighbor and I hitched up our little jumper — we called them jumpers, they looked like outside toilets, you know — and put it with a team. And set off with a lot of rugs and robes: it was very, very cold. But we had a footwarmer, so we were really very cosy. Of course we started to laugh because she'd come from London, and we thought of ourselves going down Picadilly in this outfit.

And then we got to the store, which was five miles away, to get this parcel. The store was a little tiny post office called St. Lina. And then we had a little look around St. Lina, bought a few things, and got the precious Christmas parcel.

As we were coming home, we stopped at another neighbour's and we thought we'd say hi to them because we were trying to make a date for Christmas Day so that we could all be together. Well, I tied the team up to a railing outside their place, went in to have tea, came out — fortunately didn't stay very very late — to find smoke coming out of the cutter. And what happened was: as we'd got out of the cutter, we'd tripped this footwarmer, and the charcoal had set fire to all the things in the cutter. We were just very lucky that the team didn't run away. It hadn't got to the team — it was just coming out of the cutter. So our precious Christmas parcel was burned, though it wasn't burned totally. We were able to cut off an inch of burnt cake and rescue a little. But that was heartbreaking."

A Toboggan for Christmas "My dad had four brothers and they had a number of kids. And at Christmastime everybody got together and we had a big supper on Christmas Eve, and we would have a lot of traditional Norwegian food.

And after, the big thing I really enjoyed was that we would get the old half-ton truck out, and one great big toboggan that one of my uncles had built, and we used to hook this toboggan up to the truck. It would pull us usually from my grandpa's farm to my dad's farm, which was about four and a half miles, on the road. And this was really an exciting experience for me every year.

The time I remember most was when my aunt bought me a toboggan for Christmas. And I insisted this toboggan had to be hooked up behind the truck as well as the big toboggan. And I was riding on this toboggan, for four and a half miles. Well, to say the least the toboggan wasn't that strong of a thing for this kind of treatment and after four and a half miles of travelling at about fifteen, twenty miles an hour — to me it was about sixty — there wasn't much left of my toboggan.

But I really had a tremendous evening. I can remember there was probably twenty or thirty of us, and people getting lost when we got in the field making circles, and there was people all over the snow. It was just a tremendous time."

Gatherings

The Richtfest
Michael Henry

Thanksgiving
The Indian summer sun shines down
On the prairie rippling gently in the wind.
A few children stand on the edge,
Uncertain whether to paddle into the long grasses.
Nature takes time off to sunbathe
From her near-completed cycle.
The air hangs heavy with heat.
And in the hot ovens, smelling sweetly,
Bread is baking, cake, and roast meat.
Whiffs of the approaching feast
Urge the workers on to final effort
The whole village bound in apprenticeship
To the task of building a barn.
The framework stands shakily like a newborn colt,
With each tap of the hammer, another nail is driven home.
Another board to shore up its growing confidence.

Now an age-old ritual begins
Apprentices and journeymen stand back
To the carpenter, the captain of their team.
He climbs aloft the ladder leant against the frame,
Takes out a hammer from his apron,

And bang! explodes the silence
By hitting home the ceremonial nail.
His helpers down below burst out in cheers,
The gable is now up.

They bring out food and drink,
A toast to the carpenter,
To his work that all can see,
And to the completion that no one doubts.
This is his thanksgiving, the Richtfest,
A custom brought from Germany.
After the celebration,
Like nature he will return rewarded
And encouraged to continue
His important work.

The Dance
Max Braithwaite

Over the course of the years I've attended dances in posh
wardrooms, army messes, and ballrooms twenty times as big
as Willowgreen School. I've waltzed, rhumba'd and cha cha'd
to small combos and big bands whose members are world-
renowned musicians. But the dance that sticks in my mind for
all time is the one in Willowgreen School when Orville Jackson
played the fiddle and Grandma Wilson chorded on the organ.

I first got wind of it after school on Friday when, instead
of slouching down the aisles making desultory passes at dust,
Charlie McDougall and his band of helpers began by energetically pushing all the desks to the sides, back and front of the
room.

"What's the idea?" I asked.

"Dance tonight."

"Here?"

"Yep."

"Who's coming?"

"Just about everybody in the district, I guess."

"Nobody said anything to me about it."

He merely shrugged at this and then, as an afterthought, "Oh yeah. Dad said to tell you they'll need your bed for the babies."

With that puzzling announcement he set to cleaning the floor as though he actually cared about getting the dust off it.

The bit about my bed bothered me to the extent that, after eating my supper of roast pork and bread, I got out the broom and swept my own rooms. Then I picked up the half dozen or so brown-stained cigarette butts from the edges of the table and shelves where they'd burned little black grooves. I even washed the dishes and the table top and put away the pork. Then I pulled the covers straight on my bed, hung my shirt on the back of the door and kicked dirty socks under the bed. The place looked almost tidy.

The Montgomerys were the first to arrive — and I had my first sight of Harris Montgomery who later was to become my mentor in socialism, adviser on morals, and instructor in the new economics. Seeing him then with the neat, if big, Mrs. Montgomery, I could hardly believe my eyes. He was the untidiest man I've ever seen, a sort of middle-aged beatnik. His eyes got me first, dark, wild and small beside the great bridge of his nose. Then the nose, sharp and hooked, extending down to his upper lip. His wrinkled face was lean, mouth slightly pointed, cheeks with shiny skin peeling from much exposure to wind.

He treated his wife always as a petty bourgeois and she treated him with that silent, tolerant contempt that wives have for husbands whom they've given up on.

When he saw me Harris Montgomery leaped forward, grabbed my hand, shoved his chapped face within six inches of mine, jabbed my chest with a nicotine-stained finger and demanded, "What do you think of Cole?"

"I don't know," I stammered. "I'm afraid I haven't met him yet."

"No, no, no, no! The Cole in England, I mean. The economist. G. D. H."

"Oh. That Cole?"

"Yes . . . yes. You've read him, haven't you?"

"Well . . . uh . . . "

"Great thinker. None of your mealy-mouthed bull manure about him. We'll have a talk about him. You live downstairs, don't you?"

"Well . . . yes."

"Good. We can go down there. Get away from all this damned falderal. I've been looking for somebody with some brains in his head to . . . "

But at this point Mrs. Montgomery captured him. "Hang up the Coleman," she commanded. "It's so puny dark in here, you can't see your hand before your face."

"Women!" Harris Montgomery muttered darkly. It was his most venomous expletive, and it summed up all the nonsense, muddled thinking and waste effort of the capitalist world.

But he'd lost this battle long ago. So he took a large gas lamp and hooked it on the end of a strong wire that extended down from the middle of the ceiling, and the whole room changed miraculously. I began to feel like a party.

"Now take these things downstairs." Mrs. Montgomery handed him a big wicker basket of provisions, and turned to her younger sister who came through the door carrying something bundled up in blankets. "You can put the baby downstairs in the teacher's bed. Is your fire going?"

"Uh . . . yes . . . yes, it is."

"Good. Harris, get that wash-boiler of water out of the sleigh and put it on the stove down there. And don't spill half of it on the way down the steps. Teacher, maybe you could help him."

With nothing more than my sweater on, I went out to the

sleigh to help Harris with the water. As we did so another sleigh pulled by a team of ice-flecked Clydes came slanting dangerously over the drift at the gate.

"Wahoo!" A youth in a sheepskin mackinaw and no hat leaped out of the sleigh, waving in his hand a mickey of gin. "It's a great night for the race!" he bellowed, crooking his arm over my shoulder and shoving the bottle at me. "Have a drink, pal."

Involuntarily I was reaching for the bottle when I heard Harris Montgomery's warning. "Cut it out, you damned fool Jake. That's the teacher!"

"Oh!" Jake, who was just about my age, sobered immediately. "I'm sorry, sir."

He shoved the bottle into his pocket, hurried off to unhitch the horses, and from the sleigh box came the sound of female giggles — young female giggles.

So, neatly and completely, I'd been categorized as "the teacher". Something from outer space, without feelings, Ichabod Crane. A nothing!

For a second I was swept by frustrated rage. Here was a party in my own place, and I couldn't even be a part of it. Of course, if I'd had a jug of liquor hidden down in the furnace room or in the barn as the others did, I could have invited them for a drink. But I had neither the money nor the opportunity to get a jug, and even if I had, the news would have spread like a prairie fire that the new teacher at Willowgreen was a drinker. Not that he took a drink or was sociable or a good sport. Just a drinker, and who's going to send their kids to a school run by a drunkard, I'd like to know.

So they came, the old and the young, each with their bundles, many with babies. Some had come from as far as twelve miles, a three-hour journey over a winding snow trail. In the bottoms of their sleigh boxes they'd put stones, heated in the stove and wrapped in newspaper, for foot-warmers. Some of the sleigh boxes were half filled with straw so that the children could snuggle down out of the wind like mice in a stack.

Why did they come? It was a break in the dreary drag of the winter months. They were sick to death of playing rummy and cribbage and of the sound of each other's voices. They'd had a bellyful of togetherness, babies, grandmothers, old-maid aunts, grown-up sons with no place to go, huddled in a few draughty rooms like foxes in a den, satiated with the sight and sound and smell of each other. This was their chance to break out for a few hours, see different faces, hear some gossip. Find out about that cow of Mark Brownlee's that was due to calf, the vicissitudes of fate, the shortage of feed, the uselessness of the Bennett nickel — a five-cent bonus on every bushel of wheat paid through the good offices of a prime minister who, like everyone else, was rendered confused and inept by the magnitude of the depression.

Soon the schoolhouse was full. My bed was covered with tiny bodies stacked across it like cordwood. Every so often a mother would come down the steps, listen at the closed door and, if she heard anything, tiptoe in and shove a soother into the mouth of the restless one. My kitchen-dining room was plugged with food, boilers for coffee, cups, plates and outdoor clothing. I had been dispossessed.

Upstairs were all the people in the district over the age of three. The very young squirmed on the laps of the very old. The little girls, with fresh hair ribbons and pressed print dresses, dashed about between their elders, chatted breathlessly, giggled, excited beyond comprehending by they knew not what. The little boys, on the other hand, hands shoved embarrassingly deep into knicker pockets, stood about not knowing quite what to do.

Almost to a man the male adults wore blue serge suits bought, heavens knows how many years before, through the Eaton's mail order catalogue. When the history of American costumes is finally written, the blue serge suit must surely have a special place as the worst fitting, the shiniest and most durable of all articles of clothing. Most of these were wedding suits and saw duty only at church, weddings, dances, Christmas concerts, and special political meetings. Some had been handed down from father to son to grandson.

The women, a half dozen of whom were in various stages of pregnancy, all had the same look of tired resignation. But, miraculously, as the evening progressed and the dancing became more animated, I was to notice this expression gradually change, the eyes regain a little of their sparkle, the cheeks a slight splash of colour and, from behind the tired, worried countenance, I got the occasional fleeting glimpse of what that face had been before the years — only a few, really — of drought and cold and worry and childbearing had cast them in the sad mould. The prairies are hard on women.

Of young girls there were only three. Two unbelievably homely and the other unbelievably beautiful. A dark-haired, round-cheeked, full-lipped, thick-bosomed girl whose shapely legs and thighs, which showed often as she was "swung-out", made my mouth go dry and my loins ache just to see them.

It was a gay crowd, but I wasn't part of it. Mrs. Montgomery had made a few introductions, but they'd fallen flat. They mistook my natural shyness for a stand-offish attitude, and each attempt I made at light conversation came out all wrong. Finally I found myself standing around with my hands in my pockets, trying to keep out of the people's way.

But I had my eye on the dark-haired beauty and I knew what I was going to do when the music started. I fancied myself pretty good at the flea hop, the foxtrot and the waltz, and could do a passable charleston. I'd show these damned yokels a thing or two. After all, I hadn't been nicknamed "twinkle toes" at Nutana Collegiate for nothing.

With a smattering of applause, the fiddler, Orville Jackson, took his place beside the organ in the corner. A short bandy-legged man of about sixty-five, he wore a khaki peaked cap indoors and out. I soon discovered why. Most of his front teeth were gone and, in order to keep his pipe in his mouth while playing, he hung it from the peak of his cap by a thread. He cradled his fiddle in his left arm with the butt against his chest and began tuning it.

As he did so, Grandma Wilson, who must have weighed close to three hundred pounds, came forward and sank down on the organ stool, her ample bottom overlapping on all sides. She threw her beefy hands at the organ keys and came up with a wail like a sick cat. Orville tapped his right foot twice, waved his head gently back and forth so that the suspended pipe swung in time, and drew his bow across the fiddle.

Before I could even start towards the dark young lady, four young swains swooped down upon her and bore her off. Then I noticed that the music was almost completely unfamiliar and, instead of the dancers embracing each other and shuffling around the floor as I was accustomed to do, they arranged themselves in groups of eight, facing each other. A big florid man had taken his place beside the organ and bellowed, "Two more couples wanted;" then, when a grinning farmer and his six-year-old daughter had responded, "One more couple wanted."

Then I noticed a determined, red-faced matron approaching me and, before I could duck, she had me by the hand. "Come on, Teacher," she grinned. "Be my partner."

"Yeah, get in there and fight, Teach!" somebody shouted, and, as I looked around at their grinning faces, I knew that in some crazy way I was on trial. So I suffered myself to be led to the centre of the floor, which was by now so crowded that we could scarcely get through.

Then Grandma Wilson banged the organ, Orville Jackson sawed at his fiddle, the caller shouted in a great booming voice, "Places all!" and everybody began to move in different directions.

Now, it may seem strange, but although I was born and

bred on the prairies, I had in my whole life not only never participated in a square dance, but I'd never even seen one done. As I recall it now, it was something like a football scrimmage and a basketball game combined. With women! As the music gained momentum and the caller bellowed louder and the stamping of feet became deafening, I become completely and hopelessly lost. I was shoved and pushed and chivvied about like a shopper at a bargain counter. Every so often one of the women would grab me and swing me around and then drop me. As I stomped aimlessly about I would regularly meet a six-footer in a red plaid shirt and face to match who'd take me by the shoulders with two immense hands and literally lift me into place, like a mother lifting a child. But I never stayed in place for long.

I remember once seeing an ancient book in which the evils of "round" dancing were deplored while "square" dancing was approved. This square dancing was not only indecent, it was downright perilous. Those muscular lads grabbed their partners by the nearest handle and swung them off their feet. Their dresses half the time flew up over their heads, and flying feet narrowly missed other people's jaws.

On and on, faster and faster went the dance until each couple had its turn doing whatever we were doing and then the music stopped. The panting, sweating participants sat down. My partner never even spoke to me, nor did any other member of the set. Whatever test I'd been put to, I had failed. Then the caller shouted his commands again and after a couple of "Two more couples wanted", the joint was jumping again. I can say this; that schoolhouse was mighty well built. Otherwise those dancers would have gone right through the floor and ended up in my quarters with their babies. As it was, the rhythm of the stomping feet shook the place till the desks rattled.

So it went on . . . and on . . . and on . . . square dance after square dance, with an occasional quadrille or schottische thrown in. Nobody invited me to dance again, and of course

I didn't have the nerve to ask anybody. So I watched in a sort of terrified wonder as the others whirled and swung and pranced. Occasionally I caught a glimpse of my dark lady being pawed and patted and thrown about by rawboned hands, but I realized that there was nothing there for me.

I tried again retiring to my own quarters, but found the kitchen filled with talking women preparing food. Since the bedroom was still full of babies, there was nothing for it but to return to the dance.

Around about midnight Mrs. Montgomery announced that lunch would be served and I felt like a besieged general when he sees relief coming over the hill. Big enamel pitchers of scalding coffee were brought up from the basement and served in thick, white kitchen cups. Chicken and pork sandwiches were passed around (there was virtually no market for chicken), followed by cake and cookies. I was waiting it out. Then each man rolled a fag or lighted up his pipe and the topic of economics was discussed in corners. Soon, I thought, even this will end. The kids will be cleared off my bed, everybody will go home and I'll get some sleep.

But I was greatly mistaken. Orville Jackson filled his pipe, hung it in place, and shuffled over to the organ again. Grandma Wilson draped her ample bottom over the organ stool. They struck up the music and the dance began again. And if I'd thought it lively before, now it was downright frantic. There was one slick little number where four men and four women joined hands. Then, with a quick manoeuvre, the men somehow had their arms behind the women's backs, hands clasped tight. They began to skip around in a circle, faster and faster. As the men gained momentum, the women's feet left the floor until their legs were straight out, their bodies parallel to the floor. I'd have sworn that if one had broken loose she'd have shot clear through the window.

Another feature of the after-supper session was what might be called the specialty numbers: dances performed by certain members who had become famous for them. "Dip and Dive", for instance, led by Uncle John Henry who weighed two seventy-five and was about five foot eight. Yet he had the grace and agility to lead the dancers, all holding hands, through an intricate series of dips and dives that was beautiful to watch. "Little Drops of Brandy" followed this, and a waltz quadrille.

But the specialty of specialties was when Orville Jackson and Grandma Wilson temporarily surrendered their instruments to an acne-afflicted youth and none other than our own Violet Sinclair. Then a reverent hush fell on the assembly as the two musicians took their places. Orville had set aside his peaked cap and pipe, revealing a head so bald and shiny that it gleamed beneath the gas lamp. As the music began the bald-headed man and the fat grandmother embraced each other for the only round dance of the evening. While the others formed a circle and clapped lightly and rhythmically to the tune of "Till We Meet Again", those two danced as smoothly and gracefully as any couple I've ever seen.

And the dancing went on. One o'clock, two o'clock, three o'clock plodded by and there was no sign of a break. At six o'clock a faint glow of light began to show outside and the dancers reluctantly began to make preparations to leave. They had been waiting for daylight to make the long, long sleigh ride home just a little easier.

Sleeping babies, wound in their cocoons of blankets, were carried up the basement steps and laid gently in the straw in the bottom of sleigh boxes. Horses with steam shooting from their nostrils were brought out from the barn and hitched to the sleighs. One by one they pulled out of the gate and I was left alone . . . alone with a schoolroom littered with cigarette and cigar butts, pipe ashes and tobacco juice. I thought it would never be clean again, but I was too tired to care.

I stumbled down the steps and into my bedroom, which smelled strongly of babies neglected for ten hours, peeled off my clothes and climbed beneath the covers. For half an hour the throbbing music still in my ears kept me awake, and then I sank into the deep sleep of the just.

Not for long. At nine o'clock I heard a heavy banging above me, feet on the stairs, my door being opened and somebody looking into the stove.

"It's only me," Mrs. Montgomery's voice announced cheerfully. "A few of us have come to clean up. We'll need to heat water on your stove. Some of that tobacco juice is hard to get off the floor." Then she added, "But you don't need to get up. I can find everything."

She thumped back up the stairs and, with four other ladies, tore into cleaning up the place. All morning they swept, scrubbed, scoured and, it seemed to me, played shuffleboard with the movable desks. Then, for good measure, they gave my kitchen-living room the same treatment and left.

Thus ended the one and only social event I attended during my stay at Willowgreen School.

New Year's Eve 1906
Harold F. Cruickshank

One event in my memory will never be forgotten for it was the first old-time dance in our pioneer district — New Year's Eve 1906.

I was a 13-year-old boy at the time. My father and I had felt lonely at Christmas, so far from Mother and the rest of the family back in Scotland, but the friendship and fun on that New Year's Eve helped us feel part of the community.

I can hear the screech of sleigh runners now, and the crack of frosted tamaracks in the swamps, as three or four sleigh-loads of first settlers arrived for the occasion.

It was intensely cold, and when the teams swung into the yard the icicles clinging to the nostrils of the horses gave them the appearance of huge walruses.

There was laughter and singing. Well bundled-up women and children clambered down out of the straw-filled sleigh boxes. They resembled invading Eskimos, as they untangled themselves from blankets under which they had snuggled down amidst blanket-wrapped hot rocks.

A brief exchange of greetings, then the women and children hurried to the log shack, a rambling twin building, while the menfolk stabled the teams, rubbed the horses down with hay, fed them and made them comfortable.

A couple of cows in the first stable rose and looked with wide-eyed scorn as two teams of horses were crowded in beside them.

Then, the dance!

Several layers of outer clothing had been hung up. Men and women sat a moment and chatted until, at last, the fiddler slashed his strings with bow, with the opening bars of a rollicking hornpipe which has today become a classic, played by famous orchestras. It was "The Devil's Dream", and the caller, a man from "Alabamy", called for couples.

Honor y'r pardners
Corners address
Join y'r hands
An' away to the west . . .

A boy then, I sat and stared, wide-eyed, and was amazed that in such crowded quarters there was no sign of bumping or interference, as everyone went skillfully through every measure.

"Flowers of Edinburgh"! "Wind's In the Barley"! "Macleod's Reel"! Spirited music which set even the watchers' toes tapping.

Then followed the waltz, the varsovienne, Virginia reel, "Drops of Brandy", minuet and more rollicking square dances, which persisted until the Supper Waltz was called, and I was asked by the host to take a lantern and have a look at the stock.

New Year's Eve 1906   143

The temperature was dropping rapidly and as I moved out of doors my eyelids instantly frosted shut. I had to blink a time or two before I could see. I then had to blink for another reason, for there was a display of the northern lights I've never seen bettered.

The majestic flow and brilliance frightened me as those northern merry dancers swept in almost over the rooftops.

On my way to the first stable, I stopped at a fencepost which held the thermometer. The mercury was down in the bulb, giving a reading of -60 F, as low as that thermometer registered. It was later reported by the RNWMP that much lower readings were recorded along the Pembina River flats.

Following a supper, to which most of the women had contributed, the dance was resumed and carried on almost until the first crack of dawn. Then the women moved into the bedroom part of the twin-shacks to clothe their youngsters for the trek home.

Rocks had been reheated in the oven. Horses champed cold bits and snorted protestingly as they were led out to the sleighs. A dense frost fog blanketed the area, and a distant lake boomed a hollow salvo.

Finally, sleigh runners screeched. To the accompaniment of sleigh bells, shouts and laughter, the folks were on their way and we moved on to the stables to begin the morning's chores.

We had met and talked with and laughed with almost every settler within a wide radius — and we knew we were not alone.

Box Social
Edward A. McCourt

The entertainment was announced to begin at eight o'clock. At six-thirty the first buckboard load of guests arrived. It included Mr. and Mrs. Berkslund, their three husky, teen-aged daughters, celebrated throughout the countryside for their phenomenal endurance on the dance floor, and Mrs. Berkslund's mother, aged eighty-six. Thereafter a steady stream of "rigs" poured down the narrow trails on either side of the creek — those coming from the north had to ford the stream in flood — and deposited their loads at the Stopping House door. From every point of the compass they gathered, from distances up to fifty miles or more, by buckboard, buggy, wagon, on foot and on horseback. Long before eight o'clock extra benches had been rushed from the Anglican Mission to the "auditorium" as Miss Libby Peters insisted on calling the Stopping House waiting-room, and men were standing three deep at the back. The only untoward incident occurred when Miss Libby's "Welcome" horseshoe broke from its moorings and knocked out an unfortunate cowpuncher from the Bar Five ranch. However, he regained consciousness shortly afterwards, and the disturbance which the incident had created quickly subsided.

Johnny Bradford and Linda Fraser rode over together from the Fraser ranch. Matt Fraser was suffering from a knee injury which he had sustained when a horse, only half-broken, had brushed him against the rails of the corral. "Anyway," he said, "I'm gettin' too old to be up all night. Away ye go and enjoy yoursel's."

Johnny carried a large bag containing Linda's party outfit. She herself carried, in a smaller bag, the carefully prepared and guarded box of food which, along with numerous others, would be auctioned off after the concert, the purchaser of the box enjoying the privilege of having supper with its owner. It was a convention governing the institution of the box-social that there should be no marks of identification on the boxes; the purchaser theoretically did not know whether he was spending his hard-earned money in order to eat supper with the maiden of his heart's desire or with some grandmotherly soul of eighty. In practice, however, either by some subtle form of telepathy or by downright broad hints, a girl was usually able to indicate to the man of her choice when to start bidding.

During the ride from the ranch to Pilot Creek, Johnny had made one or two attempts to secure advance information from Linda, but had been firmly rebuffed. "I shall take whomsoever the gods send me," she said. "It might be you, of course, but —"

"And it might be old man Walker or Joe Boggs," growled Johnny. "Honest, Linda, if you still have that maternal feelin' towards me you'll want to see me well fed, won't you?"

Linda chuckled thoughtfully. Then she flashed him a smile. "Well, maybe," she admitted. "We'll see." And with the vague promise of possible relenting, Johnny had to be content.

They stabled their horses in the shed behind the Anglican Mission, where some of the overflow from the livery stable was being accommodated, and went at once to the Stopping House. There they separated, and from then until the concert Johnny caught only fleeting glimpses of Linda, who was busy helping the Willing Workers. He himself was quickly wedged into a corner, between old man Walker and a puncher from the Lazy U. Old man Walker chewed tobacco continually; every two minutes his head turned with clock-like precision towards the open window behind him. He lived in a constant draught, which may have accounted for the perpetual drop of moisture which shone on the end of his nose.

At eight-fifteen the curtains — several Pilot Creek bedsheets fastened together with safety pins — parted, revealing Judith Sumner's little flock — six small girls and four small boys — shy and uncomfortable in stiffly starched frocks and unnaturally confining collars, arranged in a limp semicircle on a platform constructed of several heavy planks laid along a number of up-turned empty molasses kegs. Miss Libby Peters was at the organ — borrowed from the Anglican Mission — and the children, in response to a wheezy chord, burst into the song of welcome which Miss Libby had herself composed:

Welcome to our friends so dear,
We are glad that you are here;

May your worries fade away
And all this night be bright and gay.

And so on through twelve stanzas of similar quality and sentiment.

The response of the audience was loud and sincere. Then Mr. Bate, the Anglican Mission student, an earnest young man fresh from the east, gave the reading. His choice was perhaps unfortunate — a poem by the poet laureate, Alfred Lord Tennyson. This time the applause, in old man Walker's phrase, was "polite but not awful enthusiastic." Next Mr. Prothero, resplendent in a loud check suit across the waistcoat of which shone magnificently a mighty yardage of gold watch-chain hung with innumerable fobs and mystic charms, obliged with two vocal numbers, "Nut-Brown Maiden" and "Rocked in the Cradle of the Deep". The applause increased ten-fold when, just as Mr. Prothero was taking his bows, one of the planks slipped and the artist disappeared from view among the molasses barrels. He was extricated by Mr. Bate and as many of the audience in the front row as could crowd onto the platform. As soon as the planks had been replaced, Mr. Prothero took another bow, and brought down the house with a rendition of "The Night that Father Fell Downstairs". After he had made his exit, the juvenile chorus came on again with a number about the snows of winter being followed by the flowers of spring. Music by Mendelssohn, words by Miss Libby Peters.

But the *pièce de resistance* was the duet, "The Gypsy's Warning", sung in costume by Miss Libby and Mr. Prothero. They were called back twice, responding with two selections, "It was a Lover and His Lass", and a daring little number entitled "Will You Spark in the Park After Dark, Pretty Maiden?" during which Mr. Prothero made terrific play with eyes and moustaches, and Miss Libby responded with coy excursions and retreats. Afterwards, flushed and triumphant, she resumed her place at the organ — temporarily relinquished to Judith Sumner — and the entire cast appeared on the platform to lead the audience in the grand finale, a sing-song.

After "God Save the Queen" had been sung and the rafters had ceased to rattle, the platform was quickly cleared away and, amid a rising babble of conversation from all parts of the hall, interrupted by the shrill squeals of a score or more of excited children, preparations were begun for the auctioning off of the food boxes. Most of the men in the audience, Johnny included, took advantage of the break to slip outside for a breath of fresh air or a smoke. Meanwhile the Willing Workers, under the direction of Mr. Prothero and Mr. Bate, arranged the boxes of food on a table in front of the hall. When all was in readiness, the word was passed among the men, and they surged back into the hall in a body. As he re-entered, Johnny saw Linda, gay in her sky-blue party frock, hurrying up to the table, a swirl of white-lace petticoat showing above her trim ankles. She was carrying a box under her arm, a box ornate with ribbon and tissue-paper, and as she passed she turned and smiled significantly. Johnny grinned back in perfect understanding. There was no possibility of mistaking the box, because of the series of little silver hearts which formed a border all around the top.

As soon as the audience had settled into a semblance of order, Mr. Prothero mounted a small wooden bench that had been placed alongside the table and called for silence. He was rewarded by a mighty roar, followed by an expectant hush. Then he picked up the first box from the top of the great heap and held it high above his head. "What am I hoffered, gents?" he demanded. "Look at it — just look at it! Lovingly fashioned — hadorned with all the graces of its creator — filled to the brim with goodies moulded by 'er own fair 'ands! A lucky man 'e is 'oo gets this treasure — weights ten pounds if it weights an hounce!"

The bidding opened. The box, fashioned by the fair hands of Mrs. Joe Boggs, was finally knocked down to Slim Webber, whose face assumed the expression of a stunned ox when he caught sight of the name written on the little identification ticket attached. Then Mr. Prothero, eye alight, face already damp with sweat, seized another box, swept it aloft, and implored his fellowmen to bid, bid, bid for the love of their wives, daughters, sweethearts, and for the benefit of the Pilot Creek 'ospital. The response was enthusiastic, particularly when Mr. Prothero held up the box, generously proportioned, and artistically fashioned with a gay little sprig of artificial forget-me-nots on top. Two young cowpunchers, one from the Circle K and one from the Bar Diamond, were finally left in possession of the field, Bar Diamond winning out with a bid of twenty-eight dollars, nearly a whole month's salary.

Suddenly Johnny stiffened to attention. The box with the band of silver hearts around it was up for sale. "A bee-ootiful box!" Mr. Prothero crooned ecstatically, "a bee-ootiful box! Wot's the grandeurs that were Greece and the glories that were Rome compared to this gem — this treasure, this product of a pair of bee-ootiful and lovin' hands attached to some fair creature who will nourish the spirit as the contents of the box will nourish the body! Weights ten pounds if it weights an hounce!

"Five dollars," said Johnny.

There was a ripple of excitement through the crowd. Two dollars was the conventional opening bid. The young bloods pricked up their ears. The Circle K puncher, anxious to redeem himself, challenged Johnny's bid with a two-dollar raise, and the excitement increased until a sort of madness came upon the bidders. When the bids reached thirty dollars, Mr. Prothero interrupted to announce that cheques would be accepted for any sum above that amount. There was a prolonged burst of cheering and a renewed flurry of bids. Amid wild excitement the box was finally knocked down to Johnny for the unheard of price of fifty-seven dollars! But Linda's warm smile made him feel that the price he had paid was a small one.

The few remaining boxes were quickly disposed of, and the couples scattered into the various rooms at the back, where small tables had been set up around a long central table on which great pots of coffee steamed. Johnny, his box tucked carefully under his arm, emerged from the auditorium to find that Linda had disappeared. He paused in some perplexity. "Guess she must be out in the kitchen," he said to himself, and looked around to find a vacant table where he could wait for her.

"Oh Mr. Bradford!" It was Miss Libby Peters. There was a dazed, incredulous look on her face, but her eyes were shining.

"Why, hello, Miss Peters," Johnny smiled.

"Mr. Bradford, you were too kind. I have never been so — so —" Miss Libby was close to tears. She turned away her head, and Johnny flipped back the silver heart on the top of the box and looked at the name written underneath.

"Uh, well," he stammered, "it's — uh —"

Miss Libby slipped her arm through his. "Please don't try to explain," she said gently. "I'm really very proud."

Johnny looked down into the little, child-like face under the frame of silver hair. Then he patted Miss Libby's hand. "That makes two satisfied parties, then, Miss Libby," he said. And, suddenly, he knew he meant it.

They found a table in a quiet corner, and for half an hour Miss Libby sat enthralled, while Johnny alternately talked and ate. How it had all come about, Miss Libby had no idea, and she was wise enough not to seek too far for a solution. It was enough that a handsome young man had paid a record price for this privilege of eating supper with her. The experience was a reality of the moment—soon it would be a memory only, but one to be cherished always. And with that assurance, Miss Libby was content.

Once or twice Linda, who was eating supper with the cow-puncher from the Bar Diamond, looked in Johnny's direction.

Johnny returned her smile with a grin that extended from ear to ear. He felt no jealousy, and he was enjoying himself because Miss Libby was so obviously happy. "It's been a lot of fun, Miss Libby," he assured her, as he finished the last mouthful of a huge segment of apple pie. "Any time you want a recommend for cookin' just call on me."

"I'm glad you're enjoying yourself, Mr. Bradford," said Miss Libby gravely. Then, in response to an urgent signal from Mr. Prothero, she stood up reluctantly. "I play the organ for the dancing," she explained, with a naive pride. "I must go now."

"Well, thanks again for everythin'," said Johnny. "Food, company, concert. I'm havin' a swell time."

Miss Libby blushed delightedly. "The concert, I'm afraid, was a little lacking in body. We had hoped to present a little play, but unfortunately it fell through. Last year we did one, with Mr. Conway in the leading role. It was a very great success. But Mr. Conway is away just now — something to do with missions."

"I figger Mr. Conway would put anythin' like that over all right," agreed Johnny.

"Mr. Conway is a truly magnificent thespian," said Miss Libby. "Mrs. Prothero saw Sir Harry Irving once in the Old Country. She says that, in comparison to Mr. Conway, he is nothing — simply nothing! Now I really must go. Everyone is waiting." And Miss Libby swept out of the room with a new dignity born of the consciousness that for the past half-hour she had been the envy of almost every feminine heart in the room.

The dance got under way shortly before midnight. Children and babies were put to sleep on sofas and loveseats, for there would be no sitting-out of dances except in the case of cripples and octogenarians. Joe Sawyer, the fiddler from Macleod, provided the music, with Miss Libby chording on the organ. Their places were taken from time to time by the young Harper twins, who played duets on the mouth-organ and guitar.

However, as the twins knew only two pieces, they were able to provide only occasional relief.

This was old man Walker's hour of greatness. As caller of the dances, he stood at the front of the room beside a window that was raised sufficiently to enable him to chew in comfort without greater exertion than that occasioned by the clock-like turn of his head towards the window every two minutes. Unlike most callers, he preserved a dignified bodily immobility, except for the periodic turning of the head. But his voice had the power and quality of a foghorn, and carried to every corner of the room:

Birdie hop in,
Crow hop out,
Jine all han's,
'N' circle about.

This, too, was the great hour for the Berkslund girls. The Berkslunds had come from the States — the lumbering regions of Northern Michigan — where a girl's popularity was traditionally dependent on her endurance and the swirl of her skirts as she wove her way through the intricate figures of the dance. It was whispered that the Berkslund girls descended to unfair tactics in order to win masculine approval — that they actually sewed buckshot in the hems of their calico gowns. Whatever the reason, no skirts whirled so triumphantly as theirs, and their popularity attested to a similarity of taste between the Michigan lumber-jack and the Western cowpuncher.

The square-dances, being communal in spirit and movement, made any kind of conversation between partners impossible. Consequently, Johnny waited until Joe Sawyer struck up a waltz before claiming Linda's hand. Booking in advance was unheard of, and Johnny reached the chair in which Linda was sitting just a few inches in the van of a swarm of would-be suppliants. With a cheerful "better luck next time, boys," he led her out onto the floor.

They whirled about the room to the music of the "Skater's Waltz". Linda was an admirable dancer, having a natural, instinctive poise, and sense of rhythm, while Johnny had learned the waltzer's art in many a dance-hall between Pecos and Great Falls. "Mad at me, Johnny?" said Linda. She smiled up at him, but there was the faintest trace of apprehension in her eyes.

"Mad as a hornet," said Johnny calmly.

"Well, the Willing Workers do need money, and, besides, you made Miss Libby awfully happy."

Johnny did not answer.

"And another thing," she said. "You weren't the only one that made sacrifices."

Johnny grinned down at her. "Meanin' that eatin' with young Wilkins was a sacrifice?" he demanded.

"Well, he's awfully nice, but — but —" Suddenly she blushed. "Honestly, Johnny, you know I'd a lot sooner have had supper with you."

"Then why didn't you tip Wilkins off on the wrong box, instead of me?"

"He might not have taken it as well as you — and Miss Libby deserves a good time."

The Sundance
Faye Weasel Fatt

We have Sundance about the first week of August: we have it because it is the only time we can all get together to have our prayers.

The Sundance is held about three miles east of Stand-off.

The first one to camp at the Sundance is the Head Chief of our Reserve and the Head of the Horn's Societies. Then all the other people that want to join the Sundance start camping too.

It lasts for ten days, unless anything is holding it up: then we have it for two weeks. Rain, for instance, often holds up the Sundance.

The first to start their business are the Women's Societies. They have their prayers for four days: all this time they have ceremonial dances and prayers in their tents. They don't have their dances outside like the Horn's Societies. The fourth day, they dance early in the morning about six o'clock, and everybody gets up early to join the dance.

Then the Horn's Societies have their prayers and holy dances. They have two teepees in the centre, and nobody can go into those teepees except the members of the Horn's Societies and the people that are sick and want the Horns to pray for him or her.

They dance a lot different from the Women's Societies: they have the privilege of dancing outside, where it's nice and cool.

During the first dance, they dance around the outside of the camps, go to the centre, and sit down on the ground. Then all the people go to the centre and sit around the Horn's Societies in a circle. Then they dance for a little while. After that, they serve lunch to all the people, and after they finish lunch, they dance again. The Head of the Horn's Societies dances first, and then shoots up in the sky: that means the dance has ended.

The second dance is danced only in the centre, not on the outside of the camps. Then they serve lunch again.

The last two days, the Horn's Societies go down to the woods to chop down the biggest tree, and that tree is called 'The Medicine Lodge Pole'. The day before the big dance, they make a place where we can have our last big dance, and put the Medicine Lodge Pole in the centre. That night, all the young people that are interested in the white man's dances have their last big dance; it lasts until about two or three o'clock in the morning.

The last day, all the old people wear their Indian costumes, if they want to, to the dance. In the morning there is a parade. Everybody who wants to join the parade goes down to the woods and gets some branches of leaves, and carries them in the parade around the camp. The big dance comes about two o'clock in the afternoon. All the old people who wore their Indian costumes dance, and it ends about six o'clock that night.

Then everybody breaks up camp, and the Sundance is over until next year.

Rummage Sales
Bob Phillips

Have you ever been to a rummage sale in the basement of a church? If you have not, I can assure you it is a fine old western Canadian tradition you ought not to miss when next the chance is offered. I was invited to visit a rummage sale for a sneak preview on the night before opening, and I jumped at the offer for two reasons: it had been years since I'd been to one and my recollections were getting foggy, and this particular sale was to occur in the basement of the Regina city church I knew very well in the years before the Second World War.*

I'd had dinner that night at the home of Dr. and Mrs. Jack Boan, long-time friends in Regina. Dr. Boan is an economist at the University of Regina and had to leave soon after the meal to lecture to an evening class. Mrs. Boan, who operates an antique shop in Regina, had offered her services to the ladies of the church to help them price items for the rummage sale. She asked me to go along and I readily agreed.

I want to tell you, a rummage sale the night before opening is a busy place. Tables everywhere with ladies and their husbands running around with cartons of donated goods as they arrived. Some husbands are shouting, "Where do I put this

*First Presbyterian Church, Regina, Saskatchewan.

one?" One husband took an earned rest and came over to a table I was studying. He looked over the display quietly for some minutes and then asked, "Tell me, what is there here I simply can't live without?"

Living without is the key to all rummage sales. The ladies of this church hold one every year, attract several hundred shoppers Friday night and Saturday afternoon, and raise something like $1,500 for the church. Only they don't call their event a rummage sale but rather "an opportunity sale".

The items for sale had been donated by the ladies of the church themselves and were arranged in a dozen or so departments. I spent more than an hour wandering about, reviving memories on a number of counts.

The et cetera department: This one took my eye immediately for it contained the castoffs of people who apparently live the kind of life I have lived. There was a basinette made out of wicker and painted several times, a high chair, a stroller, two sleighs each with a box painted red, all reviving memories of the days when I was a child. Then there were tricycles and bicycles, three black-and-white TV sets each with an antenna that was bent, an old portable Singer sewing machine, four suitcases, a roll-away bed, and even a hooked rug.

Specialties: This department was equally nostalgic. There were napkin rings, pocket flasks covered with leather, candle sticks of many kinds, and assorted knick-knacks. There were ornaments representing owls, dogs and elephants, airmen and soldiers, cats, squirrels, swans and fish. There were several old tobacco pouches, some with pipe cleaners and filters thrown in. There were also trays, casserole dishes, cookie plates, lamps, and waste baskets.

Wall hangings: Discards from walls through at least half a century and more were represented in the "home-sweet-home" plaques, prayers, poems, and pictures. Some of the frames were priceless but many of their contents had become faded through age.

Jewelry: One table contained the priceless ornaments of several generations, rings, pins, beads, and brooches. There was even a grab-box special at this table: anything in sight for only fifty cents!

Staples: It has been years since I heard that name used in any other connection than food, but slowly I recalled the staple section of that old departmental store. In this corner there were bedspreads, quilts, curtains, and doilies, table mats and dresser scarfs. Many of the items had been hand manufactured by women of another generation and sold for the first time also in aid of the church.

The room: The location in the church I used to know as the "ladies' parlor" had been named "the room", and it contained the fashionable items of this decade and the last. There were long, formal gloves, lingerie, evening gowns, street-length dresses, and even pant suits. Nearby were shorter gloves, hats, and purses of all kinds.

The commode: The best item of all was simply "the commode", and it attracted the largest crowd, even at the preview. It was a piece of furniture shaped like a cube and measuring about two feet along each side. It was made of oak and nicely varnished. All of us agreed it would have made a fine front-hall piece, somewhere one might expect to sit when putting on overshoes next winter. But the most startling thing of all was that its original purpose had been perfectly preserved: the white porcelain pottie was fully operational and in place. Mrs. Boan said it ought to bring between twenty-five and fifty dollars, and I'll bet it did.

It was a wonderfully nostalgic evening, and I was told later the sale went as expected, clearing out most of the treasures in record time.

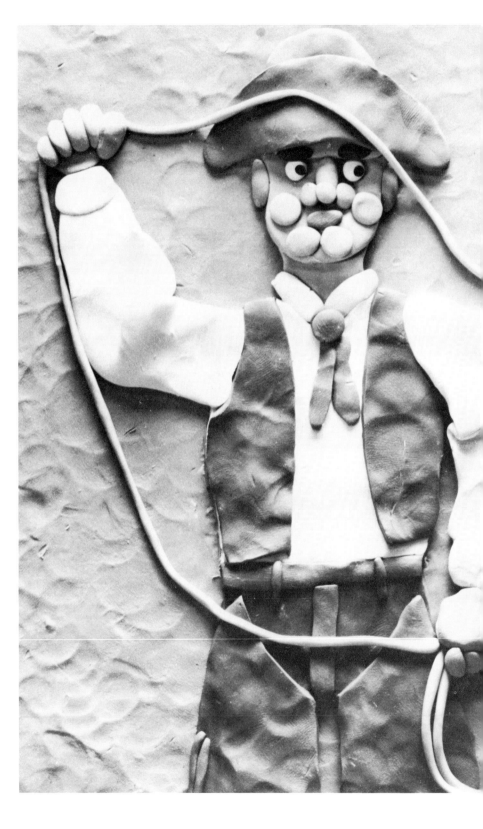

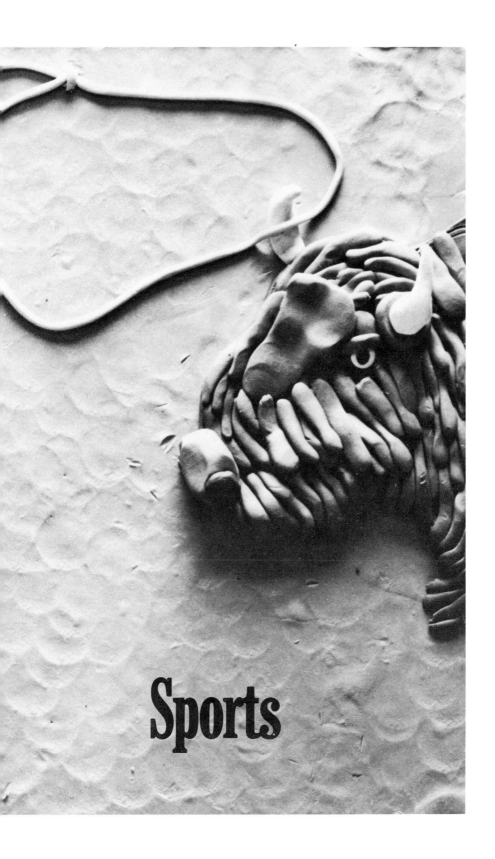

Sports

A Game of Horseshoes

David J. Wright

Anyone looking in on Amberton's leading barber and champion horseshoe player that late Saturday afternoon would hardly have guessed that Alec Brown had any thought for his forthcoming game. He was comfortably sprawled out in his barbershop chair, watching the shadow of the window ledge inch slowly toward the east wall. He figured that the shadow would reach the top of the floor moulding at just about game time.

"Lofty must be about ready by now," Alec thought. "I wonder who he's got fer a partner this time."

Lofty was Dr. Loftus Fawcett, county veterinarian and perennial challenger to the championship title held these past many years by Alec and his partner, Ole Larson. By shifting his eyes a little to the right, Alec could see the open door of Ole's office in the lumber yard. Ole would be ready when game time rolled around a few minutes from now. Alec had no fears about the outcome of this game. Lofty had teamed up with the best players for miles around, and his current partner was unlikely to change the consistent record of defeat.

Alec had just eased himself out of the chair to start closing up his shop when the phone rang. It was Lofty.

"I'm going to be about half an hour late," he said. "I've called Ole, and he says it's okay with him. But don't close your shop. I've got an old friend spending the week-end with me and he's on his way for a haircut. Also to make sure you don't chicken out on our game."

"Never run out on a game of horseshoe yet," retorted Alec, "and I'm not likely to start with you. By the way, who've you conned into being yer partner this time?"

"Same fellow — this old side-kick of mine. Name's Charlie Ovens. I'm risking his friendship sending him to you for a haircut. I've warned him, but he says he's taken worse chances in his day."

Alec chose to ignore the pretended insult. After arranging details of a side-bet on the game, he closed off the conversation.

The screen door swung open as Alec hung up the phone. The newcomer was a quiet-appearing man in his mid-thirties, about Lofty's age. "Good of you to stay open," he said. "You're Mr. Brown?"

"Alec Brown. You're Mr. Ovens, then. Let me hang yer coat up here. Lofty tells me he's got you lined up fer his partner against me and Ole Larson. Did he tell you he's been trying for five years and hasn't beaten us yet?"

"He mentioned it." Lofty's newest partner eased himself into the chair.

Alec turned back from the coat rack. "I notice you're wearing the Air Force Reserve button in yer lapel. Lofty was in the Air Force, too."

"Yes . . . I know."

Alec fastened a large white cloth over his customer's shoulders and took up his scissors. "Lofty was born and raised right here. Says he wouldn't swap his job in Amberton fer the best business in the city. Too confined there, he says. Reminds him of the prisoner-of-war camp."

Mr. Ovens closed his eyes as Alec snipped at the hair over his forehead. "I know how he feels." He gestured at the horseshoe courts across the street. "That's about the best horseshoe layout I've seen in a long time. Lofty tells me you had a lot to do with getting it organized."

"Well, Ole Larson and me call it the 'Lofty Fawcett Memorial Courts', not so much fer Lofty as fer the story he tells about his break-out from the prisoner-of-war camp. When the curling rink was put up right after the war, that lot was left vacant, fer parking and such. Ole and me used to toss the odd game of horseshoe there. Then Lofty came back with this story of his, and horseshoe kinda picked up around Amberton. Ole said we oughta do something to commem — what's the word I want?"

"Commemorate?"

"Yeah, that's it, commemorate—thanks. Anyway, Ole said we oughta commemorate Lofty's story, even if we didn't believe the half of it."

"I take it you're not sold on Lofty's tales of high adventure, then." The man in the chair smiled.

"Oh, sure, as long as they're halfway believable. And up to a point I'll go along with his yarn about this fella Cookie that got them outa that camp. But Lofty fergets I've been pitching horseshoes fer going on to fifty years. Anyway, Ole and me told folks it could be our way of saying thanks to young fellas like Lofty and the others that was in the war. Well, in no time at all, the ground there was levelled off, grassed, and them two rows of horseshoe courts strung alongside the curling rink. Sunday evenings you have to wait yer turn, they're that busy."

Mr. Ovens closed his eyes again. "What's Lofty's version of this escape from the prison camp?"

Alec laid the scissors on the shelf and started working around the ear with clippers and comb. "Well, it started when Lofty got on this Air Force Squadron overseas. Landed up there with this fella, Cookie. They'd been teamed up together as pilot and navigator. Squadron put them to work right away. Flew several missions, then bad weather set in. Crews sat around fer a day er so, playing cards, cutting up in the local villages, swapping yarns — just killing time. Lofty and Cookie borrowed bikes and explored the countryside. Came on a little town with a blacksmith shop, and they landed back at the squadron with their bikes loaded down with old horseshoes. Seems Cookie had been raised in a place where kids cut their teeth on them, and he'd been hungering fer a game ever since the weather had slowed down the flying. Lofty fell right in with the idea, too. He'd played a bit as a kid right here in Amberton. They set up pegs alongside their billets and started having a game of horseshoe."

"Just the two of them?" Artless blue eyes opened and then closed again.

"The first game. After that, there was always a crowd, according to Lofty. Seems that Cookie just couldn't miss the peg. Lofty hadn't never seen anything like it. This Cookie had the doggonedest style of throwing. Never bent his knees; stood sideways, left foot in front of the right in line with the pitch. Held the horseshoe over his head fer a second, then swung it across his body. Lofty says the shoe would look as if it was hanging in the air, lazy-like. Then it would do only half a turn and plop down over the peg neat as pins in a diaper. Couldn't believe it at first, says Lofty, but when Cookie ran up fifteen points in five throws, Lofty lets out a holler for some of the others to come see. Pretty soon there was a crowd of fliers gathered around placing bets that Cookie would miss the next one. Lofty swears he was giving odds of twenty-to-one, and cleaning up. I figger he's stretching it a bit there."

Alec switched back to the scissors. He paused for comment from the man in the chair, but Mr. Ovens was looking across the street, his face composed and expressionless.

"Well, sir, the whole squadron started playing horseshoe as if winning the war was no consequence. Flying started up again, but as soon as they had another break, they scoured the countryside fer more horseshoes. Pretty soon there was horseshoe pitches alongside every hangar, and even in front of the Officers' Mess. Aircrew, groundcrew — all went sorta horse-shoe crazy. Nobody was able to come even close to Cookie, though . . . If you'll just lean forward a bit while I'm doing the back of yer neck."

"Sorry. I was looking across at the horseshoe courts. There seems to be quite a gathering."

Alec gestured scornfully with his scissors. "Always a dozen er so out to watch our games. That's Ed Neighbor in the yellow shirt. Ole Larson and me took him and Lofty last week, three games to nothing. Fella in the Panama hat's Derwood Hartson, another of Lofty's hopefuls. Beat them two to one a month ago. They'll be pulling fer you two, of course."

"Nice of them," was the quiet comment from the chair.

Alec resumed his clipping and his narrative. "A month er so after the horseshoe fever got started, Lofty and Cookie had to bail out over enemy territory. They were captured and shoved into this prisoner-of-war camp along with several hundred other fliers. All of them itching to escape. They had a regular organization going, and everyone was expected to contribute an effort of some sort. Escape was the big thing.

"They had to scrounge a lot of things fer themselves, but some items, like sporting goods, was legal. Nevertheless, Lofty says, Cookie had quite a job persuading a set of horseshoes outa the big shot in charge of the camp — the camp com-something-er-other."

"Camp commandant."

"Yeah. This camp commandant had never heard of the game. Cookie told him to check with some of the owners of the draft horses he'd seen hauling loads of wood up to the camp. He'd be willing to bet his next Red Cross parcel against an extra bag of onions that they'd know about it. Well, the upshot was that in about a week's time the prisoners were presented with a bunch of used horseshoes."

Several more people had arrived at the courts. Alec pointed

out three more Ambertonians who had gone down to defeat along with Lofty. "Hope you don't mind spectators," he added. "In a small town the size of Amberton word gets around pretty fast." He was answered by a negative headshake.

"Well, it was just like back at the squadron. Them prisoners took to the game like kids to licorice. Some of the Canadians had played before, but to most of the Limeys and others it was brand new. That didn't stop them enjoying it. Worked off steam, you might say. Sociable, too. Always said you'd find out the best parts of a fella's make-up when you played horseshoe against him. Of course, nobody could touch Cookie, even when they made him throw sixty feet, instead of the regulation forty.

"All this time, too, they never quit thinking about how to escape. Seems this camp was surrounded by a high wire fence, with another little one a few yards inside. Any prisoner going beyond the little fence was shot, and no questions asked. They had several escape plans going, and the best of them called fer the lights to be put out and kept out long enough fer the boys to skedaddle outa there. There was poles every thirty feet er so outside the big fence, with lights, so's the guards could see if anyone went near the fence at night. The same wire that fed these lights also worked the half dozen er so searchlights located on the guards' towers. If that wire could be put on the fritz somehow, the other part of the escape plans stood a chance of working. It was outa the question fer anyone to get near enough with cutting pliers.

"That was the way things stood when Lofty and Cookie was there. The rest of the plans was working smoothly, but them prisoners was plumb stymied over the problem of the lights."

"I see we have more spectators arriving every minute."

"Let 'em come. Lofty should've kept his mouth shut, if he didn't want to be embarrassed in front of half the town.

"Well, as Lofty tells it, he was the one that spotted the answer to the light problem. Claims no particular credit — he was just lucky to be on the spot. Says he was pitching a game in the horseshoe court nearest the fence. Happened this was where the main power line came to the first light pole and led into a sorta switch-box about twenty feet up. It was fed from there to the lights around the camp, the ones around the wire. The prisoners had noticed a little fluttering of the lights the night before, but nothing steady enough to count on. There'd been a rainy spell, and they figgered some water had got into the works somewhere. Anyway, Lofty wasn't particularly surprised to see a fella wearing climbing irons come over to this pole, shinny up, open the box, and dab around in it with a bit of cloth. He closed it, came down, and went back over where he came from. Lofty figured he'd gone to throw the main switch to test the lights. Sure enough, the lights came on, but kinda fluttery-like. So back came the climber again. This time he fiddled around in the box with a screwdriver, came down, and tested once more. There was a little flurry of light, then none at all. In a minute he was back again, with a corporal — er some such — waving his arms and acting mad as a wet hen. Number One climbed the pole, disconnected the lead-in wires, unscrewed the box, and brought it down fer the other to inspect. The corporal took a look inside, yelled some more, and left, with the fella in the climbing irons trailing along behind, carrying the box. Lofty asked his chums to stretch out the game so's they could see what would happen next.

"In about five minutes, the climbing fella came back with a hammer and a couple of spikes. He went up and drove them spikes part way into the pole, three-four inches apart, where the box had been. Then he wound the bare ends of the wires around the spikes and left them like that. So Lofty knew they didn't figger on replacing the box fer that night at least.

"Right away, he broke off the game and went looking fer Cookie and a couple of the ring-leaders in the escape committee.

"The four of them came back and started a new game, so's

their real interest wouldn't be too noticeable to the guards. He'd given them the gist of his idea before they got there, and they could see fer themselves that a piece of metal laid across those spikes would short-circuit the whole kaboodle, put out the lights, and most likely blow out all the fuses to boot. Give 'em all the time they needed fer the escape, 'cause there was no telling how long it would take the guards to locate the trouble. Well, they agreed that the idea was just dandy, but how did Lofty figger to get a piece of metal over two fences and twenty feet up a pole on the other side? Lofty said that was the easy part. Cookie would throw a horseshoe there.

"I guess they looked at Lofty as if he was some kind of nut. They argued that Cookie would be shot down before he could say Jack Robinson if he stood where they were and started heaving horseshoes in the middle of the night; and it was any-ways a good fifty feet to the pole. But Lofty pointed out that it was only another fifteen feet to the corner of a building that would be in some sorta shadow. Even if it meant lofting the shoe over a high wire fence and onto a target no bigger than your hand, Lofty insisted it was worth trying. Cookie said he wasn't as sure as Lofty, but he was game to try, if the escape committee wanted to take the chance.

"Well, sir, it seems they did. The escape fellas called a meeting, and nobody came up with a better idea, so they got ready to break out that night."

The man in the chair straightened up as Alec applied his soft whisk to brushing away the bits of hair that clung to the cloth around his shoulders.

"Well, you can picture the situation Cookie was up against if he was gonna make it work. What a throw! Just as if I stood in my doorway here and tossed a horseshoe all the way across the street, aiming to make a ringer on that light fixture over the door of the curling rink. A good sixty-seventy feet, if it's an inch! And no practice beforehand. Lofty was fer riggin up some kind of a dummy layout that would give Cookie a chance to get his hand in, sort of. But the escape committee ruled that out. Afraid the guards would get wise to their plans if they saw something like that. Cookie had to go into it cold, so to speak.

"Lofty says Cookie was cool as a cucumber when the time came. They got the signal that everything was ready, and Cookie let fly with the horseshoe. Lofty stood beside him with more shoes in case they was needed; but he says that first one sailed out in a beautiful arc, crossed the wire, hanging sorta lazy-like, and made a half turn as it started to come down. Lit right across those spikes and hung there as all hell bust loose.

"There was a shower of sparks, and then the lights went out. The prisoners set up a yelling like a tribe of wild Indians, and in the confusion, Lofty and Cookie and the others got away . . ."

Mr. Ovens stood up as the cloth was removed from his shoulders and a few deft passes made at his neck with the soft brush. "I see that Lofty has arrived at the courts."

"So he has. Timed it nicely. And there's Ole Larson coming outa his office." Lofty's partner took his wallet from the coat that the barber was holding for him, but Alec told him to put it back. "Lofty and me has a side-bet on the game. Double er nothing fer the haircut. Figger I might as well make all I can outa him. One of these days Lofty might come up with somebody as good at horseshoes as he is at story-telling."

They left the barber shop and crossed the street to where a sizable crowd seemed to be waiting for them. Lofty was talking to Ole Larson but broke off to greet the new arrivals. "Hey!" he joked, "I've seen better haircuts done with a soup bowl. Maybe you've lost your touch with the horseshoes, too."

Alec laughed it off. "I'll tell you a few things about horseshoes if you'll only do yerself a favor and listen fer once. Fella can learn a lot if he keeps his ears peeled."

Lofty chuckled and introduced the other two. "Charlie Ovens — Ole Larson." Then to Alec, "Ole and I tossed for ends while we were waiting. You and Charlie take the south. Ole pitches first. Okay?"

"Jake with me," Alec replied, and walked with his

opponent to their end of the court. He noted that other games had come to a stop, and that everyone had gathered around to watch the new contest.

Ole threw first. Both shoes wound up within two inches of the peg. Ringers would come later when Ole had got warmed up. Lofty's shoes were good, too, but not good enough to beat out those that Ole had thrown. Alec picked up all four shoes and handed two to Lofty's friend. "Guess that puts us two up," he said. "Lofty will get better as the game goes on. Him and Ole are about even, as a rule."

"You toss first, since you have the lead," said Mr. Ovens.

Alec was quite happy with his first two throws. Both shoes were touching the peg; they would have been ringers if they had landed open-side on. He stepped back.

Mr. Ovens stood sideways to the direction of the throw, left foot in front of the right in line with the pitch. Never bent his knees. Held the horseshoe over his head for a second, then swung it across his body. The shoe looked as if it was hanging in the air, lazy-like, then it did a half turn and plopped down over the peg.

Alec was frozen in a half crouch. He slowly straightened up as the second shoe followed the exact pattern of the first, settling on its partner in a noisy embrace of the far peg.

As his opponent stepped back, Alec held out his hand and managed a smile — not too happy a smile, but it would do.

"I'd like to shake hands right now to show there's no hard feelings. I walked into this with my eyes open, and I gotta hand it to Lofty fer putting one over on me. Do me a favor, though. Let me call you by yer nickname from here on in."

"Please do. All my friends call me Cookie."

Skis

Bill van Veelen

The sound of skis on snow,
their continuous rhythm,
breaks the silence.
Sun shines brightly
off snow and splintered tree trunks
of an unknown avalanche.

Pine forests fall below me
as I pass the tree line.
The mountain peak
fills the sky
as I ski in its shadow.
Sky and summit meet
in a blast of icy wind
at the top.

All around me,
snowy mountain tops
push their way through a green carpet
of pine above a lonely winding road
cutting its way through the valley.
A silent world,
with only the wind to keep watch
sleeps,
waiting for spring.

Don't Just Stand There
Eric Nicol

Every article about Vancouver mentions that you can swim at
a fine bathing beach and half an hour later be skiing up the
mountain.

My pride in this remarkable civic achievement has always
been nagged by the fact that I can neither swim nor ski. The
things I do (eating, sleeping, swearing, etc.) I could do just as
well in Big Muddy, Saskatchewan. For years I have felt a
traitor to my environment, and when people asked me if I swam
or skied I have had to give them an evasive answer, such as
"Yes."

Last summer I decided to learn to swim and to ski. It was
too late in the season to learn to swim, but I got busy telling
everybody I was going to learn to ski this winter. I talked this
up so much during the fall that by the beginning of the year
I felt I *had* skied, and I became critical of the other skiers I
saw, in the newsreels.

But a couple of weeks ago at the Badminton Club, when I
was enjoying the glow of well-being that always followed my
telling somebody I was going to learn to ski, George, one of the
audience, said:

"How about coming up Hollyburn with me Wednesday?"

I may have flinched a bit, but months of ski talk had given
me a certain verbal ability, and I was able to reply smoothly:

"Well, that sounds like fun, George. Unfortunately I
haven't any skis, otherwise —"

"I can lend you skis," George said.

"I haven't any boots," I said. "Otherwise —"

"I can lend you boots, everything you need," George said.

Livid at the monstrous generosity of the man, who after all
barely knew me, I attacked his qualifications.

"I didn't know you could ski, George," I said.

"I'm an instructor for *The Daily Province* ski classes," he said.

That night I went home from badminton feeling much more tired than usual.

The next Wednesday morning it was raining. I phoned George.

"Raining, George," I said. "Rotten day for skiing, I guess, eh?"

"That's right. Next Wednesday then, okay?"

The next Wednesday brought a fine, horrible, sunny morning. George picked me up in his car and we drove to the base of the Hollyburn ski lift. He handed me my skis, which looked much lighter when he was carrying them, and we joined the cluster of skiers waiting for chairs.

When my turn came, instead of a chair whirling around the platform there came a sort of opened basket. George held me back, saying:

"That one's for the stretcher cases."

I caught the chair behind the empty stretcher basket, which preceded me slowly and confidently up the hill. Swinging 20 to 30 feet above jagged stumps, the sky-hung tumbril gave me plenty of time to brood about the blind confidence people put in mechanical engineers.

"Look at the view of the city," George shouted behind me.

Turning, I saw a magnificent panorama of the city I had been fool enough to leave. I could pick out the General Hospital very easily. I turned back and found a man waiting to catch me.

In the handsome lodge I put on the ski boots, and a *Province* photographer who happened to be up looking for funny pictures suggested he take one of me lying on my back with my skis in the air. I said I didn't want my picture taken like that, so we went out to the snow, George put on my skis, I tried to move, fell on my back with my skis in the air and the photographer took my picture.

A few attempts to keep my balance on the skis persuaded me that if skiing wasn't harder than I had thought the snow certainly was.

After I had fallen enough times to satisfy everybody around that needed a good laugh, George and I took off our skis for the hike to the Hollyburn Ski Lodge, where his class was waiting. His class was all women. The hills swarmed with women, swooping about and hammering a few more nails into the coffin of the expression "weaker sex".

Having experienced some difficulty in getting up on skis once my enormous weight hit the snow, I declined to provide burlesque comedy for a bunch of refrigerated Amazons. I retired to the cozy interior of the lodge, supplementing the group of fair, bronzed athletes with my pouchy pallor.

The young lady who gave me my coffee, with the friendliness of the fraternity said:

"There's one thing about skiing, you're never too old to learn. We have ladies of sixty up here skiing."

I said: "Uh-huh," and made a mental note to hate ladies of sixty.

As George and I started back down the trail, my legs rubbering puckishly, I took a last look at the snowy splendour of the mountainside, breathed in the deep silence that was broken only by the squeak of my vertebrae, and swore to speak of learning to swim to none but the heaviest anchors.

Curling
Eric Nicol

A number of years ago, history tells us, Englishmen used to go into Scotland to shoot deer, while Scotsmen went into England to shoot Englishmen. Later the Scots cleverly improved on this method of exchange by inventing golf, a game designed to make Englishmen go out and shoot themselves, at a very considerable saving in Scottish deer and ammunition.

Scottish thrift is likewise said to be responsible for the evolution of the sport known as "curling", a refrigerated form of lawn bowling. According to the legend, a young Highland bride was baking her first haggis for her husband when it suddenly rolled out of the oven and fell on his foot, removing it at the ankle, and proceeding through the floor into the cellar, where it wrecked part of the foundation of the house (pronounced "hoos").

Being a man of frugal habits, the husband salvaged the haggis, stuck a handle on it, and thus became the father of the first curling rock. His wife caught the first train to Reno.

Today, curling is becoming increasingly popular in Canada. Every winter more and more men, most of them perfectly normal-looking, middle-aged businessmen, respected members of their community, get together in an alley of ice to throw rocks at one another. One reason for this popularity, of course, is that the prerequisites of curling are simple. All you need is some ice, a slug of Scotch, a dash of absinthe, and three guys who are as nuts as you are, and brother, you'll be curling in no time.

The first symptom of a man being masticated by the curling bug is his sudden interest in brooms. Just ordinary brooms. His wife, for instance, watches him one night sneaking out the back door with her broom under his coat. When she tries to make him tell her what he's going to do with the broom he merely stares at her in grim silence, his eyes gleaming with the wild light of a fanatic. Or, the more cunning type of curler may take the broom out of the closet on the pretense of going out to clear the snow off the front porch. Then, as soon as he gets outside the house, a big, black sedan full of more men with brooms skids to the curb, picks him up and roars away into the night. Some women have even suspected the old man of running around with a witch, until they found out he had become a curler and shot themselves.

Until you have seen a curler in action, however, it is difficult to appreciate the importance of his broom. For, the minute a player bowls his rock down the ice, other players swoop upon it with their brooms, sweeping furiously at the ice immediately in front of the rock in what appears to be an attempt to discourage it from going any further, while the bowler runs behind, his head cocked on one side, cooing softly to the rock to ignore the bums and keep going. This is the point at which the average spectator loses his faith in humanity and is prepared to hand the world over to the insects with no questions asked.

If the rock manages to escape the sweepers, it has a good chance of landing inside one of the rings at the end of the ice. Once an opponent has succeeded in placing a rock in a ring, it becomes necessary for you to knock him out. This may be done by lifting a rock and hitting him firmly over the head with it. Should you be caught doing this, however, it will be counted as a foul, your broom will be taken away from you, and you will have to play the rest of the match with a clothes wisk.

At first glance, there seems to be little point to the sport of curling, but this is not altogether true. For one thing, it sells a lot of brooms. So far, nobody has successfully attempted to run ahead of a curling rock with a Hoover, mostly because it's harder to sneak a Hoover out of the house without the wife seeing (all the attachments fall out of the box, you know how it is).

Perhaps that is just as well, though, because with vacuum cleaners in a hot, closely-fought bonspiel, the smaller players would soon start disappearing right and left. Besides, you don't want the game to look silly, do you?

The Hometown Goalie
Jeff Brown

Under the spreading hockey net
  The hometown goalie squats;
His brow is creased with purple welts
  From taking head-high shots,
And his battered ears remind us of
  A Boy Scout's granny knots.

A row of scars conceal a face
  That sparkled once with youth;
And as he squats, he contemplates
  The ever present truth
That soon some puck may extricate
  His one remaining tooth.

One eye is blue and crossed and glazed,
  The other reddish plaid;
And though his nose is flattened out,
  You'll never see him sad —
He knows that for a first year man
  He doesn't look too bad.

Everybody Played Hockey
Barry Broadfoot

Hockey was the thing in those days. The big thing. The
Toronto Maple Leafs and Foster Hewitt on Saturday nights.
He was better known than the prime minister. It was the
touchstone to success, the way a kid could gain fame and a
little fortune, playing for Toronto or the Montreal teams,
Detroit, Chicago.

   It was like the Negro before he was allowed into organized

sports. The Negro could only enter the white man's world if he was a superb boxer, a champion. Remember Joe Louis?

So it was with hockey, and junior hockey those years was an exceedingly fast and good game. But everybody played. I've seen men of 40 going up and down the ice a full game in the intermediate leagues and every kid from the time he graduated from bob skates wanted to be a star. Corner lots were flooded and they became the rinks where the stars were produced, but this wasn't good enough. There were rarely boards, and almost never a clubhouse to change and keep warm. Then someone had an idea. I'd like to think it was my father and a few of his cronies who used to sit around the Legion on Saturday afternoons. Their one day out in the big-time. Ha! Fifty cents was a lot to spend on a beer bust those days. Or the idea might have started in a hundred places in Canada at once, like an idea whose time had come.

Look at the picture. There were hundreds of blocks of lots undeveloped and gone back to the city for non-payment of taxes in almost every city in the Thirties. So there was this land. The CPR and the CNR had thousands of boxcars lying on sidings across the west, unused from year to year, just rotting away, and those cars were of the finest construction, finest lumber, and built for the coldest weather a Canadian winter could throw at them.

There were fire hydrants everywhere, of course, and firemen sitting around doing very little. And finally, there were dozens of men idle, master carpenters, plumbers, electricians, you name it, who were willing to work for nothing, for a good cause, of course, just to feel they were doing something useful.

So put them all together and, yes, that's what you get. The neighborhood would form a legal entity called a community club, the such-and-such Community Club Association, duly constituted, officers, treasury, minutes, and all that. The city would gladly deed over the necessary land to the association. I'm not sure how the boxcar deal worked but I think they were sold to the association for a nominal sum, say, $10 each, and the association had to get the cars off their tracks and to the site. Boards were always a problem, but there was always demolition work going on somewhere and somebody always had an old truck and there were always hands to load and unload, and soon you had boards.

The fire department would come two or three times, the first to soak and freeze the ground, and the other times to build up a good thick ice surface. At our club, we used to run a garden hose from a house across the street every time we wanted a new finish on the ice. Two boxcars, fitted side by side made a good clubhouse, and two Imperial Oil barrels welded together made a fine stove.

Of course there were problems, really big problems. An association never did get things all tickety-boo until about the third year, but from the first if they started about July or so they could function quite well. Money was number one, of course. Isn't it always? But the wives would hold rummage sales or tea parties or raffles, some merchant would donate a ham and another a $5 grocery order, and the paper boys would put the hard sell on their customers at 10 cents a ticket or three for a quarter. At any one time, in Winnipeg, there must have been 40,000 raffles of one kind or another going. It was a great raffle town, and I don't know anyone who ever won anything. Maybe the raffle was a great racket too. But these clubs survived, and grew, and they had full leagues, from 4:30 after school to 10 p.m. and skating on Saturday and Sunday and broom ball for the oldsters on Saturday night and then a dance.

They were the beginnings, the rugged, small and determined Depression beginnings, of these three and four million dollar community centres you see in every city and which they are still building, because they serve a very definite need, as much now as they did back in 1934. As I said, maybe it all was just an idea whose time had come, but I like to think it all began back with my Dad and his First World War pals sitting around the Legion on Saturday afternoon.

The Slap Shot

(for Rudy Wiebe)
Steven Scriver

You see, the problem is:
to get your head above and
just ahead of the puck
to slide your forehand down
the shaft of your stick as you
pull it back
and with your back leg leaving
the ice just before your stick hits
Striking the ice just a few
inches behind the puck
hitting it about the middle
of the blade
while aiming at a corner of
the net
and if you have to think about
that, brother
it just isn't there.

World Champions

Ken McConnell

Would you like to hear about the greatest basketball game ever
played?

It happened in 1936. It was the final game between the
Edmonton Grads and the champion girls' team from the
United States, the Tulsa Stenos.

It had all started when the girls of the Commercial High
School basketball team decided to stick together after gradua-
tion, as the Edmonton Grads. They persuaded their coach, Mr.

Percy Page, to stay with them; and how he made them work! They practised shooting, dribbling, passing, and making combination plays until they played "percentage" basketball — and loved it.

The Grads won victory after victory. Soon there was no girl's team in Canada that could beat them. Three times they crossed the Atlantic to represent Canada at the Olympic Games, and won the world's championship every time. They became so famous that every year the strongest team in the United States would come to Edmonton to challenge the champions. The Grads had beaten them all; but could they beat the Stenos?

The Stenos had won their national championship three times in a row, and they were thought to be the strongest team ever produced in the United States. Their players had been brought together from the best girl athletes all over the southern and central states.

There was tremendous interest in the contest between Edmonton and Tulsa. The Edmonton Arena, which could hold 5,000 spectators, was sold out for every game. There was to be a series of five games, and the team to win three of these would hold the North American championship. In two previous series, the Grads had beaten the Stenos; the first time by three straight games, and the second by three games to one.

This time, however, it looked as if the Stenos would have the advantage. Both teams were trained to the minute; but the American girls were taller and heavier, and in basketball weight and reach count for a great deal.

Still, although the Grads were small, they had that fighting spirit which never knows defeat. They never gave up, and could score goals when they were most needed.

The first game of the 1936 series finished with Edmonton winning 53 to 49 — only four points ahead. Two nights later the Tulsa girls won by exactly the same score. In the third game the Canadians won again — this time by 37 to 30. All these three games were fought bitterly.

Now the Grads needed only one game more to keep the championship; but could they do it? For, game as they were, the Edmonton girls were small, and the weight of their visitors had worn them down. The thousands of spectators who packed the arena could see that they were weakening.

Two nights later came the big contest, the one which has been called the most exciting basketball game ever played. When the two teams took the floor, the Edmonton Arena was packed to the doors. Almost everyone believed that if Tulsa should win this fourth game, they would also win the fifth. It was simply too much to expect that the little Grads could keep up their strength much longer against these taller and heavier opponents.

Both coaches realized the importance of this game. The battle out on the floor was not the only one fought that night. The two coaches — Steve Beck of Tulsa, and J. Percy Page — were also fighting a battle of wits on the players' benches. Each was trying to outguess the other.

The Stenos started out like the champions they were. Before many minutes, they had gained a lead of eleven points. This was the greatest lead that any team had ever held over the girls from Edmonton.

It looked as if the visitors were not to be stopped. Even the loyal followers of the Grads shook their heads in despair. They thought that no team under the sun could overcome such a big lead from that big fast Tulsa team.

Still, the Canadians had not rolled up their wonderful record by accident. In many another battle they had come back from defeat to victory. Perhaps they could do it again. They did not lose heart. Instead, they fought like tigers, and slowly but surely narrowed Tulsa's long lead.

Nine points! Seven! Six! Back now to five — then three — one — and finally — just as the whistle sounded for half-time — *one point ahead!*

The arena was in an uproar! Thousands of sober citizens clapped total strangers on the back as if they were long-lost brothers.

The Last Shot

Two very tired teams went to their dressing-rooms. Both had given everything they had. In the case of the Grads at least, everyone realized that they would have to play the last half on nerve alone.

And that is exactly what they proceeded to do.

The ball was tossed up at centre. Once again the girls from Tulsa got the jump on their rivals, and began to score. As the game drew towards its end, the visitors were four points ahead. They were playing splendid ball, and it did not seem humanly possible for the exhausted little Grads to catch up. Yet, by miraculous shooting, the Canadians scored two field baskets. The game was tied again — with less than two minutes to play.

Then a visiting girl made a foul. Tiny Etta Dann of the Grads had a free shot, and promptly made it good. The score changed to 41 to 40 for Edmonton.

Now came the most exciting moment in the history of the sport. Captain Noel MacDonald of the Grads picked up the ball under her own basket. The timekeeper was already reaching for his whistle, but the ball had to be advanced over the ten-second line at once or Tulsa would be given the ball. Captain MacDonald could not risk a pass, for every other player on her team was closely guarded by a husky opponent. What if one of them were to spear the pass and flip the ball into the basket? The game would be lost.

There was only one thing to do, and Captain MacDonald did it. Although her Tulsa guard stood directly in front of her to block her, Noel shot for the basket. It was a heave of something like forty feet.

The ball had barely left her hands when the timekeeper's

whistle sounded to end the game. The exhausted Noel dropped to the floor in a dead faint, but, the shot having been started, the ball was still in play.

Thousands of spectators jumped to their feet. In dead silence they watched as the ball arched beautifully, dropped toward the basket, and fell through it — for as clean a goal as ever was scored!

Final score — 43 to 40. The Grads had done it again! They were still champions of the world; and no team in the world ever deserved the honour more.

The Ball Players
Maurice Metayer

Two groups of people lived across a river from one another. Every now and then some of the men met to play ball, those from one side of the river against those from the other side.

The same team always won and as soon as they arrived home in their kayaks they would shout and laugh with joy. In the losers' camp unhappiness and frustration prevailed.

One day, after being defeated in yet another game, an older man on the losing team took the ball used in the game and cast a spell upon it. He was certain that the winners across the river would soon be back for another game so he performed a magic rite that would make the ball disappear.

In the game that subsequently took place, the men had hardly begun to play when the ball disappeared. No one knew where to find it. The visitors recrossed the river, very unhappy at having lost the ball which had brought them such luck.

The man who had caused the ball to vanish used his magic once again. When all were sleeping in the victors' camp a curse was laid upon the ball players among them. The next morning, when these men left their tents to inspect the weather, they immediately fell to the ground. They were dead.

Joy now spread through the losers' settlement and their men, descending the river in quest of seals, cried out in triumph. They had been victorious even without the use of the ball.

We Made It
Bill van Veelen

We made it.
Looking in silence,
from the top of the pass,
we stare back
at the road
we had come up.

The grey band of asphalt
had been endless.
Pedaling was no longer automatic.
Muscles complained
of overwork,
as we we tried to conquer
gravity by heading for the sky.

We had only
52 miles left,
but we knew
it would be easy,
for it was all
downhill.

Thoughts
Marty Robillard

There are so many things in life I want to do:
But some I don't have the courage to do,
Some I don't have the ability to do,
And others nobody will let me do.
    So I fish.

Fishing Accounted For
Eric Nicol

As you travel west across British Columbia, sooner or later you discover that it disappears under the sea. For British Columbians this inconvenience is largely compensated for by the fishing industry, which employs thousands of people, all busy reaping the silver harvest of the sea, or "fishing" as it is sometimes known. In fact, the first thing the visitor sees as he enters Vancouver is the row of canneries along the waterfront, and the first thing he smells is the heady aroma of this outstanding B.C. product.

By far the most important of B. C. fish is the salmon. Of the several varieties of salmon, the most delicious is the sockeye, especially the young, or bobby-sockeye. It is indeed a stirring sight, as you sail into Vancouver, to see the dozens of tiny fishing smacks, all smacking the mouth of the Fraser, their gillnets spread around them, while the fishermen wait for the salmon run. (Of course, the salmon don't *actually* run, since they have no legs, but you just try to tell an old fisherman that!)

After the fisherman has caught a fish or, better still, several fish, he takes his catch to the cannery, where the fish are loaded onto conveyor belts manned by girls who slice off the salmon's head and tail, slit the belly, and reach in with their hand . . .

Much of the romance of the fishing industry lies in the salmon's magnificent pilgrimage upstream to spawn. Fighting fierce currents, bruised by rapids, leaping and struggling up and up, the salmon do not rest until they reach the mountain lakes far above sea level.

Beside the more formidable falls of the rivers the government has quite decently built ladders for the salmon to climb. These ladders not only help the salmon up the falls but provide the added thrill of an elopement. The salmon are all for them.

Once the spawning ground is reached, the female salmon, easily identified by her distraught expression, looks for a gravelly bit of lake bottom, and there she lays her eggs, thousands of them. After the female has laid her eggs, the male salmon swims over, stares morosely at them, and covers them up as quickly as possible. Then both salmon swim away to die.

All in all, it is undesirable to be a salmon.

Next to its own erotic impulses, the salmon's worst enemy is the sporting fisherman, who complicates the lives of steelhead, cut-throat trout, bullheads and worms. Each summer thousands of fishermen safari to some little lake inaccessible to wives, and known only to several million mosquitoes. There they pitch camp, open a bottle of whiskey, and almost catch some of the biggest fish ever seen.

The aristocrat of fishermen is the fly fisherman, who wouldn't think of fishing with a line with a worm on the end of it. It doesn't matter whether the fish is dying for a worm — all he's offered is a wad of fluff. Now, the first movement in fly fishing, after placing the lunch on the nearest anthill, is that of whirling the line behind the head and casting, and it is at this point that the novice usually finds he has already landed a fine, plump cedar. After he has chopped down the cedar and retrieved his line, the fisherman goes out into midstream in his hip-boots and makes another throw. The fly is cast. Suddenly a trout rises and snaps up the bait (some trout will do this just for a laugh). The fisherman must now play the fish, a part for which he is eminently suited, by allowing the trout to drag him into deeper water, flooding his hip-boots and requiring rescue by his companions. The main thing to remember, however, is that merely to have the fish on the hook is no reason for hauling him in and getting the whole business over and done with. There may not be another fish along for days — make him last! Even if the fish swims ashore and tries to give himself up, the sport demands that the fisherman shoo him back and tussle with him for several hours. If there's anything a true fisherman hates it's a fish that is fed up with outdoor life and tries to co-operate in its own capture.

Often, after playing the fish for some time, and just as he is about to scoop up his trout in his net, the fisherman sees his fish slip off the hook and swim away. Here we see and hear the fisherman at his best. With the first explosion of language a cauliflower-shaped cloud rises several thousand feet in the air, the river curdles around his quivering legs, and fish rise belly-upwards to the surface, to float downstream to waiting bear and otter.

But probably the happiest of all fishermen is the one who rows into the lake far enough to be unobserved, drops anchor, drops a line, and drops off to sleep. All he catches is the sun and his bites are all mosquito, but in the gentle roll of his boat, under the blue sky, the fisherman finds the peace that comes only with exclusion of the rest of the world.

The Losers
Samuel Roddan

Mr. Biggar was just about the finest track coach you could find anywhere and right now he was giving us his last minute advice before we marched out on the field and took on Lonsdale Tech for the championship of the Valley. It was pretty hot in the dressing room under the grandstand, but you could hear a pin drop when Mr. Biggar was laying it on the line —

"I want you Ogden fellows to go out there today and play up, play up, and play the game — and beat the living tar out of Lonsdale. But above all, be good sports. Remember, it doesn't matter who wins, it's the game that counts — as long as you make sure you're not the losers."

Everybody laughed. Mr. Biggar sure had a sense of humor.

Then Mr. Biggar paced back and forth. Suddenly he whirled about and fixed everyone in his stare.

"And you're going to give her all you've got. You're going to burn up the track. And you're going to fight 'em into the ground." Mr. Biggar softened his voice to a whisper and gave us a wink. "And don't anyone here forget, either, that you can be good sports into the bargain, besides."

We all laughed again. Mr. Biggar really laid things on the line. He called a spade a spade. But he wasn't stuffy and preachy. He was a real regular — and a good sport — and he sure made you feel like going out and beating the old enemy . . .

Mr. Biggar wiped his face with a big white handkerchief and snapped shut the leather bag where he carried his rubbing liniment and towels and oranges. And as we trotted out of the dressing room he clapped us on the back and spoke a few words of encouragement and advice to each of us. He told Spider Legs Beckett, our high jumper, to be sure and dust off his knee caps before he went over the bar. And he said I was to keep the old elbows sharpened for the Lonsdale hounds when they started crowding me on the curves.

"Don't let those fellows scare you, Slim," Mr. Biggar said, putting his arm around my shoulder. "They're all bluff. Once they see you can handle yourself, they'll fall back and cry like babies. You just jab away and keep going. That's the big thing. Just keep going."

I put out my hand and we shook. I could feel Mr. Biggar's great strength flowing into me through that handshake and I squeezed back as hard as I could to tell him by my own grip that I was right in there and ready to fight and give my all. I would never let the old coach down. And that was for sure. So help me.

Fats Keeler lined us up in front of the grandstand for the national anthem. I don't think the place ever looked prettier — the decorations, and the smell of the hot dogs and onions, and the bunting, and the cheer leaders turning somersaults, and all the brightly colored pompoms fluttering in the breeze. Then, at a signal from Mr. Biggar, Mary Love got Ogden going on the last verse of our famous school song. Right here we caught the Lonsdale team flat-footed because they were standing at attention waiting for the band to begin the anthem. And so we socked away at the old opposition with the sweetest school song you could ever wish to hear —

> Now triumphant, glory making
> Honors winning, records breaking
> Victory after victory taking,
> Ogden wins the fight.

Out of the corner of my eye I saw the Lonsdale coach, Mr. Howell, mumbling to himself and glaring at Mr. Biggar, who stood with his shoulders back like a real veteran and looked straight ahead as though he were taking the salute. But right after the singing of "O Canada", Mr. Howell hustled over and shouted out that Mr. Biggar was certainly commencing the track meet with a poor example of good sportsmanship. Mr. Biggar yelled back — the way anybody would under the circumstances — and Mr. Biggar got in the last word too, because he calmly advised Mr. Howell to lay off, and take it easy, since later he would be burying not only him but his whole team right under the scoreboard. Everybody laughed because Mr. Biggar really had one on poor Mr. Howell, and it was lucky for him the announcer called for quiet and introduced Mayor Nelson to the crowd. Mayor Nelson waited for silence, and then he officially declared the meet open and said, as he did every year, that not only was it a great privilege for him to be here, but that we mustn't forget the Battle of Waterloo was won on the playing fields of Eton.

A great cheer went up for the Mayor, and Mr. Biggar clapped his hands and motioned for all of us to do the same, and soon the announcer was calling for the contestants in the shot-put to report immediately to the main desk by the scoreboard. Fats Keeler, who is our hope in the weights, waved his hand and trotted forward, and Mr. Biggar gave him a couple of good pats on the back to help him do his stuff.

A little later Mr. Biggar ordered me to warm up on the grassy stretch beyond the grandstand and get ready for the 880, which always comes a little later in the meet. So I jogged up and down to loosen the muscles, and I stepped on the gas for a second or two to get the old ticker pumping, and I touched the toes and took little spurts to make sure the lungs were pulling in lots of air. But most of the time I was feeling kind of lonely and wishing the whole thing was over, but then I could hear the cheers and I could see myself coming down the home stretch giving out with the last powerful kick and really cutting the mustard and turning in a winner by at least a length and a half. Then, of course, I felt pretty proud, too, when the announcement came over the loudspeaker a few minutes later that Fats Keeler of Ogden High School had just set a new record for the shot-put with an astronomical, unbeatable heave of forty-five feet seven inches.

Nevertheless, it still is pretty lonesome just waiting around to get started on your event, and as time went by I kept watching Mr. Biggar adding up the scores in his little notebook and shaking his head. I figured the black flies must be getting bad. But I waved to him once and he waved back and that was something. And after what seemed hours, I suddenly heard the announcer calling for all contestants in the boys' 880 yards to report immediately to the starter.

Mr. Biggar hustled over to see me off and I told him I was all set and not to worry and just add another five points in his notebook for Ogden High. But Mr. Biggar was looking grim, and after he had patted me on the back a couple of times and felt the old biceps, he was telling me that we had to take the 880 or otherwise we'd lose the cup for sure. And I had to get out in front and stay there and save some strength for the last kick coming down the home stretch.

I was nodding my head but still jogging up and down with a towel over my shoulder and trying to figure out how we could be so far behind if Fats Keeler had broken the record in the shot-put. Of course I was forgetting what had happened in the pole vault and discus and the high jump, which poor Spider Legs had lost by just a hair. But I'd got the message loud and clear and I was going to be in there fighting and the last thing I'd be doing would be letting Mr. Biggar down with a second or a third. It was a first place or nothing, and no fade-out as far as I was concerned. And that was for sure.

The starter was waving his pistol above his head and shouting for everybody to be quiet and on their marks and get set and then with a bang we were off. I sprinted into an early lead and was running free and easy and out in front and lengthening my stride. I was floating along with everything going just fine and according to plan and the old lungs pumping plenty of air. Once when I glanced over my shoulder I could see the Lonsdale chaps far behind so I slowed up the pace, which was a real scorcher, and settled down to a long, even lope. And I was thinking what a good feeling it is to be way out in front for a change and not have anyone on your tail or waiting to climb your back. Then I could hear the roar of the crowd and I caught a flash of the pompoms and I gave a little kick and a spurt to show I was right in there cutting the mustard and I might possibly be trying to break the record as well as give the Lonsdale plodders a good taste of my dust. I was thinking too how sweet it was going to be in the dressing room afterward, with everybody shaking your hand and clapping you on the back and Mr. Biggar beaming and smiling and giving me a rubdown and a couple of big, juicy oranges for the old thirst.

Suddenly the crowd roared a warning. I took a quick look around and, sure enough, there was that pack of Lonsdale hounds gathering steam to steam-roller me into the cinders. I shortened my pace to shake them off but they just seemed to snort and jeer and tear ahead. I could hear them grunt and pant and they were crowding me over and I could feel the jabs in my ribs and side as they elbowed past spurting dust from the spikes of their track shoes.

And now I gave her all I had . . .

And I was running for the cup and the school . . . and I was running for my own pride and the love and the glory and to be a winner just once in my life . . . and I was running for Spider Legs who must be feeling worse than I was at this very moment . . . and I was running for Fats Keeler, the champ . . . but most of all I was running for the school and the glory and the fame and for poor Mr. Biggar who had given his all for us . . .

Then I knew I was fading . . . really fading . . . and I knew I could never catch anybody.

I heard some boos and I heard somebody yell out, "Try the sack race next time." I tried to shout back that I wasn't finished yet. I tried to get an arm up for a wave to show I was still in there cutting the mustard, no matter what. Then I felt myself going down all rubbery-legged on the black, sharp cinders . . .

Back in the dressing room everything was dead quiet, and I hobbled over beside Spider Legs who was sitting by himself staring at his knee caps. The place was hot and my mouth was dry and I could feel the muscles going into little hard lumps on my neck and back. Fats Keeler was stretched out on the table getting the full treatment and a rubdown with a special mixture of olive oil and wintergreen. He was sucking one of those big, juicy oranges that Mr. Biggar carries around in his leather bag, and Mr. Biggar was working the liniment into Fats' arms and saying that a winner always has that extra something that makes him stand out in a crowd.

"You've got pluck, Fats," Mr. Biggar said, slapping and kneading at his muscles. "And that's a scarce commodity around here. Pluck doesn't grow on trees. But you've got it, Fats. You've sure got it."

For a while I just kind of rested to get my wind back and I stared at Fats sucking his orange and watching the juice running down his chin, but now I could feel my own mouth tasting pretty bitter and the old stomach knotting up so I figured I'd better take off my strip and get into my clothes. Spider lent me a couple of Band Aids to plaster over my elbows where I had hit the cinders at the finish line, but I didn't bother putting any on the scratches on my chin. Then I got my towel and shirt and picked up my track shoes. I tied them together and slung them over my shoulder but the laces were short and the sharp spikes jabbed into my neck. As we headed for the door we took a last look around and the spikes jabbed me again and about all I could see was Mr. Biggar busy talking to the sports reporter from the *News Chronicle*. Mr. Biggar was telling him that next year he would have a lot better material and more natural talent to work with.

"Some young fellows are pretty soft," Mr. Biggar was saying. "They don't know the meaning of those old-fashioned words, like 'finish' and 'drive' and, most important, 'pluck'."

Spider and I got outside that dressing room and walked slowly down the ramp and past the empty grandstand. We waded through the clutter of paper cups and old programs and yell sheets and the torn school banners and past the broken pop bottles stacked near the exits and the trampled pompoms lying all over the ground.

Then Spider and I came to the sidewalk and went past the barbed wire fence and just moved along until we hit Hastings Street. My spikes kept jabbing me and Spider said, well, anyway, the baseball season would be starting soon, but I hardly heard him because I was still trying to pick up all the pieces . . . You can get over losing a race and coming in last but a fellow has to have somebody to look up to and when a great man like Mr. Biggar just turns out to be a phony . . . it really hurts . . . and it makes you feel lonely and lost, and all that playing-fields-of-Eton stuff seems dim and empty, and you have a letdown that's a whole lot worse than not getting a pat on the back or a fat, juicy orange.

I didn't want to explain all this to Spider because he was feeling bad enough as it was. And so I said it was just as well the baseball season would be starting soon and Spider said he had been thinking the same thing. Then we walked along until we came to Chuck Wong's Fruit Store. We went in, and we bought our own darned oranges, and they were just about the sweetest oranges I've had in a long time, but when the juices ran down my chin, it made the scratches burn and sting . . .

Discus
Grace Petrikowski

The tension is there —
countless hours of training at stake
    This is it
    The city final
    A chance for the Provincial in Calgary
    C'mon
    you can do it
Get a good grip
take a deep breath
swing the arm
spin
let it go
    Wow
    look at it fly
    It's probably the best throw so far
Try again
concentrate
    The tape measure is your friend
I'm glad it's over
    The ribbon matches your shirt
I always looked good in red.

The Hustler
Eddie Kwan

I stepped from the phone booth totally transformed. I was no longer Eddie, but Fast Eddie. In place of the calculator and armload of books, I now held a fancy two-piece cue. I placed the cue into the pouch at the back of my cape and walked into the pool room.

Closing the door behind me, I stepped into the largest billiard room I had ever seen. Thick layers of cigarette smoke hung over each of the thirty solid oak tables and I coughed. I did not like smoke. The click of balls caroming off each other assaulted my ears.

I stood silhouetted against the glass window of the door for a moment before I commandingly called out my challenge. "Excuse me, would someone here like to play a game of pool with me?" A chorus of chuckles filled the room. I have a soft and meek voice.

A girl stepped forward. "My name's Denise. Denise Sheraton." She led me to a table and said "Let's flip a coin to see who breaks. Heads I win, tails you lose." She flipped the coin and it turned out I had to break. I thought there was something odd there but I wasn't quite sure what.

I started to nose through the racks of cues but I discovered I couldn't see well enough that close so I backed up a bit. I finally selected a cue.

I had heard about this place. There were players here who could shoot looking through a mirror with an old broom handle for a cue and still win. I knew that Denise would be able to beat me easily.

I didn't remember when but Denise assured me that we had bet twenty dollars on the game. I wondered if she took Mastercharge. I hated to mortgage my shorts.

As I prepared to break, I noted that she took in every move I made with her dark brown eyes. She was a professional and clearly quite intelligent. She was also very beautiful and I did not feel comfortable around her. My cue quivered at the end. My right hand gripped it more tightly to prevent it from shaking. I knew that this would be the toughest game I had ever played and I was nervous.

My break was actually a poor one. Denise smiled and my face turned a little red. I asked her "Do you think you could give me a quick explanation of the rules? I haven't played for quite a while."

She smiled again and said "Don't worry. I'll tell you when you win."

When she bent down to shoot, I realized why she was able to play in a place like this. True, she was quite a good shot, but I noted her opponent, namely me, would require super-human effort to maintain concentration on the game. Her tactic was . . . effective.

She easily potted five of her balls. To a couple of old geezers sitting on a bench watching the game I said "This looks bad for our hero."

There are several subtle ways in which to break another pool player's concentration. I had been around for quite a while and picked up a sneaky trick here and there and now I was the master of subtle distraction. Normally I played fairly but when a twenty is on the line . . .

She stooped down for her next shot and I prepared myself. Number Two, I thought. I figured she would fall like a ton of bricks for good old Number Two.

Just before she shot, I calmly screamed out a war cry and screeched "Miss!" The ball rolled into the hole and she smirked and said "Number Two huh?" I cursed to myself. She read that book too.

She potted her second last ball and my nails dug into my cue. I pried them loose. She purposely missed her next shot though, because she wanted to play around a while. "Oh darn!" she said realistically. She knew she had my twenty bucks.

Smiling at the girl I said "That was too bad." I bent down and concentrated. This time I was really trying to make my shot. It was an easy one and I potted it. She was still watching me very closely.

I had perfect shape for my next shot. My right hand swung the cue and the ball rolled smoothly into the hole. The next shot was a moderate toughie, but I knew I could make it if I wanted to. I set up for my shot and took careful aim. Once again I tried my best to make the shot. The ball rolled toward the hole but missed and by over a foot! Naturally, because I planned it that way.

Denise said "Nice try. I have to make a tough shot here though." I smiled. It was an easy shot. But when she shot, the ball stopped just in front of the hole. If it had fallen, I would have lost. But it had not fallen because she had not intended to make it.

So far, I had made only two of the eight balls I needed to win. As well, Denise had left me pretty safe. I had to make a real tough shot, a shot considerably more difficult than my last shot, which, incidentally, I had missed by quite a distance. Denise was sure she had nothing to worry about.

I aimed very carefully and shot. Naturally the ball rolled faithfully into the hole because now I gripped the cue firmly with my left hand. From there I easily potted my remaining five balls to win the game.

Denise stared speechlessly at the spot where my winning ball fell in. But in a moment she came over laughing to congratulate me. "How did you do it? I watched you carefully and I couldn't tell." In a match she could have beaten me easily and we both knew it. I began my explanation. "When a pool player feigns poor shooting in order to suck another player in, an experienced eye can tell because a good pool player has a stroke that is smooth and flawless. Although he can aim to miss, his ease and naturalness gives him away."

Now whenever I play a fellow less talented than myself, I let him know his position to give him the opportunity to back out. But I knew that Denise was better than me and besides, she planned on taking my twenty bucks! After all, she was a hustler. I thought it only fair that she should be on the paying end for a change.

I finished my explanation. "So you see, Denise, the reason why you couldn't tell that I wasn't trying is because I *was* trying."

She gave me a quizzical look but I smiled and made like

a magician. A magician never reveals his secret.

After a little prompting, she reluctantly forked over the twenty. I laughed and said "Relax, it's tax deductible."

She laughed and asked "Weren't you taking a bit of a chance though? I could have just cleaned up on you."

I replied "I'm a hustler too, you know. I know how we like to draw a game out just to tease our opponents. I'll admit, though, there was a bit of risk involved. But for a player like me, being able to take the risks, to carry out plans like this, to hustle the hustlers is a thing of paramount importance, surpassing even money and girls. Well, maybe not girls but certainly money."

She laughed and we sat down to chat for a while. Before long, I found myself talked into buying her dinner tonight. I sighed. There's more than one way to hustle.

Carnival Procession — Calgary Stampede
Arthur Stringer

An old Chief rode along
The valley of white faces clustered where
His tribesmen once had hunted wolf and bear.
    Grim-lipped and lean and taciturn as stone,
He scorned the cheering crowds, and rode alone.
The shaggy-flanked cayuse he sat astride
Seemed but a frame of sullen bones and hide,
Yet kingly was the posture, kingly waved
The eagle feathers round a face engraved
With more than time. . . .
    Silent he rode, the sunset in his eyes,
Sadly resplendent in his foolish dyes;
A king in rags, still drowned with dignity,

An old wolf caged, yet pining to be free,
Grinding his worn fangs on the ghostly bars
That kept him from his kinship with the stars,
The curling rivers and the woodland camps
That through the mists of time went out like lamps,
The teepee clusters on the sun-washed range
That shrank and altered in a world of change,
The bellowing herd, the long sault's happy roar,
The worn portages he would know no more.
    So out along the tumult and the crowd
He passed as slow and silent as a cloud;
Remote, aloof, alone, he faltered on
To ghostlier trails from which the light had gone.

Atavists
Harold Baldwin

Out from the chutes the grunting bronchos crash
leaping, their ramrod legs like bars of steel
hit sod together. Buck and roll and squeal.
Wide sabre horns of steers that flash
their brazen tips as horse and rider dash
to hang thereon the coloured winning sash,
emblem of cowboy prowess.
Through the shivering haze,
Atavists, we are the recalled Frontier Days,
pioneer colour brushed with wanton splash.
The White-faced calves like greyhounds run,
Wise, chasing horse, his belly to the ground —
Glint of flung rope, spurs in the blazing sun,
Full is the day, saddle smell and sound.
Turn back the clock and frontier days began —
The days of the bawling herds to shipment bound.

Taming the Cyclone
Jacques Hamilton

The first Calgary Stampede in 1912 was seven days of thrills and spills — with most of the thrills and spills being provided by a snorting, spinning, wild-eyed bundle of black dynamite called "Cyclone".

Cyclone had come to the Stampede as the best bucking horse in the world, and as the show moved into its final day, his record was intact. A total of 129 men had tried to mount him and stay on him, and 129 men had ended up in the dust.

The only man in the world anyone rated as having a chance to beat Cyclone was a young Indian cowboy from Macleod, Tom Three Persons.

But as that closing Saturday dawned, Tom Three Persons wasn't available to take on the horse. Tom, lamenting his fate, was under lock and key in the Calgary jail, and staring vainly through the bars at the distant Stampede grounds.

In Victoria Park, the finals in the bucking horse contest were about to begin, and Cyclone's record of 129 to 0 was about to permit him to withdraw from the competition the undisputed champion.

But an Indian agent named Glen Campbell wouldn't hear of it. Red-faced with anger, he kept insisting that Tom Three Persons should be given a chance at the beast.

Somehow, word got to the Mounties, and they evidently agreed that a little thing like a jail sentence shouldn't keep an Alberta cowboy from showing a crowd how to ride.

With the finals already underway, a cash bond was posted and Tom Three Persons was rushed to the grounds.

A surprised crowd cheered when the announcer gave the word that Tom Three Persons of Macleod was about to ride in the finals. But the cheers gave way to apprehensive groans when the announcer added that Tom would be climbing on the back of Cyclone. Even the other competitors looked sympathetic.

Indeed, the only person who didn't seem worried about it all was Tom himself. As *The Calgary Herald* recorded the scene:

> The horse thrown to the ground, Tom jumped across him, placed his feet in the stirrups, and with a wild "whoop" the black demon was up and away with the Indian rider.
>
> Bucking, twisting, swapping ends and resorting to every artifice of the outlaw, Cyclone swept across the field. The Indian was jarred from one side of the saddle to the other, but as the crowd cheered themselves hoarse he settled every time into the saddle and waited for the next lurch or twist.
>
> His bucking unable to dislodge the redskin, Cyclone stood at rest and reared straight up. Once it looked as though Tom was to follow the fate of his predecessors. He recovered rapidly and from that time forward Cyclone bucked till he was tired. The Indian had mastered him.
>
> The thousands created a pandemonium of applause that was not equalled all week.
>
> It was a thrilling moment and in it Tom Three Persons had captured the championship of the world for himself and for Canada.

Even though Tom had to return to jail for a while, he emerged as the pride of Alberta's Indians — the only Indian to win the bronc riding championship of the world. Even today, more than half a century later, his picture hangs in the Blood reserve community hall at Standoff; a permanent tribute to a man who walked out of a jail cell to tame a Cyclone.

When the Chuckwagons Roll
Beatrice Boles Liddle

The chuckwagon race, which originated in Alberta, is the high point of the Stampede.

There are four outriders to each of the four outfits in every heat. When the starting-horn blows, one outrider holds back the team of horses fighting to be on its way. Another throws the stove in the rear of the chuckwagon. The remaining two pitch the flies and poles into the covered wagon. Now, the four entries are off — half-hidden by clouds of dust and accompanied by tumultuous cheers from the packed throng.

All outfits must make a circle-eight around two barrels before they reach the race course. Sometimes as many as three "prairie schooners" reach this point at the same time, with the fourth just behind — unless the last unit gets into serious difficulties, which often happens. The sixteen outriders keep as close as possible to their careening outfits — some alongside, some in the rear.

No whips are used and none is needed. The horses are caught up in the whirl, the same as the men. If a spill occurs, the horses keep on galloping, with or without their riders. Likewise with the teams drawing the covered wagons: the horses often continue to haul a de-wheeled or upset wagon till the cowboys cut in and spoil their fun by dragging the wrecked vehicle off the track.

Penalties are chalked up fast: when a barrel is knocked down; when a stove, fly or pole misses the wagon, or is jolted out; when outriders' horses bolt without them; or when outriders arrive "late" at the finish — twenty-five yards behind their outfits.

And when the winner boils out of the choking dust at the end of each heat, the roar from the crowd proves again the tremendous popularity of this thrilling event.

Babe's Surprise

R. Ross Annett

Joe was in an unusually happy mood as he approached the Star Store in Sanford. Ordinarily he bore himself soberly, but now he grinned at people he met, even people who were strangers to him. He had just concluded, or practically concluded, a profitable deal with Alf Bailey. All that remained was for Alf to get his brother's approval, the Bailey brothers being partners.

Joe felt that he had handled the negotiations cleverly. He had known that the Baileys wanted the purebred yearling bull which Joe had for sale. And, even more than they wanted the bull, Joe wanted to lease a section of grass from the Baileys' large holdings which bordered his present lease. He had begun by asking a thousand dollars for the bull, but had allowed Alf to dicker him down to eight hundred, which was a fair-enough price, all things considered. Finally, though with a great show of reluctance, he had agreed to the eight-hundred-dollar price, providing that the Baileys would give him a three-year grazing lease on the section of grass he coveted.

"Sometimes I ain't so awful far from bein' smart," Joe chuckled.

The annual Willow Creek rodeo was only a few weeks away, and in the Star Store window Miss Corrie was arranging an appropriate display of boots, saddles, chaps and other cowboy gear. The central feature of this display was a kid-sized cowgirl outfit — a beautiful, all-white ensemble of hat, vest, skirt and boots, all intricately embroidered and trimmed with silver. Joe stopped. He took one long look, then walked into the store.

"How much is that cowgirl outfit, Miss Corrie?" he asked.

Joe had the deep voice and slow, deliberate speech of the big-bodied man. But there must have been a betraying eagerness in his manner, for Miss Corrie gave him a rueful, understanding smile. She was an understanding person, though no knockout for looks, being a thin spinsterish redhead. She was noted for the sharpness of her tongue, but for all that she had a warm heart, especially for kids. She climbed out of the window and stood, chest-high to Joe, regarding the cowgirl costume.

"Wouldn't it look lovely on Babe!" she said. But then she shrugged regretfully. "It's priced at seventy-five dollars," she went on. "Mr. Thompson should never have ordered it, because it won't sell. None of the wealthy ranchers hereabouts happen to have little girls that size — Babe's size. And nobody else can afford to spend so much money on a child."

Miss Corrie knew Joe's circumstances well enough to include him in the "nobody else" group. But, in his present happy mood, Joe felt reckless.

"Wrap it up, Miss Corrie," he said, grinning. "I want it for Baby to wear to the rodeo."

Miss Corrie looked up at him as though she thought he was kidding. The cowgirl outfit was not only high-priced; its dazzling white made it impractical for ordinary wear. It was something for special occasions only.

"Lookit," Joe argued, "I just made a pretty good deal. Some folks would celebrate by spendin' money for liquor. So what's wrong with me lettin' myself go, spendin' it on my kids? Which reminds me, I gotta get somethin' for Little Joe too."

"Well, when you look at it that way — " Miss Corrie began. For a moment a smile lighted up her thin face. She knew, and warmly approved of, Joe's earnest desire to do right by his motherless kids. For their sake, for example — and unlike his disreputable brother, Pete — Joe did not drink. But then Miss Corrie's better judgement reasserted itself and she added sharply, "It's still crazy!"

"Wrap it up," Joe ordered. "An' please don't say a word to Baby about it. I want to surprise her at rodeo time. Now, about Little Joe — he's been wantin' a pair of chaps."

The chaps, at least, were of practical use, something that Little Joe needed for herding cattle in cold or wet weather or in the brush of the bottom lands. And Joe picked out a size large enough to allow for the boy's future growth.

I guess that's about the craziest thing I ever done, he admitted to himself, thinking about the cowgirl outfit as he drove home in the pickup. There were a hundred things he might better have spent the money for. There were dozens of things Babe needed a lot more than a fancy cowgirl costume which was not suitable for everyday wear and which she would soon grow out of. But even the soberest man has a right to kick over the traces and get extravagant once in a while. The trouble was, he told himself, he did not get to do it often enough. Surely the deal with the Baileys was sufficient excuse.

When he reached home, however, he did not let on to Uncle Pete about what he had done. He knew what Pete would say. He sneaked the parcels into the house and hid them under his bed.

By the time Babe and Little Joe came riding home from school, Joe was helping Pete brush up on his calf roping, in preparation for the rodeo. Pete could still rope and tie with the best of the young fellows, and he liked to demonstrate his prowess occasionally, along with that of Good Enough, his buckskin saddle horse.

"Me an' Good Enough's still good enough to show up the young squirts," Pete liked to brag.

When the kids arrived, Joe was holding the struggling calf, whose mother was bawling her head off in the corral, while Uncle Pete sat, rope in hand, and Good Enough waited with ears pricked forward, eager as a colt. The buckskin was no longer young, but, like Uncle Pete himself, he had the know-how that comes from long experience. The kids pulled up their pony and sat watching.

"O.K.," Big Joe called, letting go of the calf and jerking his watch out of his pocket.

The calf lifted its tail and took off for the corral. At the same instant, Uncle Pete and the buckskin took after the calf. Uncle Pete's loop went sailing out and settled over the calf's head. Good Enough stopped in his tracks, so that the tightening rope jerked the calf over in a complete somersault. By that time Uncle Pete was out of the saddle and running, hand over hand, down the rope. The calf was struggling to its feet when he reached it. He flipped it over on its side, tied it expertly, then stood erect. Babe and Little Joe clapped their hands.

"Eleven seconds, near's I can figure," Big Joe announced.

"With a second or so for you to git your watch out, it ain't fast enough," Uncle Pete grumbled. He suffered from asthma, which made his voice harsh and rasping, like the sound of an axle badly in need of grease.

"You'll get first prize, Uncle Pete!" Babe declared confidently. "and the queen is coming to the rodeo to give out the prizes!"

"Queen?" echoed Uncle Pete.

"The queen is going to be at the rodeo," Babe said.

"Aw, Babe, you got it all wrong!" Little Joe scolded.

That, of course, was obvious. A real queen would never condescend to be present at a small, back-country rodeo. Babe was just a little kid and she did not always get things straight. She was sitting behind her brother on the pony's back. The sun made a glistening crown of her fair hair, and it looked all the brighter by contrast with Little Joe's hair, which was thick and black like his pop's. The boy had his father's dark eyes, too, whereas Babe's eyes were blue. Both kids wore blue jeans and checked shirts.

Big Joe grinned at Babe fondly. She was the apple of his eye because she was fair and daintily made, like the way her mom used to be. But it bothered him, often, to think how little chance she had to be feminine and ladylike, with no mother to dress her up pretty.

"You ain't so far wrong, at that, Baby," he said. He was picturing how she would look in the beautiful cowgirl costume, and his thought was that there was going to be a little queen at the rodeo, in any case.

"They said so at school, pop!" Babe insisted. "They said that the queen would be at the rodeo."

"They said beauty queen, not a real queen!" Little Joe corrected.

"A which?" Uncle Pete demanded.

"A beauty queen," Little Joe repeated. "They're going to pick the prettiest girl to be queen of the rodeo an' give out the prizes."

Uncle Pete snorted. He said what in the aitch would they think up next? He said it was getting so that a man couldn't have a quiet drink in a bar these days, or get a haircut even, without having women bob up at his elbow. He said he had a profane good mind not to take part in the rodeo after all. This was a long speech for Uncle Pete, who usually expressed himself in grumpy monosyllables. It showed how upset he was.

"Linda Bailey thought it up," Little Joe explained. "Linda says they always have a beauty queen at the big rodeos."

Uncle Pete looked at Big Joe in disgust. Pete had the kind of face that could register disgust with very little effort. There was a hard and cynical twist to his mouth. Years of heavy drinking had given his nose and cheeks a purplish cast, and his eyes were red-rimmed and bleary.

"I get it!" Big Joe chuckled. "Linda Bailey figures she'll just naturally be the beauty queen."

Linda was a city girl, at present visiting her bachelor uncles, Alf and Bill Bailey, at the 2B Ranch. The 2B was one of the biggest ranches in the district, and Alf Bailey was the president of the Stock Growers' Association, which sponsored the rodeo. It seemed likely that his pretty niece had talked Alf into this beauty-queen foolishness, figuring that, with her uncles being local big shots, she would be a natural choice for beauty queen.

Up to that time, the Willow Creek rodeo had been a folksy

gathering of stockmen and their families for the annual picnic of the Stock Growers' Association. The picnic dinner was preceded by riding and roping events, and was followed by an open-air dance on a roofless platform set among the trees and shrubbery of the Willow Creek valley. It had never occurred to anybody that the crowning of a beauty queen would add to the general enjoyment of the occasion. Indeed, the reaction of most local people upon first hearing of the proposal was one either of scorn and derision, like Uncle Pete's, or of tolerant amusement, such as Big Joe showed. Nobody could have foreseen that the beauty-queen competition would become a veritable apple of discord and come very near to wrecking the Stock Growers' Association itself.

Joe got his first dim inkling of such a possibility when, a few days later, at the supper table, Babe announced, "Miss Carlson is going to run for beauty queen, pop!"

"Well, she's sure pretty enough," was Joe's first comment.

The school teacher was a shapely little blonde who had knocked all the local young men for a loop when she first came to the district the previous autumn. Miss Carlson had taken time to look the field over and then had cannily picked Arch Morgan for her steady boy friend. The Running M Ranch, which Arch had inherited from his father, was as big a spread as the Bailey Brothers' 2B, and Arch himself was a good-looking young bachelor.

Even then, Big Joe did not tumble to the explosive possibilities of the situation. "Looks like Linda Bailey will have some tough competition," he remarked in mild amusement.

"So they'll have to vote for beauty queen," Little Joe said.

Babe piped up eagerly, "Will you vote for Miss Carlson, pop?"

"All the school kids are goin' to work for Miss Carlson," Little Joe said. "You'll vote for her, won't you, pop!"

"Oh, sure!" Big Joe agreed, never thinking that he would soon have cause to regret making the promise.

"Will you vote for Miss Carlson, too, Uncle Pete?" Babe asked.

Uncle Pete looked at her sourly, but did not deign to answer.

"Your Uncle Pete's agin havin' a beauty queen, Baby. But you keep workin' on him," Big Joe said . . . "Say!" he went on, after a moment. "Arch Morgan is the teacher's boy friend, ain't he?"

"That's right," Little Joe answered. "Sometimes Arch comes along at recess to talk to teacher. We sure get a long recess then!"

"Arch will want his girl friend to be beauty queen," Big Joe said thoughtfully. "An' he's vice president of the Stock Growers' Association. This business could stir up some hard feelin's."

That, as it turned out, was a gross understatement. Ordinarily the Bailey brothers' attitude toward the contest would have been much the same as Uncle Pete's. They were staid old bachelors with no interest in women, beautiful or otherwise. But, with their niece prodding them, they bestirred themselves to get Linda named rodeo queen.

A day or so later it was announced that Gwen Corbett, the daughter of another rancher, would also be a candidate. Gwen was pretty and popular. She had a light foot on a dance floor, a firm seat in the saddle and a quick and knowing eye for a horse or a beef critter. She was, besides, a local girl. A lot of people thought she was a logical choice for beauty queen.

But Gwen Corbett's friends made the naive mistake of thinking that their candidate's obvious personal qualifications would ensure her election. Any practical politician could have told them different. Her nomination merely served to rouse the Bailey and Carlson supporters to active campaigning.

One evening Alf Bailey dropped in at Joe's place, riding the light-stepping blue roan that Alf called Old Blue. Alf was a tall, grim-faced man who was always chary of words and was seldom known to smile. He stepped down from his horse with a gruff "Howdy" as Joe and the kids came out on the kitchen porch, with Uncle Pete slouching along in their wake.

Joe thought that Alf had come to close the deal for the bull, but Alf said bluntly, "I come to ask you folks to vote for Linda for beauty queen."

Oh-oh! thought Joe uneasily. He had promised the kids to vote for their teacher, never for a moment thinking that the Baileys might take such an act as a personal affront. If they did so, they might refuse to go through with the deal for the bull, a deal which Joe had considered practically settled. And the grazing lease which he had shrewdly tied in with the deal was of vital importance to him. It was so important, indeed, that he might have hedged on his promise to the kids, except that Babe gave him no chance.

"Pop promised to vote for Miss Carlson, Mr. Bailey," she said.

So then Joe had to make the best of it. "You know how kids are, Alf," he said placatingly. "They were dead set I should vote for the schoolmarm, so I promised I would."

Alf did not argue the point. He gave Joe a bleak look, then turned back to his horse, without even mentioning the bull. There was, Uncle Pete noticed, a suspicious-looking bulge on Alf's hip, under his coat. Apparently Alf was electioneering in real earnest, prepared to leave no stone unturned. For Alf was not ordinarily free with liquor. So Pete fell in beside Alf and walked with him out to the gate, Old Blue stepping daintily behind them.

That done it! Big Joe was thinking vexatiously as he followed the kids into the house. "The Baileys won't lease me that grass now, that's for sure."

So everything was ruined. On the assumption that the deal would go through, Joe had splurged extravagantly on the stuff for the kids. Even then, he had had guilty qualms about it. But, if the deal was off, there was no justification whatever for spending so much money.

I gotta take the stuff back to the store, he decided regretfully. He felt worse about having to do it than about not getting the grazing lease. The thought of how Babe would look at the rodeo had kept him in a glow of anticipation. The first thing in the morning and the last thing at night, and a million times in between, he had gloated over it.

By and by Uncle Pete returned to the house. There was an expression almost benign on his hard-bitten face, and his breath was enough to pollute the air all about him. It presently appeared also that Pete's attitude toward the contest had undergone a complete change.

"It ain't a bad idee to have a beauty queen," he said.

"Then you'll vote for Miss Carlson, won't you, Uncle Pete!" Babe cried at once.

"Oh, sure, Baby!" he answered. But there was a noticeably furtive look in his eye as he said it.

"You promised Baby — an' I guess you promised Alf Bailey," Joe said accusingly after the kids had gone to bed. "You can't vote for the schoolmarm an' Linda Bailey both."

"There ain't no law says I can't," Pete argued.

Nowadays the election of a beauty queen at the Willow Creek rodeo has become an established custom and the election itself is well organized, with a ballot box and a scrutineer to see that nobody votes more than once. But that first year the queen was to be choosen merely by a show of hands. So Uncle Pete was prepared to raise a hand for any candidate whose supporters offered suitable inducement. He said, however, that he figured on raising his hand higher for Babe's teacher than for either of the others.

The next day Joe had to go to town, and he fully intended to take the chaps and the cowgirl stuff back to the Star Store. But at the last minute he got to thinking that the Baileys might be satisfied at getting one vote from Joe's family for their niece. Besides, the Baileys were influential. There was a good chance that Linda would be elected, in which case the Baileys would surely be willing to go through with the deal for the bull. This was wishful thinking on Joe's part, and he recognized it as such. But he decided to leave the parcels under his bed for a little while longer.

Immediately afterward, however, Arch Morgan began active campaigning on behalf of the schoolteacher.

He called at Joe's place one evening and, after he left, Uncle Pete's breath was as strong and his expression just as benign as it had been following Alf Bailey's visit.

Could be the schoolmarm will win out, Joe thought glumly. *I guess I better take the stuff back, after all.*

But the vision of Babe in the beautiful costume had got such a hold on him by this time that it had undermined his prudence. There were times when he caught himself thinking, *Deal or no deal, I want Baby to have somethin' extravagant for once.* Then he would try to sell himself a compromise plan; returning the high priced costume and buying, for a few dollars, one of the cowgirl outfits shown in the mail-order catalogue or in any toy store. But he hated the thought of a cheap substitute. Seemed like all Babe ever got was cheap substitutes. The upshot of it was that on the morning of the rodeo the parcels were still under Joe's bed, and Joe was still hoping against hope that the Baileys would still buy the bull. Right after breakfast he brought the parcels out.

"Here's some things I got for you kids," he said.

Babe and Little Joe shrieked with delight when they opened the parcels. It was like Christmas morning, except that they had never had such expensive presents at Christmastime. The chaps were too big for Little Joe, of course. He had to turn up the legs in wide cuffs and punch a new hole in the belt to make it fit his small waist, but he was used to having things big enough for him to grow into. The cowgirl outfit, on the other hand, might have been tailored especially for Babe. She looked so dazzlingly pretty in it that Joe's uneasy qualms were almost submerged in delight and admiration.

"You sure look like your mom, Baby!" he said huskily. "I wish your mom could see you!"

Neither the kids nor Uncle Pete had any idea how much the cowgirl stuff had cost. Pete did finger the chaps appraisingly, chaps being something that he knew the value of.

"Looks like you kind of let yourself go, Joe," he said reprovingly.

"So what?" Joe argued. "They'll last for years."

This was true about the chaps. It was the purchase of the cowgirl things that was the real extravagance. Joe felt, but could not hope to make Uncle Pete understand, that Babe's costume was cheap at seventy-five dollars. Because the memory of the way she looked, wearing it, would last for years too — like the memory he still had of the way her mom had looked in a certain blue dress at the Willow Creek dance. But he had to admit that he would feel a lot easier in his mind if the Baileys decided to go through with the deal for the bull.

They drove to the rodeo in the pickup, with the kids' pony and Uncle Pete's saddle horse trotting behind. They took the pony because, interspersed among the grownups' riding and roping events, there would be horse racing for kids. And the pony was fast enough to place Babe and Little Joe among the prize winners.

It turned out to be a proud day for Joe. But, back of all its triumphs, there was the ever-present thought that, if the Baileys proved resentful enough to renege on the deal, he would always feel that he had been foolish and improvident. He shouted himself hoarse when Babe came in first in the little kids' race. And when, leading the pony, she came skipping toward him, with her cheeks all flushed and her eyes shining, Mrs. Housman murmured in Joe's ear, "My, she's a lovely child, Joe!"

The Housmans owned the Circle H Ranch, and Mrs. Housman was chairman of the committee in charge of choosing the beauty queen.

"I've got an idea, Joe," she said. "Why don't we get Babe to crown the beauty queen? That would make a big hit with everyone."

"It's O.K. by me," Joe said. Truth to tell, he was so pleased and proud that he could hardly get the words out. Babe was shyly appalled when they put the idea to her. But Mrs. Housman finally talked her into it. "I'll be right there beside you on the platform, Babe," she promised.

After that, all the in-between events seemed of minor importance to Joe. He applauded, of course, when Little Joe won the horse race in his age group and when Uncle Pete took first prize in the calf roping. But everything else paled almost into insignificance before the thought of Babe crowning the rodeo queen before the whole crowd, looking — to Joe, at any rate — a lot prettier than the queen herself. Just thinking about it made the nagging voice of prudence almost inaudible.

When the picnic dinner was over, while people were still seated at the long tables, grouped by families or ranch parties, Mrs. Housman appeared on the platform to announce that the time had come to choose the queen. She was immediately joined by the two other members of the committee — Mr. Walton, the Sanford banker; and Mr. Jenson, the district agriculturalist.

Mrs. Housman called Gwen Corbett's name first, and Gwen stepped forth from the ladies' dressing room on the far side of the platform. She was dressed in a colorful, cowgirl costume and got a big hand from the crowd. It was apparent, as the committee members counted the raised hands, that Gwen had drawn a substantial number of votes.

Then Linda Bailey's name was called. Linda was a pretty brunette, with big brown eyes and dark, shoulder-length hair. She was wearing a wine-colored dress with a slim waist and a very full skirt. The applause for her was deafening. When the committee started counting the vote, Alf and Bill Bailey stood up in their places, grimly and ostentatiously checking the people who had their hands raised. This maneuver combined with Linda's very real charm to give the Bailey niece what seemed an overwhelming vote. Joe felt a surge of relief. He hoped that, if Linda won, the Bailey brothers would not be vindictive enough to call off the deal for the bull.

But Miss Carlson was a city girl herself and knew a thing or two about beauty contests. It turned out that she had kept a card up her sleeve — speaking figuratively only, seeing that there were no sleeves to her costume at all and very little else either. When her name was called, she came tripping out on the platform in high-heeled pumps and a skimpy, bathing-beauty getup. Everybody gasped — women in shock, the men in admiration.

Then loud arguments broke out. Alf and Bill Bailey declared that the schoolteacher had taken an unfair advantage, and most of the women in the crowd heartily agreed. But Arch Morgan retorted to the Baileys that Miss Carlson's costume was the sort of thing usually worn by candidates in beauty contests. Arch said that the Baileys were simply showing their ignorance.

"That's nothin' to what the schoolmarm is showin'!" Alf Bailey shouted. "It's indecent, that's what it is!"

"Who you callin' indecent?" Arch demanded angrily.

If Bill Housman had not rushed up to separate them, the president and the vice-president of the Stock Growers' Association would undoubtedly have come to blows. They kept hurling bitter words at each other over the heads of Bill Housman and other would-be peacemakers while, all through the crowd, loud wrangling broke out. Families were sharply divided — the scandalized wives favoring Linda Bailey, the husbands mostly bent upon voting for Miss Carlson. It was a long time before order could be sufficiently restored to get the voting resumed.

Then the uproar broke out again. Most of the men held up their hands for Miss Carlson, though some of them did it stealthily, behind their wives' backs. Some men brazenly raised both hands. There were loud accusations about some people, now voting for the school teacher, who had already been observed to vote for one of the other candidates, and counter-arguments that there was no regulation to forbid such plural voting.

True to his promise, and even though he disapproved of her costume, Joe raised his hand for the schoolteacher. He could feel Alf Bailey's somber eyes on him all the while and knew that his last faint hope was gone — because it was obvious that Miss Carlson was going to win.

In fact, without waiting for the results of the voting to be announced, Arch Morgan and his friends began to cheer. The Baileys shouted that their niece had been gypped. And Gwen Corbett's father loudly demanded that the whole election be declared void because of flagrant irregularities in the voting. Bill Housman climbed up on the platform and held a worried consultation with the committee.

Finally, Mrs. Housman raised her hand and voice, calling for order. In the ensuing, supercharged stillness, she announced that a fourth candidate had been nominated. She said that the committee deplored the squabbling that had arisen among friends and neighbors and urged people to vote for a compromise candidate. And when she announced the candidate's name, Joe was so surprised that for a moment he could not believe his ears.

Then he beheld Babe, appearing from the dressing room, looking shy and frightened, but pretty as a little blond fairy in her white cowgirl costume. Joe found out later that nominating Babe had been Mrs. Housman's idea, and it certainly saved the day — and probably the Stock Growers' Association as well. Most people were glad of the chance offered them to restore amity and good feeling. Babe's naive charm could have been a factor, and no doubt her beautiful costume also helped. At any rate, practically everyone voted for her. And when Mrs. Housman announced that Babe had been chosen queen of the rodeo, everybody cheered to the echo.

After that, Joe cast aside all lingering self-reproaches. He had been crazily extravagant, but he was glad of it. Every time he saw Alf Bailey bearing down upon him he ducked away. He did not want any unpleasantness with Alf to mar a memorable day. But Alf seemed to be relentlessly and vindictively intent upon confronting him. It spoiled Joe's enjoyment of the dance because, every now and then, he had to dodge into the crowd or into the brush to avoid coming face to face with Alf Bailey.

Alf finally did catch up to him, however, just as he and the family were ready to start for home. Alf looked sour and grim — which, of course, was the way he usually looked. By that time Joe was getting sore himself.

"Now listen, Alf — " he burst out.

"I been talkin' it over with Bill," Alf interrupted gruffly. "we'll take delivery of the bull any time, Joe."

"You — you aren't — "

"An' I'm glad that Babe got to be rodeo queen," Alf said.

Joe had no more than recovered from his surprise when Uncle Pete almost ruined everything. "That's a lot o' bull, Alf," Pete said.

Alf bristled angrily and Joe had a moment of panic.

"All Pete meant was, it's a mighty good bull," Joe hastily explained. "A lot o' bull, see? Heh-heh!"

"Oh!" grunted Alf after a moment. "That's what me an' Bill figgered. It's a lot o' bull, all right."

At the Rodeo

James M. Moir

He settles himself
in the saddle,
pulls down his hat
looks up and nods.
The gate is opened
and they plunge
into the arena.
Tossed and jerked
by the thrust
of the broncho's
powerful body,
the cowboy
with deceptive ease
rides the whirlwind.
The crowd roars its praise

Old Tom
once a top rider,
silent now
among the cheering voices,
cigarette smoke
like memories
around his head;
dazed and battered
he stands alone
riding
    still riding.

How We Climbed Cascade
Ralph Connor

Just beyond the Gap lies Banff, the capital of the Canadian National Park, a park unexcelled in all the world for grandeur and diversified beauty of mountain scenery. The main street of Banff runs south to Sulphur mountain, modest, kindly and pine-clad, and north to Cascade, sheer, rocky and bare, its great base thrust into the pine forest, its head into the clouds. Day after day the Cascade gazed in steadfast calm upon the changing scenes of the valley below. The old grey face rudely scarred from its age-long conflict with the elements, looked down in silent challenge upon the pigmy ephemeral dwellers of the village at its feet. There was something overpoweringly majestic in the utter immobility of that ten thousand feet of ancient age-old rock; something almost irritating in its calm challenge to all else than its mighty self.

It was this calm challenge, too calm for contempt, that moved the Professor to utter himself somewhat impatiently one day, flinging the gauntlet, so to speak, into that stony, immovable face: We'll stand on your head some day, old man." And so we did, and after the following manner.

We were the Professor, by virtue of his being pedagogue to the town, slight, wiry, with delicate taste for humor; the Lady from Montreal, who slight as she was and dainty, had conquered Mt. Blanc not long before; the Lady from Winnipeg, literary in taste, artistic in temperament, invincible of spirit; the Man from California, strong, solid and steady; the Lady from Banff, wholesome, kindly, cheery, worthy to be the mother of the three most beautiful babes in all the Park and far beyond it; and the Missionary.

It was a Thursday afternoon in early September of '91, golden and glowing in smoky purple hues, a day for the open prairie or for the shadowy woods, according to your choice.

Into a democrat we packed our stuff, provisions for a week, so it seemed, a tent with all necessary camp appurtenances, and started up the valley of the little Forty Mile creek that brawled its stoney way from the back of the Cascade. We were minded to go by the creek till we could get on the back of old Cascade, from which we could climb up upon his head. Across the intervening stretch of prairie, then through the open timber in the full golden glory of the September sun, and then into the thicker pines, where we lost the sunlight, we made our way, dodging trees, crashing through thickets, climbing over boulder masses, till at last the Professor, our intrepid driver, declared that it would be safer to take our team no further. And knowing him, we concluded that advance must be absolutely impossible. We decided to make this our camp.

To me a camp anywhere and in any weather is good, so that it be on dry ground and within sight, and better within sound, of water. But this camp of ours possessed all the charms that delight the souls of all true campers. In the midst of trees, tall pines between whose points the stars looked down, within touch of the mountains and within sound of the brawling Forty Mile creek and the moaning pines. By the time the camp was pitched, the pine beds made and supper cooked, darkness had fallen. With appetites sharpened to the danger point, we fell upon the supper and then reclined upon couches of pine, the envy of the immortal gods. With no one to order us to bed, we yarned and sang, indifferent to the passing of the night or to the tasks of the morrow, while the stars slowly swung over our heads.

At last the camp was still. Down the canyon came the long-drawn howl of a wolf, once and again, and we were asleep; the long day and the soothing night proving too much for the shuddering delight of that long, weird, gruesome sound. We turned over in our sleep and woke. It was morning. The Professor had already "fixed" the horses and was lighting the breakfast fire. Unhappily, we possessed the remnants of conscience which refused to lie down, and though the sun had given as yet no hint of arriving, we persuaded ourselves that it was day. A solid breakfast, prayers, and we stood ready for the climb, greener at our work than the very greenest of the young pines that stood about us, but with fine jaunty courage of the young recruit marching to his first campaign.

An expert mountain-climber, glancing down the line, would have absolutely refused to move from the tent door. With the exception of the Lady from Montreal, who had done Mt. Blanc, not one of us had ever climbed anything more imposing than Little Tunnel, one thousand feet high. While as to equipment, we hadn't any, not even an alpenstock between the lot of us. As for the ladies, they appeared to carry their full quota of flimsy skirts and petticoats, while on their feet they wore their second-best kid boots. It was truly a case of fools rushing in where angels pause. Without trail, without guide, but knowing that the top was up there somewhere, we set out, water-bottles and brandy-flasks — in case of accident — and lunch baskets slung at the belts of the male members of the party, the sole shred of mountaineering outfit being the trunk of a sapling in the hand of each ambitious climber.

As we struck out from camp, the sun was tipping the highest pines far up on the mountain side to the west. Cascade mountain has a sheer face, but a long sloping back. It was our purpose to get upon that back with all speed. So, for a mile or more, we followed the main direction of the valley, gradually bearing to our right and thus emerging from the thicker forest into the open. When we considered that we had gone far enough up the valley, we turned sharply to our right and began to climb, finding the slope quite easy and the going fairly good. We had all day before us, and we had no intention of making our excursion anything but an enjoyment. Therefore, any ambition to force the pace on the part of any member was sternly frowned down.

By 10 o'clock we had got clear of the trees and had begun

to see more clearly our direction. But more, we began to realize somewhat more clearly the magnitude of our enterprise. The back of this old Cascade proved to be longer than that bestowed upon most things that have backs, and the lack of equipment was beginning to tell. The ladies of our party were already a grotesquely solemn warning that petticoats and flimsy skirts are not for mountain climbers. And it was with some considerable concern that we made the further discovery that kid boots are better for drawing-rooms. But in spite of shredded skirts and fraying boots, our ladies faced the slope with not even the faintest sign of fainting hearts.

An hour more, and we began to get views; views so wonderful as to make even the ladies forget their fluttering skirts and clogging petticoats and fast disintegrating boots. But now we began to have a choice of directions. We had never imagined there could be so many paths apparently all leading to the mountain top, but we discovered that what had appeared to be an unbroken slope, was gashed by numerous deep gorges that forbade passage, and ever and again we were forced to double on our course and make long detours about these gulches. In the presence of one unusually long, we determined that it was time for our second breakfast, to which we sat down, wondering whether there had ever been a first. A short rest, and we found ourselves with our stock of water sadly diminished, but our stock of courage and enthusiasm high as ever, and once more we set out for the peak whose location we began to guess at, but of whose distance away we could form no idea.

By noon the Professor announced, after a careful estimate of distances, that we were more than half way there, and that in an hour's time we should halt for lunch, which double announcement spurred those of the party who had been showing signs of weariness to a last heroic spurt. It was difficult to persuade any member of the party as we sat waiting for the baskets to be opened, that we had had one breakfast that morning, not to speak of two. After lunch the Professor declared that, having been brought up on the farm, he had been accustomed to a noon spell, and must have one. Being the least fatigued, or the most unwilling to acknowledge fatigue, this suggestion of a noon spell he could afford to make. So, stretched upon the broken rocks, we lay disposed at various angles, snuggled down into the soft spots of the old bony back. We slept for a full half-hour, and woke, so wonderful is this upper air, fresh and vigorous as in the morning. We packed our stuff, passed around our water-bottles, now, alas! almost empty, tied up the bleeding right foot of the Lady from Winnipeg with a portion of the fluttering skirt-remnants of the Lady from Montreal, seized our saplings, and once more faced the summit.

Far off a slight ledge appeared directly across our path. Should we make a detour to avoid it? Or was it surmountable? The Professor, supported by the majority of the party, decided for a detour to the left. The missionary, supported by the Lady from Winnipeg, decided that the frontal attack was possible. In half an hour, however, he found himself hanging to that ledge by his toe-nails and finger-tips, looking down into a gully full of what appeared to be stone, in alpine vocabulary *scree,* and sliding out into space at an angle of forty-five degrees or less, and the summit still far above him. Hanging there, there flashed across his mind for a moment the problem as to how the party could secure his mangled remains, and having secured them, how they could transport them down this mountain side. He decided that in the present situation his alpenstock added little to his safety and could well be dispensed with. As it clattered down upon the broken rocks far below, he found himself making a rapid calculation as to the depth of the drop and its effects upon the human frame. Before reaching a conclusion, he had begun edging his way backward, making the discovery that all mountain-climbers sooner or later make, that it is easier to follow your fingers with your toes, than your toes with your fingers. The descent accomplished, the Missionary with his loyal following reluctantly proceeded to follow the rest of the party, who had by this time gone round the head of the gulch, or the *couloir* in expert phrasing, and were some distance in advance. A stern chase is a long chase, and almost always disheartening. But in this case the advance guard were merciful, and sitting down to enjoy the view, waited for the pursuing party to make up.

It is now late in the afternoon, and a council of war is held to decide whether, with all the return journey before us, it is safe to still attempt the peak. We have no experience in descending mountains, and, therefore, we cannot calculate the time required. The trail to the camp is quite unknown to us, and there is always the possibility of accident. Besides, while the climbing is not excessively steep, the going has become very difficult, for the slope is now one mass of scree, so that the whole face of the mountain moves with every step. Still, the peak is very perceptibly nearer, and the party has endured already so much that it is exceedingly loath to accept defeat. Then, too, the atmosphere has become so rare, that the climbing is hard on the wind, as the Professor says. The ladies, despite shredded skirts and torn shoes, however, are keen to advance, and without waiting for further parley, gallantly strike out for the peak. It is decided to climb for an hour. So up we go, slipping, scrambling, panting, straining ever toward the peak. We have no time for views, though they are entrancing enough to almost make us content with what we have achieved. For an hour and then for half an hour, the ladies still in advance, we struggle upward. The climbing is now over snow and often upon hands and knees, but the scree is gone and the rock, where there is no snow, is solid.

At length the Professor demands a halt. In spite of desperate attempts at concealment, various members of the party are flying flags of distress. We are still several hundred yards from the coveted summit, but the rose tints upon the great ranges that sweep around are deepening to purple and the shadows lie thick in the valleys. If we only knew about the descent, we might risk another three-quarters of an hour. The ladies begin to share the anxiety of the men, knowing full well that it is they who constitute the serious element in the situation. With bitter reluctance they finally decide that they will not ask the men to assume any greater responsibility than they already bear. It is agreed that the men shall make a half-hour dash for the summit, while the ladies await their return. Stripping themselves of all encumbrances, the Professor and the Missionary make a final attempt to achieve the peak, the Californian gallantly offering to remain with the ladies. After a breathless, strenuous half-hour, the Professor, with the Missionary at his side, has fulfilled his threat and accomplished his proud boast. Breathless but triumphant, we are standing upon the head of the old Cascade.

We dare only take a few minutes to gaze about us, but these are enough to make indelible the picture before us. Down at our feet the wide valley of the Bow with its winding river, then range on range of snow-streaked mountains, with here and there mighty peaks rising high and white against the deep blue. One giant, whose head towers far above all his fellows, arrests the eye. There he stands in solitary grandeur. Not till years after do we learn that this is the mighty Assiniboine. But there are no words to paint these peaks. They are worth climbing to see, and once seen they are worth remembering. I close my eyes any day, and before me is spread out the vision of these sweeping ranges jutting up into all sorts of angles, and above them, lonely and white, the solitary sentinel, Assiniboine.

Without a word, we look our fill and turn to the descent. A hundred yards or more and we come upon our party who, with a reckless ambition, have been climbing after us. But the whole back of the Cascade lies now in shadow, and, though half an hour will do it, we dare not encourage them to take the risk. The party has been successful, though individuals have failed.

How We Climbed Cascade   227

And with this comfort in our hearts and with no small anxiety as to what awaits us, we set off down the slope. It is much easier than we have anticipated until we strike the scree. Here, for the first few steps, we proceed with great caution, but after a short time, becoming accustomed to have the whole mountain slip with us, we abandon ourselves to the exhilaration of tobogan- ning upon the skidding masses of broken rock; and touching here and there the high spots, as the Professor says, we make the descent with seven-leagued boots till we reach the timber. It is here we meet our first accident for the day. The Lady from Winnipeg has the misfortune to turn her ankle. But there is no lack of bandages in the party. In fact, by this time the ladies' skirts consist chiefly of bandages, so that with foot well swathed, and stopping now and then for repairs to the ladies' boots, slipping, sliding, stumbling, leaping, we finally, in a more or less battered condition, arrive at camp. The indomit- able Professor, aided by the Missionary and the Man from California, set about supper. But long ere it is ready the rest of the party are sound asleep. They are mercilessly dragged forth, however, to the refreshment of tea, toast and bacon, for which they are none too grateful, and after which they drop back upon their pine beds into dreamless sleep.

It takes us a full week, the greater part of it spent in bed, to realize that mountain-climbing, *sans* guides, *sans* mountain- eering boots, *plus* petticoats, is a pastime for angels perhaps, but not for fools.

On the upper part of the mountain, the Professor and I were greatly excited over what appeared to be the fossil remains of a prehistoric monster, and if its jawbone had not weighed several hundred pounds — the backbone must have weighed several tons — we would have carried it down as a present to the Museum. We left them behind us, and they are there to this day for some anthropologist to see.

The Coming of Mutt

Farley Mowat

An oppressive darkness shadowed the city of Saskatoon on an
August day in 1929. By the clock it was hardly noon. By the
sun — but the earth had obliterated the sun. Rising in the new
deserts of the southwest, and lifting high on autumnal winds,
the desecrated soil of the prairie drifted northward, and the sky
grew dark.

In our small house on the outskirts of the city my mother
switched on the electric lights and continued with the task of
preparing luncheon for my father and for me. Father had not
yet returned from his office, nor I from school. Mother was
alone with the sombre day.

The sound of the doorbell brought her unwillingly from the
kitchen into the hall. She opened the front door no more than
a few inches, as if expecting the menace of the sky to thrust its
way past her into the house.

There was no menace in the appearance of the visitor who
waited apologetically on the step. A small boy, perhaps ten
years of age, stood shuffling his feet in the grey grit that had
been falling soundlessly across the city for a day and a night.
He held a wicker basket before him and, as the door opened,
he swung the basket forward and spoke in a voice that was
husky with the dust and with the expectation of rebuff.

"Missus," he asked in a pale, high tone, "would you want to buy a duck?"

Mother was a bit nonplussed by this odd echo of a catch phrase that had already withered and staled in the mouths of the comedians of the era. Nevertheless, she looked into the basket and to her astonishment beheld three emaciated ducklings, their bills gaping in the heat, and, wedged between them, a nondescript and bedraggled pup.

She was touched, and curious — although she certainly did not want to buy a duck.

"I don't think so," she said kindly. "Why are you selling them?"

The boy took courage and returned her smile.

"I gotta," he said. "The slough out to the farm is dry. We ate the big ducks, but these were to small to eat. I sold some down to the Chinee Grill. You want the rest, Lady? They're cheap — only a dime each."

"I'm sorry," Mother replied. "I've no place to keep a duck. But where did you get the little dog?"

The boy shrugged his shoulders. "Oh *him,*" he said without much interest. "He was kind of an accident, you might say. I guess somebody dumped him out of a car right by our gate. I brung him with me in case. But dogs is hard to sell." He brightened up a little as an idea struck him. "Say, lady, you want him? I'll sell him for a nickel—that way you'll *save* a nickel for yourself."

Mother hesitated. Then almost involuntarily her hand went to the basket. The pup was thirsty beyond thirst, and those outstretched fingers must have seemed to him like fountains straight from heaven. He clambered hastily over the ducks and grabbed.

The boy was quick to sense his advantage and to press it home.

"He likes you, lady, see? He's yours for just *four* cents."

If there was one drawback to the new life in Saskatoon, it was that we had no dog. During my lifetime we had owned, or had been owned by, a steady succession of dogs. As a newborn baby I had been guarded by a Border collie named Sapper, who was one day doused with boiling water by a vicious neighbour, and who went insane as a result. But there had always been other dogs during my first eight years, until we moved to the west and became, for the moment, dogless. The prairies could be only half real to a boy without a dog.

I began agitating for one almost as soon as we arrived and I found a willing ally in my father — though his motives were not mine.

For many years he had been exposed to the colourful tales of my Great-uncle Frank, who homesteaded in Alberta in 1900. Frank was a hunter born, and most of his stories dealt with the superlative shooting to be had on the western plains. Before we were properly settled in Saskatoon my father determined to test those tales. He bought a fine English shotgun, a shooting coat, cases of ammunition, a copy of the *Saskatchewan Game Laws,* and a handbook on shotgun shooting. There remained only one indispensable item — a hunting dog.

One evening he arrived home from the library with such a beast in tow behind him. Its name was Crown Prince Challenge Indefatigable. It stood about as high as the dining-room table and, as far as Mother and I could judge, consisted mainly of feet and tongue. Father was annoyed at our levity and haughtily informed us that the Crown Prince was an Irish setter, kennel bred and field trained, and a dog to delight the heart of any expert. We remained unimpressed. Purebred he may have been, and the possessor of innumerable cups and ribbons, but to my eyes he seemed a singularly useless sort of beast with but one redeeming feature: I greatly admired the way he drooled. I have never known a dog who could drool as the Crown Prince could. He never stopped, except to flop his way to the kitchen sink and tank up on water. He left a wet and sticky trail wherever he went. He had little else to recommend him, for he was moronic.

Mother might have overlooked his obvious defects, had it not been for his price. She could not overlook that, for the owner was asking two hundred dollars, and we could no more afford such a sum than we could have afforded a Cadillac. Crown Prince left the next morning, but Father was not discouraged, and it was clear that he would try again.

My parents had been married long enough to achieve that delicate balance of power which enables a married couple to endure each other. They were both adept in the evasive tactics of marital politics — but Mother was a little more adept.

She realized that a dog was now inevitable, and when chance brought the duck boy — as we afterwards referred to him — to our door on that dusty August day, Mother showed her mettle by snatching the initiative right out of my father's hands.

By buying the duck boy's pup, she not only placed herself in a position to forestall the purchase of an expensive dog of my father's choice, but she was also able to save six cents in cash. She was never one to despise a bargain.

When I came home from school the bargain was installed in a soap carton in the kitchen. He looked to be a somewhat dubious buy at any price. Small, emaciated, and caked liberally with cow manure, he peered up at me in a near-sighted sort of way. But when I knelt beside him and extended an exploratory hand he roused himself and sank his puppy teeth into my thumb with such satisfactory gusto that my doubts dissolved. I knew that he and I would get along.

My father's reaction was of a different kind.

He arrived home at six o'clock that night and he was hardly in the door before he began singing the praises of a springer spaniel bitch he had just seen. He seemed hardly even to hear at first when Mother interrupted to remark that we already had a dog, and that two would be too many.

When he beheld the pup he was outraged; but the ambush had been well and truly laid and before he could recover himself, Mother unmasked her guns.

"Isn't he *lovely,* darling?" she asked sweetly. "And so *cheap.* Do you know, I've actually saved you a hundred and ninety-nine dollars and ninety-six cents? Enough to pay for all your ammunition and for that *expensive* new gun you bought."

My father was game, and he rallied quickly. He pointed scornfully at the pup, and in a voice sharp with exasperation he replied:

"But — that — that 'thing' isn't a *hunting* dog!"

Mother was ready for him. "How do you *know, dear,*" she asked mildly, "until you've tried him out?"

There could be no adequate reply to this. It was as impossible to predict what the pup might grow up to be, as it was to deduce what his ancestry might have been. Father turned to me for support, but I would not meet his eye, and he knew that he had been out-manoeuvred.

He accepted defeat with his usual good grace. I can clearly remember, and with awe, what he had to say to some friends who dropped in for a drink not three evenings later. The pup, relatively clean, and already beginning to fatten out a little, was presented to the guests.

"He's imported," Father explained in a modest tone of voice. "I understand he's the only one of his kind in the west. A Prince Albert retriever, you know. Marvellous breed for upland shooting."

Unwilling to confess their ignorance, the guests looked vaguely knowing. "What do you call him?" one of them asked.

I put my foot in it then. Before my father could reply, I forestalled him.

"*I* call him Mutt," I said. And I was appalled by the look my father gave me.

He turned his back on me and smiled confidentially at the guests.

"You have to be rather careful with these highly bred specimens," he explained, "it doesn't always do to let them know their kennel names. Better to give them a simple bourgeois name like Sport, or Nipper, or — " and he gagged a trifle — "or even Mutt."

During his first few weeks with us Mutt astonished us all by his maturity of outlook. He never really was a puppy, at least not after he came to us. Perhaps the ordeal with the ducks had aged him prematurely; perhaps he was simply born adult in mind. In any case he resolutely eschewed the usual antics of puppyhood. He left behind him no mangled slippers, no torn upholstery, and no stains upon the rugs. He did not wage mock warfare with people's bare feet, nor did he make the night hideous when he was left to spend the dark hours alone in the kitchen. There was about him, from the first day he came to us, an aura of resolution and restraint and dignity. He took life seriously, and he expected us to do likewise.

Nor was he malleable. His character was immutably resolved before we ever knew him and, throughout his life, it did not change.

I suspect that at some early moment of his existence he concluded there was no future in being a dog. And so, with the tenacity that marked his every act, he set himself to become something else. Subconsciously he no longer believed that he was a dog at all, yet he did not feel, as so many foolish canines appear to do, that he was human. He was tolerant of both species, but he claimed kinship to neither.

If he was unique in attitude, he was also unique in his appearance. In size he was not far from a setter, but in all other respects he was very far from any known breed. His hindquarters were elevated several inches higher than his forequarters; and at the same time he was distinctly canted from left to right. The result was that, when he was approaching, he appeared to be drifting off about three points to starboard, while simultaneously giving an eerie impression of a submarine starting on a crash dive. It was impossible to tell, unless you knew him very well indeed, exactly where he was heading, or what his immediate objective might be. His eyes gave no clue, for they were so close-set that he looked to be, and may have been, somewhat cross-eyed. The total illusion had its practical advantages, for gophers and cats pursued by Mutt could seldom decide where he was aiming until they discovered, too late, that he was actually on a collision course with them.

An even more disquieting physical characteristic was the fact that his hind legs moved at a slower speed than did his front ones. This was theoretically explicable on the grounds that his hind legs were much longer than his forelegs — but an understanding of this explanation could not dispel the unsettling impression that Mutt's forward section was slowly and relentlessly pulling away from the tardy after-end.

And yet, despite all this, Mutt was not unprepossessing in general appearance. He had a handsome black and white coat of fine, almost silky hair, with exceptionally long "feathers" on his legs. His tail was long, limber and expressive. Although his ears were rather large and limp, his head was broad and high-domed. A black mask covered all of his face except for his bulbous nose, which was pure white. He was not really handsome, yet he possessed the same sort of dignified grotesquerie that so distinguished Abraham Lincoln and the Duke of Wellington.

He also possessed a peculiar *savoir faire* that had a disconcerting effect upon strangers. So strong was Mutt's belief that he was not simply "dog" that he was somehow able to convey this conviction to human onlookers.

One bitterly cold day in January Mother went down town to do some post-Christmas shopping, and Mutt accompanied her. She parted from him outside the Hudson's Bay Department Store, for Mutt had strong antipathies, even in those early months, and one of these was directed against the famous Company of Gentlemen Adventurers. Mother was inside the store for almost an hour, while Mutt was left to shiver on the wind-swept pavement.

When Mother emerged at last, Mutt had forgotten that he had voluntarily elected to remain outside. Instead he was nursing a grievance at what seemed to him to be a calculated indifference to his comfort on my mother's part. He had decided to sulk, and when he sulked he became intractable. Nothing that Mother would say could persuade him to get up off the frigid concrete and accompany her home. Mother pleaded. Mutt ignored her and fixed his gaze upon the steamed-up windows of the Star Cafe across the street.

Neither of them was aware of the small audience that had formed around them. There were three Doukhobors in their quaint winter costumes, a policeman enveloped in a buffalo-skin coat, and a dentist from the nearby Medical Arts Building. Despite the cold, these strangers stood and watched with growing fascination as Mother ordered and Mutt, with slightly lifted lip and *sotto voce* mutters, adamantly refused to heed. Both of them were becoming exasperated, and the tone of their utterances grew increasingly vehement.

It was at this point that the dentist lost touch with reality. He stepped forward and addressed Mutt in man-to-man tones.

"Oh, I say, old boy, be reasonable!" he said, reproachfully.

Mutt replied with a murmur of guttural disdain, and this was too much for the policeman.

"What seems to be the matter here?" he asked.

Mother explained. "He won't go home. He just won't go!"

The policeman was a man of action. He wagged his mittened paw under Mutt's nose. "Can't you see the lady's cold?" he asked sternly.

Mutt rolled his eyes and yawned and the policeman lost his

temper. "Now, see here," he cried, "you just move along or, by the gods, I'll run you in!"

It was fortunate that my father and Eardlie came by at this moment. Father had seen Mutt and Mother in arguments before, and he acted with dispatch, picking them both up almost bodily and pushing them into Eardlie's front seat. He did not linger, for he had no desire to be a witness to the reactions of the big policeman and of the dentist when they became aware of the fact that they had been arguing with a dog upon a public street.

Arguments with Mutt were almost invariably fruitless. As he grew older he became more vocal and more argumentative. When he was asked to do something that did not please him, he would begin to mutter. If he were pressed, the muttering would grow in volume, rising and falling in pitch. It was not a growl, nor was it in the least threatening. It was a stubborn bumbling sound, quite indescribable.

It happened that Father was writing a novel that first winter in the west, and he was extremely touchy about being disturbed while working on it.

One evening he was hunched over his portable typewriter in the living room, his face drawn haggard with concentration, but he was getting very little actually down on paper. Mother and I, recognizing the symptoms, had discreetly retired to the kitchen, but Mutt had remained in the living room, asleep before the open fire.

Mutt was not a silent sleeper. He snored with a peculiar penetrating sound and, being a dog who dreamed actively, his snores were often punctuated by high-pitched yelps as he galloped across the dream prairie in pursuit of a rabbit.

He must have been lucky that evening. Perhaps it was an old and infirm rabbit he was chasing, or perhaps the rabbit slipped and fell. At any rate Mutt closed with it, and instantly the living room reverberated to a horrendous conflict.

Father, blasted so violently from his creative mood, was

enraged. He roared at Mutt, who, awakened harshly in the very moment of victory, was inclined to be surly about the interruption.

"Get out, you insufferable beast!" Father yelled at him.

Mutt curled his lip and prepared to argue.

Father was now almost beside himself. "I said *out* — you animated threshing machine!"

Mutt's argumentative mutters immediately rose in volume. Mother and I shivered slightly and stared at each other with dreadful surmise.

Our apprehensions were justified by the sound of shattering glass, as a volume of *Everyman's Encyclopedia* banged against the dining-room wall, on the wrong side of the French doors. Mutt appeared in the kitchen at almost the same instant. Without so much as a look at us, he thumped down the basement stairs — his whole attitude radiating outrage.

Father was immediately contrite. He followed Mutt down into the cellar, and we could hear him apologizing — but it did no good. Mutt would not deign to notice him for three days. Physical violence in lieu of argument was, to Mutt, a cardinal sin.

He had another exasperating habit that he developed very early in life, and never forgot. When it was manifestly impossible for him to avoid some unpleasant duty by means of argument, he would feign deafness. On occasions I lost my temper and, bending down so that I could lift one of his long ears, would scream my orders at him in the voice of a Valkyrie. But Mutt would simply turn his face toward me with a bland and interrogative look that seemed to say with insufferable mildness, "I'm sorry — did you speak?"

We could not take really effective steps to cure him of this irritating habit, for it was one he shared with my paternal grandfather, who sometimes visited us. Grandfather was stone deaf to anything that involved effort on his part, yet he could hear, and respond to, the word "whisky" if it were whispered inside a locked bedroom three floors above the chair in which he habitually sat.

It will be clear by now that Mutt was not an easy dog to live with. Yet the intransigence that made it so difficult to cope with him made it even more difficult — and at times well-nigh impossible — for him to cope with the world in general. His stubbornness marked him out for a tragicomic role throughout his life. But Mutt's struggles with a perverse fate were not, unfortunately, his alone. He involved those about him, inevitably and often catastrophically, in his confused battle with life.

Wherever he went he left deep-etched memories that were alternatively vivid with the screaming hues of outrage, or cloudy with the muddy colours of near dementia. He carried with him the aura of a Don Quixote and it was in that atmosphere that my family and I lived for more than a decade.

After several years in Saskatoon, my family moved into a new neighbourhood. River Road was on the banks of the Saskatchewan River, but on the lower and more plebeian side. The community on River Road was considerably relaxed in character and there was a good deal of tolerance for individual idiosyncrasies.

Only three doors down the street from us lived a retired schoolteacher who had spent years in Alaska and who had brought with him into retirement a team of Alaskan Huskies. These were magnificent dogs that commanded respect not only from the local canine population but from the human one as well. Three of them once caught a burglar on their master's premises, and they reduced him to butcher's meat with a dispatch that we youngsters much admired.

Across the alley from us lived a barber who maintained a sort of Transient's Rest for stray mongrels. There was an unkind rumour to the effect that he encouraged these strays only in order to practise his trade upon them. The rumour gained stature from the indisputable fact that some of his oddly assorted collection of dogs sported unusual haircuts. I came to know the barber intimately during the years that followed, and he confided his secret to me. Once, many years earlier, he had seen a French poodle shaven and shorn, and he had been convinced that he could devise even more spectacular hair styles for dogs, and perhaps make a fortune and a reputation for himself. His experiments were not without artistic merit, even though some of them resulted in visits from the Humane Society inspectors.

I had no trouble fitting myself into this new community, but the adjustment was not so simple for Mutt. The canine population of River Road was enormous. Mutt had to come to terms with these dogs, and he found the going hard. His long, silken hair and his fine "feathers" tended to give him a soft and sentimental look that was misleading and that seemed to goad the roughneck local dogs into active hostility. They usually went about in packs, and the largest pack was led by a well-built bull terrier who lived next door to us. Mutt, who was never a joiner, preferred to go his way alone, and this made him particularly suspect by the other dogs. They began to lay for him.

He was not by nature the fighting kind. In all his life I never knew him to engage in battle unless there was no alternative. His was an eminently civilized attitude, but one that other dogs could seldom understand. They taunted him because of it.

His pacific attitude used to embarrass my mother when the two of them happened to encounter a belligerent strange dog while they were out walking. Mutt would waste no time in idle braggadocio. At first glimpse of the stranger he would insinuate himself under Mother's skirt and no amount of physical force, nor scathing comment, could budge him from this sanctuary. Often the strange dog would not realize that it *was* a sanctuary and this was sometimes rather hard on Mother.

Despite his repugnance toward fighting, Mutt was no

coward, nor was he unable to defend himself. He had his own ideas about how to fight, ideas which were unique but formidable. Just how efficacious they actually were was demonstrated to us all within a week of our arrival at our new address.

Knowing nothing of the neighbourhood, Mutt dared to go where even bulldogs feared to tread, and one morning he foolishly pursued a cat into the ex-schoolteacher's yard. He was immediately surrounded by four ravening Huskies. They were a merciless lot, and they closed in for the kill.

Mutt saw at once that this time he would have to fight. With one quick motion he flung himself over on his back and began to pedal furiously with all four feet. It looked rather as if he were riding a bicycle built for two, but upside down. He also began to sound his siren. This was a noise he made — just how, I do not know — deep in the back of his throat. It was a kind of frenzied wail. The siren rose in pitch and volume as his legs increased their RPMs until he began to sound like a gas turbine at full throttle.

The effect of this unorthodox behaviour on the four Huskies was to bring them to an abrupt halt. Their ears went forward and their tails uncurled as a look of pained bewilderment wrinkled their brows. And then slowly, and one by one, they began to back away, their eyes uneasily averted from the distressing spectacle before them. When they were ten feet from Mutt they turned as one dog and fled without dignity for their own back yard.

The mere sight of Mutt's bicycle tactics (as we referred to them) was usually sufficient to avert bloodshed, but on occasion a foolhardy dog would refuse to be intimidated. The results in those cases could be rather frightful, for Mutt's queer posture of defence was not all empty bombast.

Once when we were out hunting gophers, Mutt was attacked by a farm collie who, I think, was slightly mad. He looked mad, for he had one white eye and one blue eye, and the combination gave him a maniac expression. And he acted mad, for he flung himself on the inverted Mutt without the slightest hesitation.

Mutt grunted when the collie came down on top of him, and for an instant the tempo of his legs was slowed. Then he exerted himself and, as it were, put on a sprint. The collie became air-borne, bouncing up and down as a rubber ball bounces on the end of a water jet. Each time he came down he was raked fore and aft by four sets of rapidly moving claws, and when he finally fell clear he was bleeding from a dozen ugly scratches, and he had had a bellyful. He fled. Mutt did not pursue him; he was magnanimous in victory.

Had he been willing to engage deliberately in a few such duels with the neighbourhood dogs, Mutt would undoubtedly have won their quick acceptance. But such was his belief in the principles of nonviolence — as these applied to other dogs, at least — that he continued to avoid combat.

The local packs, and particularly the one led by the bull terrier next door, spared no pains to bring him to battle, and for some time he was forced to stay very close to home unless he was accompanied by Mother or by myself. It was nearly a month before he found a solution to this problem.

The solution he eventually adopted was typical of him.

Almost all the back yards in Saskatoon were fenced with vertical planking nailed to horizontal two-by-fours. The upper two-by-four in each case was usually five or six feet above the ground, and about five inches below the projecting tops of the upright planks. For generations these elevated gangways had provided a safe thoroughfare for cats. One fine day Mutt decided that they could serve him too.

I was brushing my teeth after breakfast when I heard Mutt give a yelp of pain, and I went at once to the window and looked out. I was in time to see him laboriously clamber up on our back fence from a garbage pail that stood by the yard gate. As I watched, he wobbled a few steps along the upper two-by-four, lost his balance, and fell off. Undaunted, he returned at once to the garbage pail and tried again.

I went outside and tried to reason with him, but he ignored me. When I left he was still at it, climbing up, staggering along for a few feet, then falling off again.

I mentioned this new interest of his during dinner that night, but none of us gave it much thought. We were used to Mutt's peculiarities, and we had no suspicion that there was method behind this apparent foolishness. Yet method there was, as I discovered a few evenings later.

A squad of Bengal lancers, consisting of two of my friends and myself armed with spears made from bamboo fishing rods, had spent the afternoon riding up and down the back alleys on our bicycles hunting tigers (alley cats). As suppertime approached we were slowly pedalling our way homeward along the alley behind River Road when one of my chums, who was a little in the lead, gave a startled yelp and swerved on his bike so that I crashed into him, and we fell together on the sun-baked dirt. I picked myself up and saw my friend pointing at the fence ahead of us. His eyes were big with disbelief.

The cause of the accident, and of my chum's incredulity, was nonchalantly picking his way along the top of the fence not fifty yards away. Behind that fence lay the home of the Huskies, and although we could not see them, we — and most of Saskatoon — could hear them. Their frenzied howls were punctuated by dull thudding sounds as they leaped at their tormentor and fell back helplessly to earth again.

Mutt never hesitated. He ambled along his aerial route with the leisurely insouciance of an old gentleman out for an evening stroll. The Huskies must have been wild with frustration, and I was grateful that the fence lay between them and us.

We three boys had not recovered from our initial surprise when a new canine contingent arrived upon the scene. It included six or seven of the local dogs (headed by the bull terrier), attracted to the scene by the yammering of the Huskies. They spotted Mutt, and the terrier immediately led a mass assault. He launched himself against the fence with such foolhardy violence that only a bull terrier could have survived the impact.

We were somewhat intimidated by the frenzy of all those dogs, and we lowered our spears to the "ready" position, undecided whether to attempt Mutt's rescue or not. In the event, we were not needed.

Mutt remained unperturbed, although this may have been only an illusion, resulting from the fact that he was concentrating so hard on his balancing act that he could spare no attention for his assailants. He moved along at a slow but steady pace, and having safely navigated the Huskies' fence, he jumped up to the slightly higher fence next door and stepped along it until he came to a garage. With a graceful leap he gained the garage roof, where he lay down for a few moments, ostensibly to rest, but actually — I am certain — to enjoy his triumph.

Below him there was pandemonium. I have never seen a dog so angry as that bull terrier was. Although the garage wall facing on the alley was a good eight feet high, the terrier kept hurling himself impotently against it until he must have been one large quivering bruise.

Mutt watched the performance for two or three minutes; then he stood up and with one insolent backward glance jumped down to the dividing fence between two houses, and ambled along it to the street front beyond.

The tumult in the alley subsided and the pack began to disperse. Most of the dogs must have realized that they would have to run halfway around the block to regain Mutt's trail, and by then he might be far away. Dispiritedly they began to drift off, until finally only the bull terrier remained. He was still hurling himself at the garage wall in a paroxysm of fury when I took myself home to tell of the wonders I had seen.

From that day forth the dogs of the neighbourhood gave up their attempts against Mutt and came to a tacit acceptance of him — all, that is, save the bull terrier. Perhaps his handball game against the fence had addled his brain, or it may be that he was just too stubborn to give up. At any rate he continued to lurk in ambush for Mutt, and Mutt continued to avoid him easily enough, until the early winter when the terrier — by now completely unbalanced — one day attempted to cross the street in pursuit of his enemy, and without bothering to look for traffic. He was run over by an old Model T.

Mutt's remarkable skill as a fence walker could have led to the leadership of the neighbourhood dogs, had that been what he desired, for his unique talent gave him a considerable edge in the popular game of catch-cat; but Mutt remained a lone walker, content to be left to his own devices.

He did not give up fence walking even when the original need had passed. He took deep pride in his accomplishment, and he kept in practice. I used to show him off to my friends, and I was not above making small bets with strange boys about the abilities of my acrobatic dog. When I won, as I always did, I would reward Mutt with candy-coated gum. This was one of his favourite confections and he would chew away at a wad of it until the last vestige of mint flavour had vanished, whereupon he would swallow the tasteless remnant. Mother thought that this was bad for him, but as far as I know, it never had any adverse effect upon his digestive system, which could absorb most things with impunity.

Just This Once
Carol Rose

The little pup waddled happily towards him. Ricky was able to smother any misgivings he had, under the desire to have that warm, lovable little creature for his own.

"You're sure he's ready to leave his Mom?" Ricky asked.

"Yep, you can take him right now, if you want."

"Gee, Bob, I can't believe it; a puppy of my very own. I'm going to take him home to show Mom!"

Ricky scooped up the curly little fat pup, and hugging him, started off at a trot for home. The pup was squirming with excitement, licking Rick's face and nipping playfully at his fingers.

"Hey, cut it out," admonished Rick in mock anger, and nestled his face in the downy-soft fur of the fuzzy little head.

Minutes later he burst through the back door and lunged up the steps into the kitchen.

"Mom," he bellowed, "Look what I've got!"

"Oh, isn't it cute?" cooed his mother, as she put down her paint brush and proceeded towards the pair. "Where did you get him?"

"Bobby gave him to me, isn't he neat?" The words rushed out in a mad flurry of excitement.

"He's real neat, but what will Daddy say about you having a puppy?"

"The last time I asked him, he said I could *someday,* so can I keep him Mom, please? Can I? Mrs. McInson says he's ᵒ house-trained already."

"You're sure Dad said you could?"

"Honest, Mom. He said I could someday, and I'm big enough to look after him now."

"You can keep him till Daddy comes home, but I'm not as sure as you are that he'll let you keep him."

"Thanks, Mom!" Rick exclaimed, and enveloped her in a bear hug. "I'm going to go get Bob," he called over his shoulder, as he headed back outside.

Before returning to her painting, Janet stood gazing reflectively after the boy. What a crushing disappointment it would be to Ricky if Graham made the boy give up the pup when he returned, two weeks hence. The father-son relationship left something to be desired, and Janet wondered if they would ever reach a comfortable level of mutual understanding.

Ricky and Bobby returned and noisily began preparations to make the new guest as comfortable as possible. A cardboard box with a soft cushion was carried to Rick's room, and was to serve as his bed. When all was in readiness Bobby left, promising to return "first thing in the morning", to check and see how the pup made out away from his Mom.

"Can I have something to eat, Mom?" Rick asked and headed for the fridge.

"Yes; did you wash?" came the reply from behind the easel.

"Forgot," Ricky replied and hastily passed soap and water over his chapped, grubby hands, blackening the towel as he quickly dried them.

"Hey, I bet you're hungry, too," he said to the pup, who was prancing at his feet, as he thrust his head in the fridge.

"Hamburger!" he crowed joyously. "I bet he loves hamburger."

"What's his name, Rick?"

"I'm not sure what I'll call him. He looks like . . . he looks like . . . " Rick mused as he gazed into the pup's face. "Hey, I know. You know in that movie, where that curly-headed fat guy burned Rome?"

"Curly-headed fat guy? You don't mean Nero?" she asked incredulously.

"That's it! That's what I'll call him. Nero! With all that curly hair around his face he reminds me of him, and nobody but me will have a dog called Nero."

Happily he pulled a hamburger patty from the fridge and broke it up for Nero to eat, while he noisily chomped on an apple.

"Eat hearty, oh king, for tomorrow you won't get hamburger."

"Ricky, I hope you're not forgetting that Nero may not be able to stay?" Janet voiced the doubts gnawing at her.

"You don't think Dad will let me keep him, do you?" Rick accused.

"I really don't know."

"He probably won't. He never lets me have stuff I want. And he's never home!" he cried as he warmed to the topic. "He just comes home and tells me what I can't do, every once in a while."

"Now Ricky, that's not true. You get a lot of things. Didn't you get new skis and boots for Christmas, so you could have fun skiing?"

"Yeah, I got new skis at Christmas. But I woulda sooner kept my old skis, and had Dad come skiing with me. He never does stuff with me like other Dads do."

"We've been through this before."

"It's true! He's never here! How many times have you had to be my 'Dad' at father-and-son banquets? Every time!" he interjected before she could reply. "And he's never here to help me with my cub projects, and when I need my bike fixed or something, I gotta get Bobby's Dad to do it. Why can't he get a different job, so we can do stuff together?"

"It's what he's trained to do, Ricky."

His heart in his eyes, he gazed imploringly at his Mom. "Mom, I hope just this once he'll try to understand me, and to know how much I need Nero." Ricky pulled the pup to him and hugged him fiercely.

"Why don't you hop on your bike and go to the Red Rooster and get him a can of dog food?" his mother tactfully changed the subject.

"Okay. You take good care of Nero while I'm gone!"

Life held no end of joy for Ricky during the next two weeks, as he and Nero became inseparable buddies. During the day, Ricky taught him to lead, and to come when he was called. He even bought a box of Puppy Treats out of his allowance, to reward his small chum for his successes. At night Ricky would sit on the rug and Nero would crawl onto his knee and the two would enjoy an hour of TV together. Luckily Nero had no "accidents" in the house, and the only item he had chewed up was a pencil, accidentally left lying on the floor. Ricky had donated an old leather mitt for Nero to chew, and between the mitt and his rawhide bone, the chewing instinct was pretty well satisfied. Ricky was as proud of Nero as if he had created him with his own two hands, and constantly reminded his mother what a good pup he was. In actual fact, the curly little rascal had already won Janet's heart, but Rick was not completely aware of it. With the Easter holidays over, Ricky had reluctantly returned to school and Janet and Nero had developed a "mutual admiration society". Each day when Ricky returned home at 3:30, a joyful reunion would take place as the boy and the pup tumbled and wrestled together with the total abandon and energy of youth.

The night before Graham was due to return, Janet went in to say a final goodnight to her son. The scene was typical of a nine-year-old boy's room; "treasures" strewn about at random, pennants plastering the walls; a pup curled up in a box near the bed, and a tousled blond head bent over his pet, crooning a final goodnight before going to bed.

"Did you remember your prayers, son?"

"Not yet. But Mom?"

"Yes," she replied softly.

"Is it okay if I ask God to make Daddy let me keep Nero?"

"No, honey, we can't ask God for personal favors. We'll have to leave Him out of this. Look! Nero's asleep already, maybe you should go to sleep now, too. Okay? Daddy will be home tomorrow, and the suspense will be over. Night, Ricky."

"Night, Mom."

"Anybody home?" Graham walked into the kitchen, just as Ricky was unsuccessfully trying to teach Nero to sit up. There seemed no way that fat little bottom would ever do anything but roll around on the slippery floor. Before either Janet or Ricky could speak, Graham thundered; "What's that dog doing in the house?"

"Bobby gave him to me, Dad. Isn't he cute?" he added hopefully.

"He's so hairy, he looks more like a dust mop than a dog."

"I can brush him, Dad."

"You can't keep him here, Rick. I won't have an animal in my house."

"I'll keep him in the yard, and he can sleep in the garage, Dad. He's already trained," he offered eagerly, and grabbed the offending pup and hustled him outside. When Ricky returned to the kitchen, Graham seemed to have forgotten the episode completely, as he gave Janet a final squeeze and asked Ricky how he was doing in his spelling tests lately. Ricky decided not to push the issue.

"Hey, I brought something for you, Rick." He reached into his pocket and brought out a little wrench on a key chain. "For your collection."

"Thanks, Dad. That's neat!" Rick exclaimed. "Look, Mom."

"Boy, you're going to have a real collection! Does that make fifteen or sixteen?"

"I'll check," Rick called, already on his way to his room with the latest addition to his collection.

Around nine o'clock that night a meek little boy, clad in baggy flannel pyjamas, appeared at his Dad's elbow.

"Dad, about my dog . . . "

"Not now, son; I'm trying to sort through this mountain of mail." Graham frowned deeply at the bill he held in his hand, his normally stern countenance becoming even more forbidding.

"Going to bed?"

"Yeah, if I have to."

"Have a good sleep. See you in the morning." He slapped Ricky playfully on the seat, and once more became absorbed in the bills.

After Ricky had left, Janet re-opened the topic. "Graham, I'm not sure you realize how much the pup means to Ricky."

"Now, Janet, you're always looking for a problem where one doesn't exist. You're a born worry-wart," he bantered. "I'll take care of it! But first, let's enjoy the weekend; I've been away a long time, and I don't feel like 'talking dogs' as soon as I arrive." When he noticed her continued look of concern, he reassured her once again: "Believe me, there's no problem."

The weekend passed happily. On Sunday they went for a drive and got thick chocolate milk shakes on the way home. The subject of Nero's future never entered the conversation and Ricky began to relax. Maybe everything was okay now that the pup was out of the house; and Nero would get used to being alone in the garage at night. Several times during the night Ricky had crept quietly out to check on him.

At lunch time on Monday, Ricky bade his mother and father a hasty farewell and hurried out for a last minute romp with Nero before heading for school. "See you after school, Nero. You be a good dog, while I'm gone!" With that he was gone, carefully latching the gate behind him.

When the bell rang to herald the close of school that day, Ricky couldn't get ready to leave fast enough.

"I'll meet you over in the field, Bobby, after I pick up Nero."

"Okay, see you later."

Cheerfully, Ricky started home, not dillydallying the way he usually did, wrestling with friends and teasing girls.

He opened the gate expecting an extravagant welcome from his little canine buddy.

Nothing.

He whistled and called.

Still nothing.

The silence was unbearable.

"I bet Dad stuck him in the garage," he muttered and jerked open the door. He looked hopefully towards Nero's bed. It was empty.

"Come, Nero!" he called desperately.

"What's all the shouting about?" Graham asked, as he poked his head around the garage door.

"I'm looking for Nero." Ricky looked up with a worried frown. "You've got him! Oh, Dad!" There were no words for Ricky's joy, as he hugged the little pup in his arms.

"If we're going to have a dog in this family, there's no way he's going to go around looking like a dust mop. Nero and I just paid a visit to the barber. Looks pretty good, doesn't he?"

"Neato, Dad!" Ricky's face was split in a happy grin. "Come on, let's show Mom!"

Mock-death

Jon Whyte

Out of the house
    I walked beside him slowly
watching his limp hind legs
    waddle torment to his drooped tail
before I turned my eyes away
    for a moment . . . to find he had
disappeared
    from both walk and lawn
I found him
    curled into a questionmark of silence
against a shaded wall
    beneath the low boughs of a fir
his dull eyes
    not gladdened to see me

by my uncovery
       of him in his mute misery
and of what he had hoped
       his last place to lie in patience
our brown dachshund
       who was dying who needed
more than the love
       and the care we could provide
less than the loneliness
       he needed for dying
the assistance for solitude
       not solace we could not give
"You can't die,"
       I murmured . . . he lay his brown muzzle
deep in the leafmould
       worming deeper into the shadow
afraid to look at me
       who should have been consoled
"You've got to walk,"
       with no knowledge of words' work
"and then perhaps
       it will move what's bothering you . . .
You can't die." Again.
       He'd eaten too much of a bone
and the dry matter
       had dammed his intestines so
he vomited water and oil
       and the enemas couldn't urge a thing
What could he know
       except he was hurting
his poor brown body
       arching and agonying his efforts
to die and that hurting
       means aching and death can prevent
the aching and that
       he must die in loneliness?

Talking Down the Cat
Eric Nicol

"This being National Cat Week," I said to the Captain, "I suppose I should put in a plug for cats."

Captain Fracas is our cat. Or perhaps it would be more accurate to say that we are his people. The Captain is part Persian and part sawdust. He brings the sawdust up from the basement in his fur, since he uses the sawdust bin as his bathroom. He is very tidy about going to the bathroom, but not so tidy coming back. In fact he is a mess. He is why the living-room floor sometimes looks like the Last Chance Saloon.

The Captain is ten years old now, pretty senior for a cat. He's had time to learn English, which he speaks with a slight accent that he knows people find charming. I have a smattering of Felinese, but we find it easier to converse in my own language.

"Cats don't need plugging," yawned the Captain. "Cats can look after themselves."

"A lot of people don't like cats," I said.

"A lot of cats don't like people," he murmured. "But we haven't started a National Humans Week yet."

"What cats don't like people?" I demanded.

"The cougar, the panther, the leopard, the lion . . ."

The Captain is always dragging in his influential relatives like this. Almost as annoying as the sawdust.

"You wouldn't know," I said tartly, "but some cats need protection. Alley cats, for instance . . ."

"Rank socialism," he interrupted (another bad habit). "Survival of the fittest keeps the species strong," and he belched in the manner of Charles Laughton.

"Survival of the fittest," I hooted. "You lie around on a soft rug all day, get fed the best grade liver, wear a fur coat that didn't cost you a penny, never do a stroke of work, and you talk about survival of the fittest!"

The Captain calmly licked a paw before replying. Then he said:

"If I am so useless, why do you keep me?"

"Well . . ." There had to be some reason. "You're a good-looking animal. And you have a lot of personality. You hand us some laughs."

"Exactly. The talents of a first-rate insurance salesman. A good salesman makes six or seven hundred a month. I get a couple of dollars' worth of liver, padded with the cheap cat food you buy." The Captain blinked. "Sometimes I envy the alley cat's integrity, but balancing on the rim of a garbage can is not my idea of the way to eat dinner."

"It's not just a matter of hardship," I said quickly, noticing that the Captain was beginning to doze. "Some people just can't stand any kind of cat. They hate cats. They prefer dogs, that are open and friendly and wag their tails because they are happy, not because they are sore."

"Escapists," murmured the Captain. "Need their ego bolstered. Dogs make people feel important and necessary. Cats make them feel just like another mammal. Dogs make people feel that it's love that makes the world go around. Cats prove that it's fresh meat. We're bound to be unpopular with the romantics." His eyes closed, his chin nestled in his paws.

"In that case," I said with some asperity, "I shall not plug National Cat Week and alienate a section of my readers. I shall write about something else."

"You're not going to use that confounded typewriter!" cried the Captain, fully awake. He has sensitive eardrums.

"I certainly am," I crowed, sliding in a sheet of copy paper. "Like this."

I started banging away. Cursing, the Captain got up and went into the bedroom. I had beaten him again.

The Cat
Judy D'Angio

The cat waits
Its tail switching;
Whipping the air furiously.
The muscles in its back legs
Tense . . .

The ears are pricked
Listening, Listening,
For what? The object of interest
Does not make a sound.
Silence . . .

Slowly, Suppley
Its hind quarters lowered
An unseen fraction of an inch.
The cat is ready —
He springs!

Another piece of tinsel falls from the tree.

My Pet Owls
Farley Mowat

Wol and Weeps were with us long enough to be well known in Saskatoon. Particulary Wol. As my father said, Wol never quite realized that he was an owl. Most of the time he seemed to think he was people. At any rate, he liked being with people and he wanted to be with us so much that we finally had to stop trying to keep him out of the house. If we locked him out he would come and bang his big beak against the window panes so hard we were afraid the glass would break. Screens were no good either, because he would tear them open with one sweep of his big claws. So eventually he became a house owl. He was always very well mannered in the house, and he caused no trouble — except on one particular occasion.

One midsummer day we had a visit from the new minister of our church. He had just arrived in Saskatoon, so he didn't know about our owls. Mother took him into the living room, he sat down on our sofa with a cup of tea balanced on his knee, and began to talk to Mother about me skipping Sunday School.

Wol had been off on an expedition down the riverbank. When he got home he ambled across the lawn, jumped up to the ledge of one of the living room windows and peered in. Spotting the stranger he gave another leap and landed heavily on the minister's shoulder.

Mother had seen him coming and had tried to warn the minister, but she was too late. By the time she had her mouth open, Wol was already hunched down on the man's shoulder, peering around into his face, making friendly owl noises.

"Who-who?" he asked politely.

Instead of answering the minister let out a startled yelp and sprang to his feet. The tea spilled all over the rug, and the teacup shot into the fireplace and smashed into a million pieces.

It was all so sudden that Wol lost his balance; and when he lost his balance his talons just naturally tightened up to help him steady himself. When Wol tightened his grip the minister gave a wild Indian yell, and made a dash for the door.

Wol had never been treated this way before. He didn't like it. Just as the minister reached the front porch, Wol spread his wings and took off. His wings were big, and they were strong too. One of them clipped the man a bang on the side of his head, making him yell even louder. But by then Wol was airborne. He flew up into his favourite poplar tree, and he was in such a huff at the way he had been treated that he wouldn't come down again till after supper.

Riding on people's shoulders was a favourite pastime with

Wol. Usually he was so careful with his big claws that you couldn't even feel them. Sometimes when he was on your shoulder and feeling especially friendly, he would nibble your ear. His beak was sharp enough to have taken the ear right off your head at a single bite, but he would just catch the bottom of your ear in his beak and very gently nibble it a little. It didn't hurt at all, though it used to make some people nervous. One of my father's friends was a man who worked for the railroad, and he had very big, red ears. Every time he came to visit to our house he wore a cap — a cap with ear flaps. He wore it even in summertime because, he said, with ears as big as his and an ear-nibbling owl around he just couldn't afford to take chances. Wol was usually good-natured, but he *could* get mad. One morning Mother sent me to the store for some groceries. My bike had a flat tire so I had to walk, and Wol walked with me. We were only a little way from our house when we met the postman coming toward us. He had a big bundle of letters in his hand, and he was sorting them and not watching where he was going. Instead of stepping around Wol, he walked right into him.

Worse still, he didn't even look down to see what it was he had stumbled over. He just gave a kind of kick to get whatever it was out of his way.

Well, you could do a lot of things to Wol and get away with it — but kicking him was something different. Hissing like a giant teakettle, he spread his wings wide out and clomped the postman on the shins with them. A whack from one of his wings was like the kick of a mule. The postman dropped his handful of letters and went pelting down the street, yelling blue murder — with Wol right on his heels.

After I got hold of Wol and calmed him down, I apologized to the postman. But for a month after that he wouldn't come into our yard at all. He used to stand at the gate and whistle until one of us came out to get the mail.

Our owls were so used to going nearly everywhere with me

now that when school started that fall I had a hard time keeping them at home. I used to bicycle to school, which was about two miles away across the river. During the first week after school opened, I was late four times because of having to take the owls back home after they followed me part way.

Finally Dad suggested that I lock them up in the big pen each morning just before I left. Wol and Weeps hadn't used that pen for a long time, and when I put them in they acted as if it was a jail. Wol was particularly furious, and he began to tear at the chicken wire with his beak and claws. I sneaked off fast. I was almost late anyway, and I knew if I was late once more I'd be kept in after school.

I was nearly halfway over the river bridge when a man on the footpath gave a shout and pointed to something behind my back. At the same time a car, coming toward me, jammed on its brakes and nearly skidded into the cement railings. Not knowing what was going on, I put on my brakes too, and I just had time to stop when there was a wild rush of air on the back of my neck, a deep "HOOO-HOOO-HOO!" in my ear, and Wol landed on my shoulder.

He was out of breath — but he was so pleased with himself that I didn't have the heart to take him home. Anyway, there wasn't time. So he rode the handle bars the rest of the way to school.

I skidded into the yard just as the two-minute bell was ringing and all the other kids were going through the doors. I couldn't decide what on earth to do with Wol. Then I remembered that I had some twine in my pocket. I fished it out and used it to tie him by one leg to the handle bars.

The first class I had that morning was French. Well, between worrying about Wol and not having done my home-work, I was in trouble with the teacher (whom we called Fifi behind her back). Fifi made me come up in front of the class so she could tell me how dumb I was. I was standing beside her desk, wishing the floor would open and swallow me up, when there was a whump-whump-whump at the window. I turned my head to look, and there sat Wol.

It hadn't taken him long to untie the twine.

I heard later that he had banged on the windows of two or three other classrooms before he found the right one. Having found the right room at last, he didn't waste any time. Unluckily Fifi had left one of our windows open. Wol ducked down, saw me, and flew right in.

He was probably aiming to land on my shoulder, but he missed and at the last second tried to land on Fifi's desk. It was a polished hardwood desk; he couldn't get a grip on it. His brakes just wouldn't hold; he skated straight across the desk scattering papers and books all over the floor. Fifi saw him coming and tried to get up out of her chair, but she wasn't fast enough. Wol skidded off the end of the desk and plumped right into her lap.

There were some ructions after that. I was sent to the principal's office and Fifi went home for the rest of the day.

Vulture
Jay Ames

The vulture
Is grossly repulsive
his manners
are far from urbane
and yet if
he had me for dinner
I'd be far
Too dead to complain.

Leisure
Postscripts

Circus in Town

Sinclair Ross

It was Jenny's first circus. A girl in purple tights, erect on a galloping horse, a red-coated brass band, a clown, an elephant ripped through the middle. "And did you see the elephant?" she asked her brother Tom who had found the piece of poster in the street when he was in town marketing the butter and eggs. "Was it really there? And the clown?"

But the ecstatic, eleven-year-old quiver in her voice, and the way she pirouetted on her bare toes as he led the horse out of the buggy shafts, made him feel that perhaps in picking up the poster he had been unworthy of his own seventeen years; so with an offhand shrug he drawled, "I could see the tents and things but I didn't bother going over. Good shows never stop off at the little towns." And then, in a softer voice, as if suddenly touched by her white eagerness, "Everybody said it wouldn't amount to much. A few ponies and an elephant or two — but what's an elephant?"

She wheeled from him, resenting his attempt to scoff away such wonders. The bit of poster had spun a new world before her, excited her, given wild, soaring impetus to her imagination; and now, without in the least understanding herself, she wanted the excitement and the soaring, even though it might stab and rack her, rather than the barren satisfaction of believing that in life there was nothing better, nothing more vivid or dramatic, than her own stableyard.

It was supper-time, her father just in from the field and turning the horses loose at the water-trough, so off she sped to greet him, her bare legs flashing and quick like the pink spokes of a wagon wheel, her throat too tight to cry out, passionate to communicate her excitement, to find response.

But the skittish old roan Billie took fright at the fluttering poster, and her father shouted for her to watch what she was doing and keep away from the horses. For a minute she stood quite still, cold, impaled by the rebuff; then again she wheeled, and this time, as swiftly as before, ran to the house.

A wave of dark heat, hotter than the summer heat, struck her at the door. "Look — " she pierced it shrilly — "what Tom brought me — a circus," and with her poster outstretched she sprang to the stove where her mother was frying pork and eggs and potatoes.

There was no rebuff this time. Instead, an incredible kind of pity — pity of all things on a day like this. "Never mind, Jenny." A hot hand gentle on her cheek a minute. "Your day's going to come. You won't spend all your life among chickens and cows or I'm not the woman I think I am." And then, bewilderingly, an angry clatter of stove-lids that made her shrink away dismayed, in sudden dread of her father's coming and the storm that was to break.

Not a word until he had washed and was sitting down at the table. Then as the platters were clumped in front of him he asked, "What's wrong" and for answer her mother hurled back "Wrong? You — and the farm — and the debts — that's what's wrong. There's a circus in town, but do we go? Do we ever go anywhere? Other children have things, and see things, and enjoy themselves, but look, look at it! That's how much of a circus my girl gets!"

Jenny dared to be a little indignant at the scornful way her mother pointed to the piece of poster that furtively she had hung over the kitchen calendar while waiting for her father. A beautiful poster — a band and half an elephant — and she felt exasperated and guilty that there should be a quarrel about it, her father looked so frightened and foolish, her mother so savage and red.

But even had she been bold enough to attempt an explanation it would have been lost in the din of their voices. Her mother shouted about working her fingers to the bone and nothing for it but skimping and debts. She didn't mind for herself but she wanted Jenny to have a chance. "Look at her clothes and her bare feet! Your own daughter! Why don't you take hold — do something? Nothing ahead of her but chickens and cows! Another ten years — can't you just see the big, gawky know-nothing she's going to be?"

Jenny gulped, startled. Ten years from now it was a quite different kind of young lady she intended to be. For a moment there was a sick little ball of consternation down near her midriff, a clammy fear her mother might be right — and then she was furious. So furious that for the next minute or two the quarrel passed over her. She wasn't gawky and she wasn't know-nothing. She was farther on in school than any other girl her age. She could do fractions and percentages and draw a map of North America with her eyes shut. Her mother to talk, who, only last Sunday when she was writing a letter had to ask her to spell "necessary"!

But suddenly the din between her mother and father split apart, and it was Tom speaking. Tom unruffled and magisterial, rising to his seventeen years and the incumbency of maintaining adult dignity at their table. "Can't you hold on and let us eat in peace? We've heard all that before. Jenny and I are hungry."

Jenny shivered, it was so fine and brave of Tom, but there was a long terrible minute while she watched her father's face to see what was going to happen. Two or three years ago, she remembered, for just such bravery, Tom had been sent reeling through the door with a welt across his face.

But today, instead of the oath and whack of knuckles, there was Tom's voice again, steady and quiet, a little scornful. "Come on Jenny, you're not eating anyway. We'll go out and leave them to it."

It was dangerous, she thought swiftly — taking sides was always dangerous, parents weren't to be flouted — but she couldn't help herself. Her pride in Tom was uncontrollable, mastering her discretion. Eyes down, bare feet padding quick and silent, she followed him.

They walked gravely across the yard and sat down on the edge of the water-trough, as if their destination had been agreed upon before they started. "It's too bad all right you couldn't go to the circus," Tom consoled her, "but everybody said it wouldn't be worth the money. And maybe some Saturday night before long you can come to town with me."

She glanced up puzzled, impatient. Pity again! If only they would just keep quiet and leave her alone — join her, if they liked, to see the circus.

That was all, for she wasn't wishing yet. It was too soon. There was a sudden dilation of life within her, of the world around her — an elephant, a brass band in red coats, half a poster blown from a billboard — and to recapture the moment of its impingement against her was all she wanted, to scale the glamour and wonder of it, slowly, exquisitely, to feel herself unfurl.

"There's Dad now, starting for the barn," Tom nudged her. "Better go and finish your supper. I don't want any more."

Neither did she, but to escape him she went. Uneasily, apprehensive that when she was alone with her mother there might be a reckoning for her having taken sides with Tom. And she was afraid of her mother tonight. Afraid because all at once she felt defenceless, perishable. This sudden dilation of life — it was like a bubble blown vast and fragile. In time it might subside, slowly, safely, or it might even remain full-blown, gradually strengthening itself, gradually building up the filmy tissues to make its vastness durable, but tonight she was afraid. Afraid that before the hack of her mother's voice it might burst and crumple.

So when she found the kitchen deserted, her mother down cellar putting food away, there was a cool, isolated moment of relief, and then a furtive poise, an alert, blind instinct for survival and escape. She glided across the kitchen, took down the poster from where it still hung over the calendar, and fled with it to the barn.

There was a side door, and near it a ladder to the loft. No one saw her. She lay limp in the hay, listening to her heart-beat subside, letting the little core of pain in her breast that had come from running slip away through her senses like cool grains of wheat that sometimes she sat in the granary trickling through her fingers. It was a big, solemn loft, with gloom and fragrance and sparrows chattering against its vault of silence like boys flinging pebbles at a wall. And there, in its dim, high stillness, she had her circus. Not the kind that would stop off at a little town. Not just a tent and an elephant or two. No — for this was her own circus; the splendid, matchless circus of a little girl who had never seen one.

"You'll catch it," Tom said when he found her, "hiding up here instead of helping with the dishes."

Catch it she did, but for once the threats of what would happen next time failed to touch her. The circus went on. All night long she wore purple tights and went riding Billie round and round the pasture in them. A young, fleet-footed Billie. Caparisoned in blue and gold and scarlet, silver bells on reins and bridle — neck arched proudly to the music of the band.

Stanislowski *vs.* Grenfell*
Stephen Scriver

It is noted
without metrics or mourning
that the world's foremost violinist
played in Grenfell
to assembled chairs of the Legion Hall

while two-thirds of the populace
was attending a four-pointer
between the Spitfires and Whitewood
at the Community Recreation Centre

*Grenfell, Saskatchewan.

The Bijou Theatre
Tony Cashman

Movies are bigger now. They're longer. They're wider. They're louder. They're in colour. But would anyone say they're more fun than they were in 1908 when Pop Lawrence came to Edmonton to open our first movie house?

Mr. Lawrence wasn't too sure about the future of movies or the future of Edmonton when he came here, so he was careful to bring a return ticket, with which he could beat a retreat to Fremont, Ohio, if necessary. The return portion boosted the total price of the ticket to twenty-three dollars. Pop Lawrence had a projector in his luggage, and his historical bit of entertainment hardware slipped into Canada unnoticed. At any rate it was unnoticed by the customs. Pop was afraid the tariff demand of the border guards might doom the project economically, so when an official glared at his trunk and said "Anything to declare?" Pop decided he should not begin with his brother-in-law's movie projector. He began instead with a pair of shoes he had bought in Detroit. "Have to charge you duty on those," said the customs man. He collected and moved on, and the historic progression moved on towards Edmonton.

Pop had a partner in the venture, a chap named Bill Hamilton.When he and Bill arrived in August 1908, they found Edmonton talking excitedly about the streetcar system (which was about to acquire a streetcar), but there was no excited talk about movie houses. Al Cameron, manager of two legitimate theatres, the Orpheum and the Opera House, said he wouldn't take five thousand dollars to run a movie theatre. Movies could never compete with the living stage. For one thing, movies were so dreadfully lowbrow.

Pop found out about this feeling. He had two backers for his movie house, and the wife of one of them would never come near the place. The place was called The Bijou — a favourite name for such halls of entertainment — and it was on 100th Street, across from the site of the present Centennial Library.

Patrons of the Bijou paid a dime and got two reels of entertainment. The second reel was the feature film. The first combined a comedy and educational feature. Now the films which came to the manager of such a place were less than simply "silent". They were totally devoid of subtitles or of any aid to understanding the flealike hopping of the pale figures on the screen.

Much of the production on a movie was done right in the house. As a first step in production, Mr. Lawrence hired an orchestra to accompany the action on screen and fill in the gaps when the reels were being rewound. This was quite a gap, because movie machines had to be cranked by hand, in both directions. It was against the law to use an electric motor; the owners of legitimate theatres had insinuated this law into the statutes.

The feature films were uncomplicated action-packed affairs, full of to-ings and fro-ings in which the good guys were easily distinguished from the bad guys. But when a full house of 205 patrons paid a dime apiece, Pop figured they were entitled to sound effects. So in addition to the orchestra, Pop would provide a play-by-play commentary, standing beside Joe Elwood, the projectionist. To enhance a drama of the Wild West, Pop and Bill once decided to give the crowd the sound of real shooting. Bill went behind the screen with a pistol and blank cartridges, intending to synchronize his bangs with the action on the screen. The first bang went off on schedule, but then the pistol jammed. As a chase flickered across the screen, Pop jumped to his feet and shouted, "Believe me, folks, there are a lot more shots than that being fired."

The comedies required little narration from the manager but the educational shows were a problem. When the distributor sent ten minutes of film on coal mining or lumbering or growing tobacco, Mr. Lawrence had to go to the library and read up on coal mining or lumbering or growing tobacco until he could speak for ten minutes on the subject.

By 1909, Mr. Lawrence was able to bring his family from Ohio. Soon after their arrival, Mrs. Lawrence and the two young daughters went to the Bijou. The daughters watched the show and listened to the voice of the narrator for a while. Then one turned around to see whence the voice was coming. "Oh, look. There's papa hollering the show!" To give the audience a chance to holler, the Bijou then added singsongs to the bill of fare. The words of popular songs like "Shine on Harvest Moon" or "Only an Outcast" were flashed on the screen, and the hollering of the tune was led by local singers. Three of them used to alternate, a girl and two men.

He introduced another innovation — the first newsreel. On May 6, 1910, word came over the telegraph that King Edward VII had died. That night Mr. Lawrence went back downtown to the telegraph office and sent a cable to London ordering a film of the king's funeral to be sent "right away, C.O.D." He knew the film would take two weeks to get here and would arrive on a Friday afternoon, along with the Old Country mail for Mike's Newsstand. Just waiting for the fateful day was tense enough, and it became worse when two rival theatres announced that they would show the king's funeral, starting the following Monday. The theatre that was the first with the newsreel would gain an unassailable prestige. Tuesday passed . . . and Wednesday. And Thursday almost passed. Then at 3:30 p.m. the Bijou was advised by wire that the funeral films had reached Calgary.

Mr. Lawrence had five thousand hand bills printed in a hurry, advertising the Bijou's scoop. On Friday morning he rounded up thirty kids, at one dollar each, to be ready to rush handbills through the town. Then, early Friday afternoon, he went over to the CPR station in Strathcona to get the precious film straight off the train. The train arrived on time, at 3:30, and the film was on it. Clutching the package under his arm, Mr. Lawrence ran to the butcher's shop and phoned the theatre to send the boys out with the handbills. Well, no, he didn't exactly phone the theatre; the Bijou didn't have a phone. He called Connelly and McKinley's funeral home, which was then next door. When Mr. Lawrence got back to the north side, people were already drifting into the Bijou to see the king's funeral. And it ran over and over again for six day's, from one o'clock in the afternoon to eleven at night, while Mrs. Jack Bartley played Chopin's "Funeral March" over and over on the theatre piano.

But then it was back to business as usual, with the comedy, the feature on industry, the action-packed Western and Pop Lawrence hollering the show. Movies were more fun in those days.

Back-Yard Barbecue
Eric Nicol

My rejoicing in the coming of summer's sun is always modified
by the knowledge that I must suffer the torture of the damned.
Namely, roasting.

I don't tan. The sun doesn't transform me into a bronzed
god. It turns me into a braised beet. Little Red Writhing Hood.

People tell me that the sun does this because I am fair.
That's what they say. What they mean is I'm the sort of thing
that should only come out at night. Me and the dew worms. I
know what they're thinking, blast them.

I wouldn't bother with the whole ugly business, except that
these days everybody gets a tan. I see them on my way to the
office, dozens of them, sprawled about on Kitsilano Beach in
their bathing suits, baking as much as the law will allow. I
understand that even more of them go off into the hills and
bake what the law won't allow, as well. These people may just
want to look healthy, but they seem to me to go to unusual
lengths to make sure that they will look well done from any
angle. Anyhow, by midsummer all these people will be running
around black as Othello, so that a Desdemona like me can't
appear in public without being suffocated socially.

It's all very well saying that you have a fine white skin.
Nobody wants to see a lily on thy brow these days. Thighs of
alabaster are out. These days you're supposed to look like Aunt
Jemima, if you have to carry a stack of pancakes to do it.

So, to avoid looking like something disturbed under a rotten
log and running to save its eggs, I shall have to incinerate
myself. Every year I try a different sun-tan lotion, something
that my friends have told me will enable me to tan without
burning. And every year I confront these friends, my little blue
eyes glaring out of a boiled ham.

Olive oil was the thing, they told me. Complete protection.

So I covered myself with olive oil, took a magazine into the back yard, lay down, and started reading about how the Italians do all their cooking with olive oil. I got up, went into the house and washed off the olive oil. Nobody is going to catch me looking like an Italian entree.

Next I was persuaded to try a jar of a cream advertised by posters of a young woman pouting prettily over her third degree burns. She had dropped one strap of her bathing suit to show how white she was before she blundered into the sun without the cream.

The dropped shoulder strap was an inspired piece of advertising. I bought the cream. I smeared it over me like a Channel swimmer and waded stickily into the back yard. Lying on my back on some newspapers I quickly became a death trap for a large variety of bugs that became mired in the ventral ooze. The cream evidently made me smell like hollyhocks or something. A sizeable insect of a species I didn't recognize tried to breast-stroke its way into the relative safety of my shorts. I got up and went into the house with the newspapers stuck to my back.

Since then I have tried several other lotions and creams. Some of them left me whiter than I was before I put them on, cleansing the pores, of all the dirty tricks. One made me brown but bumpy, and when the bumps went so did the brown.

Now I have resigned myself to peeling. I peel beautifully. If anybody wanted to make out a case for my having a dash of reptile in my make-up he'd only have to see me cast off my skin and wiggle away gleaming in the new one. With me epidermis is no problem. I've got skin to burn.

And by the middle of September I'll begin to look almost brown. Then the sun will disappear and in two weeks I'll be shark's belly again. It hardly seems worth it.

Besides, the doctors say that excessive exposure to the sun is bad for the skin. I wish you'd speak up a little louder, doctors. These blighters don't seem to hear you.

The Boy Who Blew It

Dave Reid

Up to now I've been hesitant to come out and tell this story because I didn't think anyone would really take me seriously. But now my English teacher is telling me to write a short story from experience, and this is the first thing that comes to mind. So . . . .

FIRST ANNUAL CANADIAN BUBBLEGUM BLOWING CONTEST! That's what the poster said in big, bold print. Beneath it, in smaller letters, was additional information: $100 regional prize, $300 provincial prize, $500 national prize, and the sponsor's name, Blo-Brite Gum, a new one. Now that's for me, I thought, as I was immediately reminded of Owen Quib.

Owen Quib was weird. Looking back on his, ah, misfortune, I suppose it is only logical and fitting that he died the way he did. I remember when I first met him. I think it was in grade eight, four years ago. I was skipping math. Just walking down the hall minding my own business when, suddenly, I heard a very odd sound, or rather sequence of sounds. It's kind of hard to describe, that sound. First, there was a series of sibilant fizzes; then a few quiet pops like rain on a house roof; finally a dry slurp. Then the sequence started over.

Glancing up, I saw the funniest looking kid I have ever seen. He was of average height, but that was the only average thing about him. He was skinny. Not slight or thin, skinny. He must have weighed all of seventy pounds. He had long arms that hung down his sides like two bleached jungle vines. His cream-colored hair set off large, dark blue eyes.

As I stared at him, and he returned the gaze, I saw how he was making those sounds. He was slumped in a corner, chewing on what I assumed was either bubble gum or a large hunk of rubber. This, in itself, wasn't too bad, but what really made me stare was the way he would periodically expel a gigantic, thin-walled sphere of this . . . stuff from his mouth. Then he would proceed to somehow fold it up into a perfect square and flip it back into his mouth.

I stood there for a few minutes, fascinated with his oral dexterity; then, realizing what I was doing, I perked up and introduced myself. At this point I got my first inkling of this . . . this person's third and final quirk. Quib launched into a solid, five-minute monologue, giving me what seemed to be his entire life story. He did this with perfect articulation, except for a slight muffle, yet he continued to blow those gigantic bubbles without skipping a syllable.

During the next three years, I had a few classes with this kid, Owen Quib, and we became almost friends. I never saw him that he wasn't doing tricks with gum. He once confided to me that he was so good because he practised in his sleep. The times were also rare that he wasn't talking, and I often wondered how he kept from getting kicked out of all his classes. As it was, his nickname among the teachers was "Hot Air Owen". It's ironic . . . but never mind that now. Another thing during those few years was the way Owen kept growing up, but not out. By the spring of last year, he was skinnier, if anything.

Anyway, it should be obvious why I thought of Quib when I read that poster. To make a long story short, I managed to get in touch with Owen and conned him into entering the contest. What really made me happy was the way I convinced him that I would make a great manager and trainer and, since he was getting more of an emotional reward out of the contest, that I was entitled to at least seventy per cent of the prize money.

The regional trials were no problem at all. Owen and I just stood there chatting and when the judges came by they immediately called Owen a winner. Not only was he blowing bubbles averaging nine inches in diameter, but he was talking as always. This win made me happy, to say the least, and it whetted my appetite for more. After all, it's surprising how much can be bought with $70, yet how quickly it runs out.

The win included a free trip for Owen to Edmonton for the provincial semi-finals. I'm still not sure how, but I managed to convince the organizers that it was essential to Quib's success that I go to Edmonton as well, in the role of trainer. We stayed in the Edmonton Plaza hotel, and here we started a preliminary training program. I decided that Owen's main problem would be a lack of stamina and staying power. So I had him blowing bubbles in the sauna and pool. Understandably, it didn't take long until we were the only ones in there. Anyway, by the time the contest day came around, Owen could stay under water blowing bubbles for two minutes.

The regional trials had been held in our own high school auditorium, but the provincials were class. They were held in the Jubilee Auditorium! Owen's bubble grew and grew until he finally ended up with a sixteen-inch diameter globe — a tremendous bubble, even for him. He beat his nearest competitor by over an inch.

We were both happy. My 70 percent of the provincial first prize worked out to $210. I put this into the bank to wait for the rest of the money which I'd decided we had to win. Owen was happy as an athlete is happy.

The provincials led to the last, and most important, competition, the national finals in Winnipeg. We had two weeks in Winnipeg to get ready, and I was faced with a dilemma. What could I do to make Owen better? We both realized that my underwater training program had served its purpose. Finally, I decided that the only way Quib could get better would be to simply blow into his bubbles instead of talking into them. But by this time Owen was so overconfident that he just kept telling me not to worry. I was worried though, I had $350 riding on this guy!

However, the two weeks passed and the big day came. The competitions were held at Rainbow Stage, an open air auditorium. With the cloudless blue sky hanging above, it seemed absolutely gigantic. To say that we were a bit nervous up there would be a lot like saying Owen was a slightly offbeat person.

This time we had some real competition, but Owen managed to defeat everyone in the preliminaries and ended up vying for the championship against Fred Mackenzie, a Maritimer whose personal best was 17 inches. This guy was a direct and striking contrast to Owen. He was rotund and jolly looking, yet he spoke very rarely, and when he did, it was in monosyllables and short, clipped sentences. It was hard not to stare at them as they got ready for this, their most important competition. They'd both get two tries, and the largest bubble would win.

They started blowing, intense concentration on both faces, as Owen's ever-present voice seemed to tighten to the breaking point. The bubbles grew . . . 10 inches . . . 12 inches . . .14 . . . 15 . . . 16½ . . . POP! The snap of defeat and the sudden clarity of Quib's words shattering the tense air as, with agonizing slowness, I watched his beautiful orb age and shrivel and finally sag to its death. Meanwhile Mackenzie's sphere kept growing . . . 18½ inches . . . 19 . . . I could see myself standing alone on one side of that great void, with all that beautiful prize money on the other side, and the emptiness growing bigger between us. Finally, at 20½ inches, Mackenzie gestured that he wanted this size taken for his final measurement, and he wanted to dispense with his other try. This left Owen with one more try at what had become the single goal in his life, and more to the point as far as I was concerned, one more try at my money.

He worked his mouth for a few minutes to get exactly the shape he wanted in the gum. Then he started blowing, while telling himself that he knew perfectly well he could do it and what was he worried about anyhow? The bubble grew from its first thick pink beginnings. It took on form and seemed almost alive.

Suddenly, when the bubble reached 11 inches, Owen did something I had never seen him do before. It was something which caused his death, and I have a nagging feeling it was partly my fault. He looked pointedly in my direction, said something I didn't quite catch, then quit talking and simply blew into the bubble! But his mouth and throat muscles kept supplying all the energy needed for talking, as they had done for years. This energy was no longer being used, and it turned into heat. The bubble was filling with extremely hot air, and as it grew over 17 inches it started to rise. And, in consequence, Owen Quib rose too.

Just for the record, I'm sure that by the time Quib's shoes were five feet off the ground, the bubble was over 21 inches in diameter. Yet the whole situation seemed to have some weird effect on Owen; he seemed to be in some kind of daze. He just kept on blowing superheated air into the bubble, and it kept on dragging him up and up until he must have been at least 200 feet in the air.

Suddenly everything grew calm, a hush fell over Rainbow Stage, and I felt like I wasn't really there at all. I saw the bubble stop growing, hang for a moment, then ever so slowly develop wrinkles that grew and deepened. And then Owen Quib was falling, and I looked down, and he was going to hit the cement, and here he comes . . . Oooohh!

The half crunch, half splat as Owen hit the platform brought me out of my stupor. I ran over to where he was, but he was spread over about twelve square feet. I just stood there with thoughts running through my mind, thoughts of how badly he had wanted to win and how I wanted to win, thoughts of training and Owen not bothering to try blowing bubbles normally, thoughts of my first meeting with Owen, and a million other, very trivial things about my relationship with Owen Quib.

After that it was pretty gruesome. Someone had called an ambulance, but there wasn't much they could do except clean up that mashed puddle that had been Owen Quib. The judges decided that, despite all, Quib's bubble had beaten Mackenzie's, and I got all the prize money. After a day or two everyone went home, and I've just been trying to forget about it since.

Well, that's my story. Reading it, I'll admit that it does sound a bit farfetched, especially to a lot of people who've never even heard about the contest because of the way the gum company quashed publicity after Quib's death. Nonetheless, I'll vouch for the fact that that's how it really happened. I suppose there is some twisted moral in what happened: Owen Quib just got carried away; then, when his bubble burst, he had to come back down to earth.

Acknowledgements

The editor wishes to thank the authors and publishers for permission to include the following in this anthology:

R. Ross Annett for "Babe's Surprise" from *The Saturday Evening Post* (June 7, 1958).

D. P. Barnhouse for "An Angel After All".

Calgary Power for "Taming the Cyclone" by Jacques Hamilton from the radio spot from "Our Alberta Heritage".

The Canadian Publishers, McClelland and Stewart Limited for "The Dance" and for "Hark, the Herald Angels . . . Sing?" by Max Braithwaite from *Why Shoot the Teacher?* For "Lutiapik" by Betty Lee from *Lutiapik*. For "The Coming of Mutt" by Farley Mowat from *The Dog Who Wouldn't Be*. For "My Pet Owls" by Farley Mowat from *Owls in the Family*. For "The Curtain Goes Up" by Myra Paperny from *Wooden People*. For "Circus in Town" by Sinclair Ross from *The Lamp at Noon and Other Stories*.

Clarke, Irwin & Company Limited for "Christmas" by Emily Carr from *A Little Town and a Little Girl* (1951).

Agnes Copithorne for "Summer Vacation, or Nothing Ever Happens Around Here".

Copp Clark Pitman for "World Champions" by Ken McConnell from *All Sails Set*.

Harold F. Cruickshank for "New Year's Eve 1906" from *Heritage Magazine*.

Judy D'Angio for "The Cat".

Doubleday Canada Limited for "Everybody Played Hockey" by Barry Broadfoot from *Ten Lost Years* (1973).

Gage Publishing Limited for "Vulture" by Jay Ames, for "Happiness, Hard Won" by Roy Devore, for "The Losers" by Samuel Roddan, and for "A Game of Horseshoes" by David J. Wright, all from *Rubaboo*. For "At the Rodeo" by James M. Moir from *Family Chronicle* (1978).

Tom Gee for "A Moment's Silence".

Michael Henry for "The Richtfest" from *Heritage Magazine.*

Hurtig Publishers for "The Bijou Theatre" by Tony Cashman from *The Best Edmonton Stories.* For "The Ball Players" by Maurice Metayer from *Tales from the Igloo.*

Mervin J. Huston for "Holiday Handicapping" from *The Great Canadian Lover.*

Eddie Kwan for "The Hustler".

Beatrice Boles Liddle for "When the Chuckwagons Roll" from the *Alberta Golden Jubilee Anthology.*

Margaret McCourt for "Box Social" by Edward A. McCourt from *The Flaming Hour.*

The Macmillan Company of Canada Ltd. for "Christmas on the Farm" by Allan Anderson from *Remembering the Farm.*

McGraw-Hill Ryerson Limited for "Curling" by Eric Nicol from *Sense and Nonsense* (1947). For "Backyard Barbecue", for "Don't Just Stand There" and for "Fishing Accounted For" by Eric Nicol from *Still a Nicol* (1972). For "Talking Down the Cat" and for "Thieving Raffles" by Eric Nicol from *Twice Over Lightly* (1953).

W. O. Mitchell for "Melvin Arbuckle's First Course in Shock Therapy". For "Miss Henchbaw" from *Jake and the Kid.*

Grace Petrikowski for "Discus".

Dave Reid for "The Boy Who Blew It".

Carol Rose for "Just This Once".

Summerthought Ltd. for "Arby's Pinocchio" by Charles Noble, for "Another Hallowe'en" by J. O. Thompson, and for "Mock-death" by Jon Whyte, all from *Three: Noble, Thompson, Whyte.*

Thistledown Press Ltd. for "The Slap Shot" and for "Stanislowski *vs.* Grenfell" by Stephen Scriver from *Between the Lines.*

Bill van Veelen for "Skis" and for "We Made It".

Western Producer Prairie Books for "Special Occasions" by J. C. Charyk from *The Little White Schoolhouse.* For "A Boy's Unforgettable Christmas Dinner" by J. G. MacGregor from *Northwest of Sixteen.* For "Rummage Sales" by Bob Phillips from *Out West: Stories About Persons and Places on the Canadian Plains*. For "Horror of Haunted Hallowe'en" by Eleanor Pronik from *Glistening in the Sun: An Anthology of YC Verse*.

Since the first printing of this anthology, we have been granted permission to reprint the following copyrighted material:

"Stage Fright" by Ken Wotherspoon

While every effort has been made to trace the owners of copyrighted material and to make due acknowledgement, we regret having been unsuccessful with the following selections.

"Atavists" by Harold Baldwin
"The Hometown Goalie" by Jeff Brown
"Carnival Procession — Calgary Stampede" by Arthur Stringer
"Thoughts" by Marty Robillard
"The Sundance" by Faye Weasel Fatt